A guide to leisure activities in

CAMBRIDGESHIRE   ESSEX

NORFOLK   SUFFOLK

SERIES EDITOR CATHERINE BAKER

·K·U·P·E·R·A·R·D·

Going Places

Going Places – the most comprehensive coverage in one volume of the leisure and sporting activities to be enjoyed in the cities, towns and villages of these adjoining counties. An invaluable source of information and ideas for visitors and residents alike, this guide offers all age groups the opportunity to pursue a favourite pastime or discover a new one regardless of the weather or season.

The activities section gives you detailed information on over sixty leisure activities, the names and addresses of their governing bodies and a list of all the places where you can enjoy them arranged alphabetically under county headings. To find out more details look up the places in the second section of the guide.

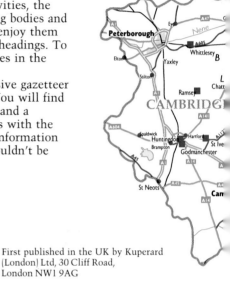

The second section is a comprehensive gazetteer of one hundred places in the region. You will find a description, some local information and a detailed list of all the leisure activities with the telephone number, address or access information and any other interesting details. It couldn't be easier.

Acknowledgements

We are very grateful for the help we have received from the county, district and local councils, the tourist information centres and the individual establishments we have included in this guide. Every effort has been made to obtain accurate details at the time of going to press, however it is advisable that you telephone your destination before embarking on a long journey. Corrections, alterations or additional entries should be sent to The Editor, c/o The Publisher, for inclusion in a new edition.

We would like to thank the following for supplying the photographs included in this guide:

Anglia Balloons; Babergh District Council; Borough of Great Yarmouth, Department of Publicity; Cambridge Evening News; Chris Ridgers; County Visuals, Kent County Council; East Cambridgeshire District Council; Epping Forest District Council; Essex County Council; Fenland District Council; FlyPast Magazine; Forest Heath District Council; Gloucestershire County Planning Department; Huntingdon District Council; Ian Meredith; Jen Harvey; Mid Suffolk Leisure Centre; North Norfolk District Council; North Weald Aerodrome; Norwich Ski Club; Peterborough City Tourist Information Centre; Peterborough District Council; Solar Wings Limited; Southend-on-Sea Borough Council; St Edmundsbury Borough Council; Suffolk Coastal District Council; Suffolk County Council, Planning Department (Tourism); Waveney District Council; Wild Type Productions Ltd.

First published in the UK by Kuperard (London) Ltd, 30 Cliff Road, London NW1 9AG

First published 1991

© Research and text
J & J Entertainment Ltd.
© Design and production
The Pen & Ink Book Company Ltd.

ISBN 1-870668-57-X

Design and production

Printed and bound in Great Britain

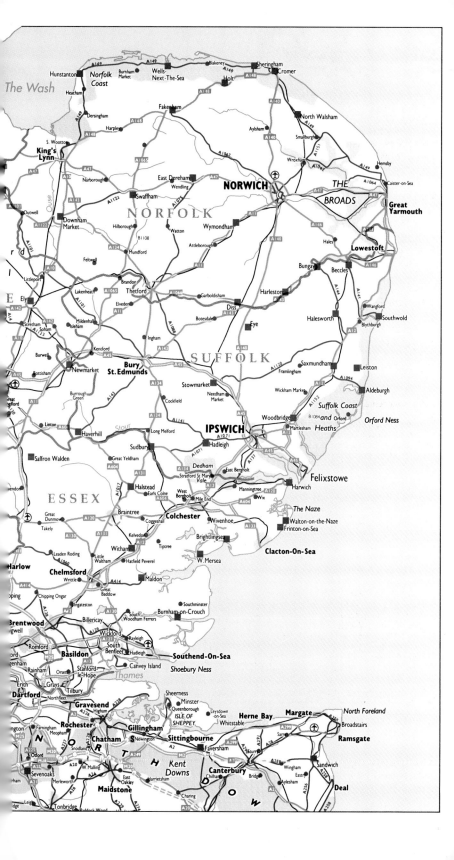

Contents

Activities

However you like to spend your time, whether ballooning or birdwatching, microlight flying or messing about in boats, playing a round of golf or soaking up the history and tradition found in historic houses, churches and castles, then the eastern counties have much to offer and they are all listed in this section. Look up the leisure or sporting activity you are interested in, they are arranged alphabetically, and you will find a list of all the locations where you can pursue your interest, these are again listed alphabetically. To find out more details about these venues look up the town or village in the second section and under the relevant activity heading you will find the telephone number, address or access information and more details. It couldn't be easier and browsing through this section you might even discover a new sport or activity to try as well as a new appreciation and enjoyment of the leisure facilities offered in the eastern region.

Climbing

Climbing can test your nerves and physical abilities to their limits. It is an exhilarating and rewarding sport that is easy to start. There are climbs to suit all ages and abilities, local clubs to join and accompany on expeditions and for the committed climber there are training courses to go on for a weekend or longer.

The eastern counties are not noted for their hills and do not encompass any good climbing country within their borders. However many sports centres throughout the region do have indoor climbing walls where the interested beginner can learn basic hand and footholds, which muscles to use and how to use them correctly. The experienced climber can keep in shape in between their climbing expeditions elsewhere.

The national body for climbing is listed below, they will give advice on all aspects of mountaineering, climbing and mountain safety. They supply lists of clubs and courses on request.

British Mountaineering Council (BMC)
Crawford House
Precinct Centre
Booth Street East
Manchester
☎ 061 273 5835

CAMBRIDGESHIRE

Cambridge: Kelsey Kerridge Sports Hall
St Ives: St Ivo Recreation Centre

ESSEX

Basildon: Terry Marsh Sports Centre
Colchester: University of Essex Sports Centre

Harlow: Harlow Outdoor Pursuits Centre
Southend-on-Sea: Clements Hall Leisure Centre
Witham: Bramston Sports Centre

NORFOLK

Norwich: University of East Anglia Sports Centre

SUFFOLK

Bury St Edmunds: Bury St Edmunds Sports and Leisure Centre
Haverhill: Haverhill Sports Centre

Shooting

Shooting, whether rifle, game or clay pigeon shooting, is a popular sport for many. Gun licences are required by anyone owning or using a rifle or shotgun, they are obtained from the police headquarters or the Chief Constable of your area of residence. Game licences are required for certain quarry, pheasant, deer, grouse and partridge for instance, but not for rabbits provided permission has previously been obtained from the landowner or owner of the shooting rights. Game licences are available from local post offices before shooting. Rifle clubs and sporting agencies will usually organise gun and game licences when necessary.

Many of the individual clubs included here are Shooting Clubs (SC), Gun Clubs (GC), Clay Pigeon Shooting Clubs (CPSC) or Clay Pigeon Clubs (CPC). More detailed information about shooting and clay pigeon shooting can be obtained from the associations below.

British Association for Shooting and Conservation
National Headquarters, Marford Mill
Clwyd
☎ 0244 570881

Clay Pigeon Shooting Association
107, Epping New Road, Buckhurst Hill
Essex
☎ 081 505 6221

CAMBRIDGESHIRE

Cambridge: Cambridge Shooting Association; Cambridge SC Ground; Cambridge University CPSC Ground; Cottenham CPC Ground; Kelsey Kerridge Sports Hall
Chatteris: Fenland GC Ground
Ely: Isleham GC Ground; The Mepal Clay Target Centre Ground
Gamlingay: Bassingbourne Rod and GC Ground
March: Greenend Shooting Ground
Peterborough: Manor Leisure Centre
St Neots: Waresley and District GC Ground
St Ives: St Ivo Recreation Centre
Waterbeach: Denny GC Ground

ESSEX

Dedham: Kings Arms Clay Club
Epping: Epping Sports Centre
Southend-on-Sea: Clements Hall Leisure Centre
Witham: Bramston Sports Centre

NORFOLK

East Dereham: Wayland GC Ground
Downham Market: Greenend Holiday and SG Ground
Fakenham: Creake CSC Ground
Hunstanton: Heacham and North West Norfolk Wildfowlers Association Ground
King's Lynn: Pentney Abbey SG Ground; Sandringham SS Ground
Norwich: Deighton Hills GC Ground; Michael C Litton

Swaffham: Beeston GC Ground; Marham Guns Ground
Thetford: Ashill CPC Ground
Wells-next-the-Sea: Burnham Overy and Norton Wildfowling Ground

SUFFOLK

Bury St Edmunds: Bury St Edmunds Sports and Lesiure Centre
Dedham: Kings Arms Clay Club Suffolk Ground
Framlingham: Framlingham CPSC Ground
Hadleigh: East Anglia Shooting
Haverhill: Haverhill Sports Centre
Mildenhall: Hereward CS Ground; Lakenheath Road and GC Ground
Newmarket: Newmarket GC Ground
Southwold: High Lodge SS Ground
Stowmarket: ICI GC Ground
Woodbridge: East Suffolk Gun Club; RAF Bentwaters/Woodbridge Rod and GC Ground

Ballooning

The romantic appeal of hot air ballooning captivates many – if the idea of drifting through bright, clear skies appeals then this might be the pursuit for you. To gain your private pilot's licence tuition from a qualified pilot is necessary. A minimum of twelve hours flying experience and a test flight with a qualified examiner are the prerequisites necessary for you to make a solo flight. Additional examinations in navigation, meteorology, and air law will safely extend your ballooning skills.

The British Ballooning and Airship Club is the governing body of the sport and they will provide information on ballooning meets and local clubs.

The British Ballooning and Airship Club
Barbara Green, Information Officer
P.O. Box 1006
Birmingham
☎ 021 643 3224

NORFOLK

Diss: Thomas Holt Wilson
Norwich: Anglia Balloons

Flying

To take to the skies has been man's aspiration for centuries and the appeal of flying often leads enthusiasts into a fascination with aviation history and vintage aircraft – there are many places such as North Weald Airfield where collections of operational and historic aircraft can be seen in action at 'fly-in' days.

To obtain a private pilot's licence requires a minimum of 40 hours flight training at a local flying club, five multiple-choice examinations in meteorology, aviation law, technical aspects, radio telephony and navigation and two flight tests with an examiner to observe both general handling and navigational skills. For anyone interested in taking up flying the Student Pilot Association, their address is below will supply both information and a list of flying schools on request.

For those who either own a plane or who might be interested in building a plane then the Popular Flying Association will be a valuable source of information, their address is below.

Student Pilots Association
30 Tisbury Road
Hove
East Sussex
☎ 0273 204080

Popular Flying Association
Terminal Building
Shoreham Airport
Shoreham-by-Sea
☎ 0273 461616

CAMBRIDGESHIRE

Cambridge: Cambridge Aero Club
Peterborough: Peterborough Airfield

NORFOLK

Cromer: Norfolk and Norwich Aero Club
Norwich: Norwich School of Flying

ESSEX

Epping: North Weald Airfield
Clacton-on-Sea: Clacton Aero Club
Southend-on-Sea: Park Sports Centre;
Southend Flying Club

SUFFOLK

Cromer: Norfolk & Norwich Aero Club
Ipswich: East Anglian Flying Club;
Ipswich School of Flying; Suffolk
Aero Club

Fly Past Fly-in 90 at North Weald Airfield

Gliding

Gliding is a graceful and exciting way to explore the skies. Learning to control a glider is easily and quickly mastered whilst learning to soar is the art every glider pilot seeks. A skilful pilot can cover over two hundred miles or climb to tens of thousands of feet.

Trial flights are available to give you a taste of the air and no age restrictions exist other than pilots under sixteen not being able to fly solo. Dual-control training gliders are used for training and an average of 50 take-offs and landings accompanied by a qualified instructor will take you to solo flying standard. To fly cross-country you must acquire your Bronze badge which will test not only your flying ability but also your knowledge of air law, meteorology and the theory of flight.

The governing body of gliding is the British Gliding Association, they will provide you with information about gliding and details of gliding clubs.

The British Gliding Assocation
Kimberley House
Vaughan Way
Leicester
☎ 0533 531051

CAMBRIDGESHIRE

Cambridge: Cambridge University
  Gliding Club
Peterborough: Peterborough and
  Spalding Gliding Club
Ramsey: Nene Valley Gliding Club

ESSEX

Colchester: Essex & Suffolk Gliding
  Club
Epping: Essex Gliding Club

NORFOLK

Thetford: Norfolk Gliding Club

SUFFOLK

Bury St Edmunds: Rattlesden Gliding
  Club

Hang Gliding

Hang gliding has an element of adventure and excitement, all the senses are used to master three planes of movement simultaneously when you 'take to the skies'. Hang gliding attracts people of all ages and backgrounds – the minimum age to fly solo is 16, there is no maximum age. Basic training at a school registered with the British Hang Gliding Association (BHGA) is the first step to solo flying. A minimum of a week's course is required to obtain the Pilot One licence needed to fly your own hang glider. The BHGA set out and maintain high standards of instruction, equipment and service at the 21 schools registered with them.

The governing body of hang gliding is the British Hang Gliding Association listed below. Information about hang gliding and a list of registered schools is available from them on request.

British Hang Gliding Assocation (BHGA)
Cranfield Airfield
Cranfield
Bedfordshire
☎ 0234 751688

NORFOLK

King's Lynn: Flexiwing Training.

10

Microlight Flying

Microlights are small aircraft that are great fun to fly. They are single or two seater hi-tech planes that have been flown as far afield as Africa and Australia and at speeds of over 100 mph. They are definitely not toy aeroplanes yet they need none of the facilities of a conventional aeroplane, your garage can be your hangar and any fair-sized field your aerodrome. If you are interested try an 'air experience' flight from one of the listed schools. Learning to fly then involves a training course to acquire your flying licence, this usually takes between one and six months. You need to be 17 and reasonably fit to fly your own microlight, patience and perserverance will enable you to learn the art of flying so you can escape into the air and enjoy this safe and exhilarating form of flying.

The British Microlight Aircraft Association is the governing body of the sport and can be contacted for more information at the address below.

British Microlight Aircraft Association
Bullring
Deddington
Oxford
☎ 0869 38888

CAMBRIDGESHIRE

Chatteris: Air School Instruction
Ely: Pegasus Flight Training

ESSEX

Chelmsford: Micro-Air Flying Club
Grays: Essex Airports

NORFOLK

East Dereham: David Clarke Microlight Aircraft

Parachuting

Parachuting is exciting, exhilarating and dynamic, it offers you the joy and freedom of the sky. You can experience the thrill of your first jump by static line parachuting where your parachute opens automatically as soon as you leave the aircraft, by accelerated free-fall (AFF) where your first descent is from 12,000 feet with two highly qualified instructors, or by tandem parachuting where you jump using a dual harness system with an instructor who controls your free-fall and landing – a quick and easy introduction to free-fall. You can progress from beginner to complete parachutist by one of two systems depending on how you made your first jump, and then go on to take up sport parachuting, a highly skilled sport offering many personal and competitive challenges.

The British Parachute Association is the governing body of the sport and will supply you with information both about the sport and courses offered by its affiliated clubs.

The British Parachute Association
Mr C Port (General Secretary)
5 Wharf Way
Glen Parva
Leicester
☎ 0533 785271

Peterborough: Action Enterprise Ltd;
Peterborough Parachute Centre

Chelmsford: East Coast Parachute
Centre

Ipswich: Ipswich Parachute Centre

Paragliding

Paragliding or parascending is parachuting without an aircraft. Parascenders are tow-launched over land and water or foot-launched from a hillside to experience the exhilaration of flying under a canopy, square or round. You can join an introductory course at one of the British Assocation of Parascending Clubs where you will be given thorough ground training as well as learning how to fly yourself, usually in a day. Further courses are tailor-made to local conditions and your choice – you can learn to make flights last for hours, try aerobatics or take part in competitions, meets or fun events. Whatever you do there will be a qualified BAPC expert to supervise and help you decide within strict safety guidelines. Parascending is an exciting and inexpensive sport that will place the world at your feet.

The British Association of Parascending Clubs, the governing body of the sport, will provide details of their clubs and a full information pack on request.

**British Association of Parascending
Clubs Ltd**
18 Talbot Lane
Leicester
☎ 0533 530318

Epping: North Weald Paragliding Club;
The Brigade Paragliding Club

Norwich: Pegasus Scouts Paragliding
Club
Great Yarmouth: Apollo Tavern
Paragliding Club

Sudbury: Suffolk Eagles Paragliding Club

Leisure Centres

Excellent opportunites exist throughout the region to pursue a range of indoor sports options including the increasingly popular racket sports of squash and badminton as well as ice skating, roller skating and tenpin bowling. For the fit, not so fit and those who wish to relax there are the more varied facilities offered by the sports and leisure centres listed, these include saunas, solariums, fitness centres, swimming pools, splash pools, badminton courts and bodybuilding gyms. The range of facilities offered by different leisure centres is so diverse that it would be advisable to contact individual centres to discover what they offer.

CAMBRIDGESHIRE

Cambridge: Kelsey Kerridge Sports Hall
Chatteris: Cromwell Community College
Ely: Paradise Centre; Soham and District Sports Hall
Peterborough: Bushfield Sports Centre; Manor Leisure Centre; The Cressett; Werrington Sports Centre
St Ives: St Ivo Centre
St Neots: St Neots Sports Centre
Wisbech: Hudson Sports Centre

ESSEX

Basildon: Basildon Sports Centre; Bromford Sports Centre; The Markhams Chase Sports Centre
Brentwood: Brentwood Centre; The Courage Hall
Canvey Island: Runnymede Sports Hall; Waterside Farm Sports Centre
Chelmsford: Riverside Ice and Leisure Centre; William de Ferrers Sports Centre
Chipping Ongar: Ongar Sports Centre
Clacton-on-Sea: Clacton Leisure Centre
Colchester: Colchester Sports Centre; Monkwick Sports Hall; University of Essex Sports Centre
Epping: Epping Sports Centre
Grays: Grays Park Leisure Centre
Halstead: Halstead Sports Centre
Harlow: Harlow Sportcentre
Harwich: Harwich Sports Hall
Maldon: Tiptree Sports Centre
Saffron Walden: Lord Butler Leisure Centre
Southend-on-Sea: Clements Hall Leisure Centre; Park Sports Centre; Westcliff Leisure Centre
Tilbury: Tilbury Leisure Centre
Waltham Abbey: Waltham Abbey Sports Centre
Witham: Bramston Sports Centre

NORFOLK

Great Yarmouth: Great Yarmouth Marina Leisure Centre
Hunstanton: Oasis Leisure Centre
Kings Lynn: Kings Lynn Sports Centre
North Walsham: North Walsham Sports Hall
Norwich: Crome Recreation Centre; Duke Street Centre; Long Stratton Leisure Centre; The Norman Centre Norwich Sports Village; University of East Anglia Sports Centre; Wensum Lodge Sports Centre
Swaffham: Swaffham Leisure Centre
Thetford: Breckland Sports Centre

SUFFOLK

Beccles: Beccles Sports Centre
Bungay: Bungay Sports Hall
Bury St Edmunds: Bury St Edmunds Sports and Leisure Centre
Felixstowe: Felixstowe Leisure Centre
Haverhill: Haverhill Sports Centre
Ipswich: Gainsborough Sports and Community Centre; Maidenhall Sports Centre; Northgate Sports Centre; Whitton Sports and Community Centre
Leiston: Leiston Sports Centre
Lowestoft: Waveney Sports and Leisure Centre
Mildenhall: Dome Sports Centre
Newmarket: Newmarket Sports Centre
Stowmarket: Mid Suffolk Leisure Centre
Sudbury: Great Cornard Sports Centre; Sudbury Sports Centre

13

Leisure Sports

ICE SKATING

CAMBRIDGESHIRE

Peterborough: Peterborough Ice Rink

ESSEX

Chelmsford: Riverside Ice and Leisure Centre

ROLLER SKATING

CAMBRIDGESHIRE

Cambridge: Kelsey Kerridge Sports Hall
St Ives: St Ivo Recreation Centre

ESSEX

Southend-on-Sea: Roller City

SUFFOLK

Bury St Edmunds: Rollerbury

TENPIN BOWLING

CAMBRIDGESHIRE

Peterborough: Peterborough Bowl

ESSEX

Colchester: Colchester Sports Centre
Southend on Sea: Pavilion Lanes
Walton-on-the-Naze: Pier Bowling

NORFOLK

Great Yarmouth: Regent Bowl
Kings Lynn: Kings Lynn Bowl
Norwich: Crome Bowl; Norwich Club Bowl

SUFFOLK

Ipswich: Kingpin Bowling Centre; Solar Bowl

Squash

Squash is one of the racket sports that has flourished over the past twenty years, a popular sport for the busy executive or for the sports enthusiast who enjoys the challenge it provides and the fitness it requires. Squash courts are a prominent feature of most leisure and sports centres and many hotels also offer squash facilities so it is unlikely that you will ever be far away from somewhere to play in the eastern counties.

CAMBRIDGESHIRE

Cambridge: Kelsey Kerridge Sports Hall
Ely: Paradise Centre; Soham and District Sports Hall
Peterborough: Bushfield Sports Centre; The Cressett; Werrington Sports Centre
St Ives: St Ivo Centre
St Neots: Abbotsley Golf and Squash Club

ESSEX

Basildon: Basildon Sports Centre; Bromford Sports Centre; The Markhams Chase Sports Centre
Braintree: Riverside Pool
Brentwood: Brentwood Centre; The Courage Hall
Burnham-on-Crouch: Royal Corinthian Yacht Club
Chelmsford: Dovedale Sports Centre; Riverside Ice and Leisure Centre
Chipping Ongar: Ongar Sports Centre
Colchester: Colchester Sports Centre; University of Essex Sports Centre
Epping: Epping Sports Centre; Loughton Hall
Grays: Grays Park Leisure Centre
Great Dunmow: Helena Romanes School
Halstead: Halstead Sports Centre
Harlow: Harlow Sportcentre
Harwich: Harwich Sports Centre
Maldon: Tiptree Sports Centre
Saffron Walden: Lord Butler Leisure Centre
Southend-on-Sea: Clements Hall Leisure Centre; Park Sports Centre
Tilbury: Tilbury Leisure Centre
Waltham Abbey: Waltham Abbey Sports Centre
Witham: Bramston Sports Centre

NORFOLK

Great Yarmouth: Great Yarmouth Marina Leisure Centre
Hunstanton: Oasis Leisure Centre
Kings Lynn: Kings Lynn Sports Centre
Norwich: Crome Recreation Centre; Duke Street Centre; Long Stratton Leisure Centre; Norwich City Baths; The Norman Centre; Norwich Sports Village; University of East Anglia Sports Centre; Wensum Lodge Sports Centre
Swaffham: Swaffham Leisure Centre
Thetford: Breckland Sports Centre

SUFFOLK

Beccles: Beccles Sports Centre
Bungay: Bungay Sports Hall
Bury St Edmunds: Bury St Edmunds Sports and Leisure Centre
Haverhill: Haverhill Sports Centre
Ipswich: Maidenhall Sports Centre; Northgate Sports Centre; Whitton Sports and Community Centre
Leiston: Leiston Sports Centre
Lowestoft: Waveney Sports and Leisure Centre
Mildenhall: Dome Sports Centre
Newmarket: Newmarket Sports Centre
Stowmarket: Mid Suffolk Leisure Centre

Mid Suffolk Leisure Centre - squash courts and a pool to cool off in

Adventure Centres

Choose from a wide range of sports and activities to build up your own programme at one of the special interest or multi-activity centres listed. The range of activities offered by multi-activity centres is diverse whilst special interest centres cater for one activity or type of activity. Accommodation and prices vary so send for a brochure to compare facilities before you make your choice.

The British Activity Holiday Association monitors instruction and safety standards, they offer a consumer advisory service that can be contacted via the address below.

Special activity break packages for families are offered by many hotels and guesthouses, details of these have not been included but can be obtained from the East Anglia Tourist Board or from local Tourist Information Centres.

British Activity Holidays Association
Chief Executive
Rock Park Centre
Llandrindod Wells
Powys
Wales
☎ 0597 3902

East Anglia Tourist Board
Toppesfield Hall
Hadleigh
Suffolk
☎ 0473 822922

CAMBRIDGESHIRE

SPECIAL INTEREST CENTRES

Cambridge: The Windmill Stables
Chatteris: Mepal Outdoor Centre
Huntingdon: Grafham Water Centre

ESSEX

MULTI-ACTIVITY CENTRES

Burnham-on-Crouch: Bradwell Field Studies and Sailing Centre
Dedham: Flatford Mill Field Centre

SPECIAL INTEREST CENTRES

Castle Hedingham: Four Seasons Cycling Holidays
Chelmsford: New Hall Riding Centre
Colchester: Dorian Tours

NORFOLK

MULTI-ACTIVITY CENTRES

North Walsham: Broadland Outdoor Adventure

SPECIAL INTEREST CENTRES

Ludham: How Hill Trust
Kings Lynn: Norfolk Cycling Holidays
Norwich: Wensum Lodge
Wells-next-the-Sea: Ilex House Residential Bird Courses

SUFFOLK

MULTI-ACTIVITY CENTRES

Brandon: Centre Parcs
Lowestoft: Gunton Hall Holidays
Stowmarket: Kids Club Activity Holidays

SPECIAL INTEREST CENTRES

Aldeburgh: Snape Maltings
Ipswich: Newton Hall Equitation Centre
Woodbridge: Poplar Park Equestrian Centre; Deben Junior Tennis Club

Birdwatching

Birdlife in Britain is rich and varied and birdwatching is an extremely popular activity as borne out by the current membership figures of the Royal Society for Protection of Birds (RSPB) - over half a million. The RSPB have many reserves, often exceptionally beautiful locations where visitors can enjoy the relaxing atmosphere and observe the wealth of birds and wildlife from covered hides. The RSPB will supply information about their reserves, about bird watching holidays and their work on request from the address below.

The Royal Society for the Protection of Birds (RSPB)
The Lodge
Sandy
Bedfordshire
☎ 0767 80551

CAMBRIDGESHIRE

Chatteris: Ouse Washes Reserve
Duxford: Fowlmere
Ely: Wicken Fen Wetland Reserve
Huntingdon: Grafham Water
March: Welney Wildfowl Refuge
Peterborough: Nene Washes
St Neots: Little Paxton Gravel pits

ESSEX

Burnham-on-Crouch: Bradwell Field Studies Centre
Brightlingsea: Brightlingsea Creek; River Colne
Colchester: Abberton Reservoir; Fingringhoewick Nature Reserve
Dedham: Flatford Mill Field Centre
Harwich: Stour Wood and Copperas Bay
Maldon: Northey Island

NORFOLK

Blakeney: Cley Marshes
Brancaster: Scolt Head Island; Titchwell Marsh
Great Yarmouth: Breydon Water
Hunstanton: Snettisham
Ludham: Hickling Broad; Horsey Mere; How Hill Nature Reserve Centre
Norwich: Strumpshaw Fen; Surlingham and Rockland Marshes
Wells-next-the-Sea: Ilex House Residential Bird Courses

SUFFOLK

Aldeburgh: North Warren
Hadleigh: Wolves Wood
Leiston: Minsmere
Orford: Havergate Island
Saxmundham: Minsmere

17

Camping & Caravanning

Camping and caravanning have long been enjoyed by families and individuals of all ages as an inviting way of getting out into the countryside. The Camping and Caravanning Club will supply details about membership and their activities on request.

The Camping and Caravanning Club
G A Cubitt (Director General)
Greenfield House
Westwood Way
Coventry
☎ 0203 694995

CAMBRIDGESHIRE

Cambridge: Great Shelford Camping and Caravanning Club Site; Highfield Farm Camping and Caravanning Club Site; Roseberry Tourist Park
Godmanchester: Park Lane (Touring)
Waterbeach: Landbeach Marina Park

ESSEX

Brentwood: Kelvedon Hatch Camping and Caravanning Site
Brightlingsea: Caravan Club
Burnham-on-Crouch: Creeksea Place Caravan Park; Silver Road Caravan Park
Canvey Island: Kings Holiday Park
Clacton-on-Sea: Brook Farm Caravan Park; Highfield Holiday Park; Hutleys Caravan Park; Leisure Glades Touring Park; Point Clear Holiday Park; Seawick Holiday Lido Ltd; Tower Caravan Park; Valley Farm Caravan Park
Colchester: Colchester Camping; Colchester Camping Caravan Park; King's Vineyard
Epping: Debden House Camp Site
Halstead: Gosfield Lake Caravan Park
Harlow: Roydon Mill Caravan Park
Harwich: Greenacres Caravan Park
Maldon: Barrow Marsh Camping Site; Beacon Hill Leisure Park; St Lawrence Caravans
Manningtree: Strangers Home Inn
Southend-on-Sea: Hayes Farm Caravan Park; Lansdowne Country Club; Riverside Village Holiday Park
Walton-on-the-Naze: Naze Marine Holiday Park; Willows Caravan Park
West Mersea: Waldegraves Farm Holiday Park

SUFFOLK

Lowestoft: Beach Farm Caravan Park; Touring Caravan Park
Saxmundham: Lakeside Caravan Park

Cricket

Cricket conjures up images of English village greens on lazy Sunday afternoons in summer for people throughout the world. The tradition of county cricket in England is long and distinguished and can be appreciated and enjoyed by a visit to any of the county grounds. You might even be lucky enough to see some records shattered if the summer of 1991 is as long and dry as that of 1990.

ESSEX

Chelmsford: Essex County Cricket Club

Cycling

Cycling – what better way to explore the eastern counties. This is certainly cycling country with its flat landscape and network of winding roads to entice you from village to village – gentle touring countryside for the solo or tandem cyclist. Cycles are often available for hire, several hire shops are listed in this guide and others may be listed in leaflets available from the Tourist Information Centres who also produce maps and cycle routes for many areas. Some of the cycling holiday centres will provide a luggage porter and many offer cycling weekends to give you a taste of the 'cyclers view' of the countryside – a good introduction.

The Cyclists' Touring Club, their address is below, will provide information about touring and local cycling groups as well as technical and legal information.

The Cyclists' Touring Club
69 Meadrow
Godalming
Surrey
☎ 04868 7217

CAMBRIDGESHIRE

Cambridge: Armada Cycles; Town Centre
Huntingdon: Solec
Peterborough: Surface Watersports

ESSEX

Braintree: Braintree District Council Routes

Castle Hedingham: Four Seasons Cycling Holidays
Colchester: Dorian Tours
Dedham: Flatford Mill Field Centre
Harlow: Harlow Cycling Club; Harlow Velodrome
Saxmundham: Byways Bicycle Centre

NORFOLK

Hunstanton: A E Wallis
Kings Lynn: Norfolk Cycling Holidays
Wroxham: Just Pedalling

Fishing

Fishing is divided into coarse fishing, game fishing and sea fishing.

Coarse fishing is very popular, the species usually caught are bream, carp, chub, dace, gudgeon, perch, pike, roach, rudd and tench. There are many fine opportunities for excellent coarse fishing in the eastern counties, the Broads being particularly good. The close season for coarse fishing is between March 15th and June 15th. Permission in the form of a rod licence is necessary from the water authority in charge of the water you are planning to fish, these are usually obtainable from local tackle shops and are issued by the National Rivers Authority for rivers and by the Regional Water Company for still waters such as lakes and reservoirs. After obtaining the rod licence permission must be obtained from the owner of the water, this might be an angling club in which case it is usual to pay a membership fee or it might mean buying a ticket, again local tackle shops are usually the best places to enquire about water ownership.

The eastern counties are not noted for their game fishing waters but there are opportunities to fish for trout at some of the region's reservoirs. The close season for trout lasts from October 1st to March 24th and for salmon between November 1st and January 31st although these could vary depending on the different water authorities. The miles of coastline that form the eastern boundary of Norfolk, Suffolk and Essex provide excellent opportunities for sea fishing trips.

General information, licences and leaflets are available from the National Rivers Authority, Anglian Region, their address is listed below. The National Anglers' Council will also provide information about fishing in the area.

National Rivers Authority Anglian Region
Information Unit
Kingfisher House
Goldhay Way
Orton Goldhay
Peterborough
☎ 0733 371811

National Anglers' Council
11 Cowgate
Peterborough
☎ 0733 54084

CAMBRIDGESHIRE

COARSE FISHING
Cambridge: River Ouse
Ely: River Ouse
Godmanchester: River Ouse; Stanjays Tackle Shop
Huntingdon: Hinchingbrooke Country Park; Grafham Water; Rivers Ouse and Nene; Tim's Tackle
March: River Nene
Peterborough: River Nene
Ramsey: River Nene
St Ives: River Ouse; Gravel Pits
St Neots: River Ouse; Little Paxton Gravel Pits
Wisbech: River Nene

GAME FISHING
Huntingdon: Grafham Water

ESSEX

COARSE FISHING
Basildon: Berwick Ponds: Cobblers Mead Lake; Old Hall Lake; Stanford-le-Hope
Braintree: Rivers Blackwater and Pant; The Right Angle Tackle Shop
Brentwood: Moor Hall Farm; South Weald Lakes
Chelmsford: Boreham; Danbury Park Lakes
Clacton-on-Sea: Lake Walk; Brian Dean Tackle Shop
Coggeshall: River Stour at Bures; P Emson Tackle Shop
Colchester: Birch Hall Lake; Layer Pits
Dedham: River Stour at Dedham; Flatford Mill and Nayland
Epping: Epping Forest
Great Dunmow: Roding
Halstead: Gosfield Lake
Harlow: Rivert Stort; Roydon; Ryemeads
Maldon: River Blackwater; Beeleigh Lock; Chigborough Gravel Pits; Railway Pond; Totham Pit; Totham Reservoir

Fishing

Manningtree: River Stour
Southend-on-Sea: Eastwood Pit; Essex Carp Fishery; Shoebury Park Lake
Witham: Witham Lake; Bovington Mere; Hatfield Peverel; River Stour; Rivenhall Lake, Kelvedon

GAME FISHING

Chelmsford: Hanningfield Reservoir
Colchester: Ardleigh Reservoir Trout Fishery
Maldon: Chigborough Trout Fishery; Chigborough Gravel Pits

SEA FISHING

Burnham-on-Crouch: Creeksea
Clacton-on-Sea
Harwich
Southend-on-Sea
Walton-on-the-Naze

NORFOLK

COARSE FISHING

Aylsham: Bure Valley Lakes
Cromer: Felbrigg Hall Lake, Gunton Lake
Diss: Diss Mere; River Waveney; Zoe's Tackle Shop
Fakenham: River Yare; Willsmore Lake
Great Yarmouth: Ormesby; River Yare
Kings Lynn: River Ouse
North Walsham: Norfolk Broads
Norwich: Norfolk Broads and River Yare
Thetford: River Ouse

GAME FISHING
East Dereham: Bintree Mill Trout Fishery; Roosting Hills Trout Fishery; Tannery House Fishery

SEA FISHING
Cromer
Hunstanton
Sheringham

SUFFOLK

COARSE FISHING

Aldeburgh: River Alde
Beccles: River Waveney
Bungay: Broome Pits; Bungay Cherry Tree Angling Club; River Waveney
Bury St Edmunds: Rivers Stour, Colne, Blackwater, Chelmer and Crouch
Eye: River Waveney
Ipswich: Alton Water; River Stour
Kessingland: River Waveney
Lowestoft: River Waveney
Mildenhall: River Lark
Needham Market: Needham Lake
Saxmundham: Henham Dairy Ponds; River Alde
Sudbury: River Stour
Woodbridge: River Deben

GAME FISHING

Bungay: Halcyon Lake Fishery
Saxmundham: River Wang at Peasenhall (trout)

SEA FISHING

Aldeburgh
Felixstowe
Lowestoft
Southwold

Football

Football has always been a popular sport both to play and to watch. This popularity has reached unparalleled proportions in recent years with professional players reaching the status previously accorded only to stars of the screen or the pop world. Always colourful and often exciting the league teams are worth a visit one Saturday afternoon - you might well be watching a soccer star of the future in action!

CAMBRIDGESHIRE

Cambridge: Cambridge United
Peterborough: Peterborough United

ESSEX

Colchester: Colchester United
Southend-on-Sea: Southend United

NORFOLK

Norwich: Norwich City

SUFFOLK

Ipswich: Ipswich Town

Golf

Golf is a relaxing and increasingly popular sport for a wide range of people. The golf clubs listed welcome visitors but it is advisable that you contact the club in advance of playing in order to check if they have any restrictions - some require a handicap certificate or will only accept visitors who are members of another club. It is also worthwhile checking what the fees and hire charges are and what facilities are available. Most clubs have a pro-shop on the course where clubs and other equipment can be hired and the professional will give tuition.

CAMBRIDGESHIRE

Cambridge: Cambridgeshire Moat House Hotel Golf Club; Girton Golf Club; The Gog Magog Golf Club
Ely: Ely City Golf Course
March: March Golf Club
Peterborough: Burghley Park Golf Club; Milton Golf Club; Orton Meadows Golf Course; Thorpe Wood Golf Course
Ramsey: Ramsey Golf Club
St Ives: St Ives Golf Club
St Neots: Abbotsley Golf and Squash Club; St Neots Golf Club

ESSEX

Basildon: Basildon Golf Club; Basildon Golf Course; Aquatels
Braintree: Braintree Golf Club; Towerlands Golf Club

Brentwood: Bentley Golf and Country Club; Hartswood Golf Course; Orsett Park Golf Club; Thorndon Park Golf Club; Upminster Golf Course; Warley Park Golf Club
Burnham-on-Crouch: Burnham-on-Crouch Golf Club
Canvey Island: Boyce Hill Golf Club; Castle Point Golf Club
Chelmsford: Channels Golf Club; Three Rivers Golf Club; Widford Golf Course
Clacton-on-Sea: Clacton-on-Sea Golf Club
Colchester: Birch Grove Golf Club; Colchester Golf Club; Stoke-by-Nayland Golf Club
Epping: Chigwell Golf Club; High Beech Golf Club; Theydon Bois Golf Club
Frinton-on-Sea: Frinton Golf Club; The Club House

Grays: Belhus Park Golf Club
Harlow: Canon's Brook Golf Club; Four Provinces Driving Range
Harwich: Harwich Golf Club
Maldon: Bunsay Downs; Maldon Golf Club; Quietwaters Golf Club; Three Rivers Country Club; Warren Golf Club
Saffron Walden: Saffron Walden Golf Club
Southend-on-Sea: Ballards Gore Golf Club; Belfairs Golf Club; Rochford Hundred Golf Club; Thorpe Hall Golf Club

NORFOLK

Brancaster: Royal West Norfolk Golf Club
Caister-on-Sea: Great Yarmouth and Caister Golf Club
Cromer: Links Country Park Golf Club; Royal Cromer Golf Club
Diss: Diss Golf Club
Downham Market: Ryston Park Golf Club
East Dereham: Dereham Golf Club
Fakenham: Fakenham and District Golf Club
Great Yarmouth: Gorleston Golf Club; Great Yarmouth and Caister Golf Club

Hunstanton: Hunstanton Golf Club
Kings Lynn: Granary Golf Club; King's Lynn Golf Club; Middleton Hall
Mundesley: Mundesley Golf Club
Norwich: Costessey Park Golf Course; Eaton Golf Club; Norwich Golf Course; Royal Norfolk Golf Club
Sheringham: Sheringham Golf Club
Swaffham: Swaffham Golf Club
Thetford: Thetford Golf Club

SUFFOLK

Aldeburgh: Aldeburgh Golf Course
Beccles: Wood Valley Golf Club
Bungay: Bungay and Waveney Valley Golf Club
Bury St Edmunds: Bury St Edmunds Golf Club; Flempton Golf Club; Fornham Park Golf and Country Club; Royal Worlington Golf Club
Felixstowe: Felixstowe Ferry Golf Club
Haverhill: Haverhill Golf Club Ltd
Ipswich: Ipswich Golf Club; Rushmere Golf Club
Lowestoft: Rookney Park Golf Club
Newmarket: Newmarket Golf Course
Southwold: Southwold Golf Club
Stowmarket: Stowmarket Golf Club
Sudbury: Newton Green Golf Club
Woodbridge: Waldringfield Heath Golf Club; Woodbridge Golf Club

Horse Racing

Horse racing is a sport enjoyed by many but riding is not always the way in which race lovers participate, watching and betting are very often the form their involvement takes. The eastern counties can boast a racing heartland in Newmarket where the Racecourse and the nearby National Stud Museum are world famous. It is also home to the National Horseracing Museum and the Jockey Club, founded in 1751 and the controlling body for British racing. A 'day at the races' can be enjoyed by all at any of the regions racecourses.

CAMBRIDGESHIRE

Huntingdon: The Racecourse

ESSEX

Colchester: Marks Tey Racecourse

NORFOLK

Fakenham: The Racecourse
Great Yarmouth: The Racecourse

SUFFOLK

Newmarket: July Racecourse; Rowley Mile Racecourse; The National Stud

Horse Riding

Riding is a very popular pursuit in Britain and there are many riding schools and equestrian centres throughout the eastern region offering a range of facilities from residential instructional holidays to basic instruction and horse and pony hire. Some centres specialise in trail riding, some place a greater emphasis on horse care and stable management whilst others provide courses on a variety of equestrian skills such as show jumping, cross country and side saddle. The range of facilities provided may include an indoor school, a dressage ring or a cross country course. To discover more about the schools and riding in general you should contact the British Horse Society, address below, who will send you detailed information on request as well as a list of their many publications.

British Horse Society
British Equestrian Centre
Stoneleigh
Kenilworth
Warwickshire
☎ 0203 696697

Huntingdon: Great Gransden; Mill Cottage Riding and Livery Stables
March: Knightsend Farm
Peterborough: Lynch Farm Equitation Centre
Ramsey: Ramsey St Marys

CAMBRIDGESHIRE

Cambridge: Broadway Farm; Gransden Hall Riding School; Haggis Farm Stables; New Farm Stables; Park House Stables Ltd; Sawston Riding School; The Windmill Stables

ESSEX

Basildon: Longwood Equestrian Centre
Billericay: Brook Farm Equestrian Centre; De Beauvoir Farm Livery Yard; Park Lane Riding and Livery Stables

Braintree: Rayne Riding Centre; Wethersfield Riding Stables
Brentwood: Folkes Farm Riding and Livery Stables; Foxhound Riding School Ltd; Lillyputts Equestrian Centre
Burnham-on-Crouch: Medway Riding Centre; Elmwood Equestrian Centre
Chelmsford: Hill Farm
Colchester: Colchester Riding School; Park Farm Riding and Livery Centre
Epping: Epping Forest; Woodredon Riding School
Finchingfield: Moor End Stables
Harlow: Churchgate Farm
Saffron Walden: Brook Farm Equestrian Centre
Southend-on-Sea: Belfairs Riding School
Waltham Abbey: High Beech Riding School
Witham: Glebe Equestrian Centre

Aylsham: Rectory Road Riding School
Cromer: West Runton Riding Stables

Diss: Reeves Hall; Rosebrook Farm
Fakenham: North Norfolk Riding Centre
Great Yarmouth: Belton Riding Centre; Hillcrest Riding School Ltd; Willow Farm Riding School
Hunstanton: Home Farm Riding Stables
King's Lynn: Runcton Hall Stud
Lowestoft: Pakefield Riding School
Mundesley: Rose-Acre Riding Stables
Norwich: Newin Equestrian Centre; Salhouse Equestrian Centre; Strumpshaw Riding Centre
Thetford: Hockwold Lodge Riding School; Stanbrook Riding Centre

SUFFOLK

Beccles: Barnby Training Centre
Clare: The Stoke-by-Clare Equitation Centre
Felixstowe: Kembroke Hall Riding School; Tollgate Livery Centre
Ipswich: Newton Hall Equitation Centre
Lowestoft: Pakefield Riding Centre
Woodbridge: Poplar Park Equestrian Centre

Orienteering

Orienteering is a wonderful way to get out into the countryside no matter what your age or level of fitness. You can run, jog or walk as you read your map and choose your route to the red and white markers. You can go solo or share your experiences with friends and family – there's a course for everyone and groups of two and four are welcome on beginners courses. It costs very little and you can try it out at one of the permanent orienteering courses. If you like maps, fresh air and exploring the countryside then this could be the leisure activity for you. The British Orienteering Federation, address below, will supply you with details of clubs and future events as well as a list of the permanent orienteering courses around the country.

British Orienteering Federation
Riversdale
Dale Road North
Darley Dale
Matlock
Derbyshire
☎ 0629 734042

CAMBRIDGESHIRE

Huntingdon: West Anglian Orienteering Club

ESSEX

Colchester: Essex Stragglers
Southend-on-Sea: Havering and South Essex Orienteering Club
Waltham Abbey: Lee Valley Park

NORFOLK

Holt: Holt Country Park
King's Lynn: Wash Orienteers
Norwich: Mousehold Heath; Norwich Orienteering Club

SUFFOLK

Brandon: Brandon Country Park
Framlingham: Suffolk Orienteering Club

Tennis

Britain might not have produced a top-class tennis player in recent years but that cannot be attributed to a lack of facilities. There are excellent indoor and outdoor courts, floodlit all-weather courts and expert tuition is also available. Complete beginners to experienced players concentrating on advanced techniques are catered for by the professional coaches in some of the coaching programmes. There are public tennis courts, usually hard, in most parks, recreation areas and leisure centres. You can usually hire them for a small fee and only have to turn up to play.

For anyone interested in lawn tennis the Lawn Tennis Association will supply you with information about their clubs and play opportunities if you approach them at the address below.

Lawn Tennis Association
J C U James (Secretary)
The Queen's Club
West Kensington
London
☎ 071 385 2366

Tennis and Rackets Association
Brigadier A D Myrtle (C.B., C.B.E.)
c/o The Queens Club
Palliser Road
London
☎ 071 381 4746

CAMBRIDGESHIRE

Cambridge: Cambridge Indoor Tennis Centre; Cambridge Lawn Tennis Club; Christ's Pieces; Jesus Green; Lammas Land; Queen Edith's Way
Peterborough: Court Tennis Centre

ESSEX

Brentwood: Clearview
Southend: Chalkwell Park; Priory Park

NORFOLK

Norwich: Norwich Sports Village

SUFFOLK

Woodbridge: Deben Junior Tennis Club

Walking & Rambling

Walking, rambling or, perhaps, ambling will provide everyone, no matter what their age, with the opportunity to discover the charms of the countryside and the country inns that provide ideal stopping places for refreshments. The pace is entirely up to the walker and the route could be one selected from the OS map or one suggested in any of the innumerable books and leaflets of walks and nature trails. Many popular routes are signposted and footpaths, byways and bridlepaths have been linked in certain areas to form long distance routes which are well marked and easy to follow. The local Tourist Information Centres usually have a good selection of leaflets on local walks and if you would like to join a planned programme of walks the Ramblers' Association will provide you with details of their activities and club walks. The Long Distance Walkers Association will provide OS maps and guidebooks for recommended walks on request.

The Ramblers' Assocation
1/5 Wandsworth Road
London
☎ 071 582 6878

Long Distance Walkers Association
Mr P Dyson (Secretary)
30 Park Avenue
Roundhay
Leeds
West Yorkshire
☎ 0532 657029

CAMBRIDGESHIRE

Cambridge: Coe Fen and Paradise Nature Trails; Devil's Dyke; Gog Magog Hills; Roman Road Circular Walk; Shepreth Riverside Walk; Wimpole Way
Ely: Bishops Way; Ely-Little Thetford-Ely; Ely to Witchford; Roswell Pits
Godmanchester: Port Holme Meadow
Huntingdon: Huntingdon Amble/Town Trails; Ouse Valley Long Distance Footpath
Linton: Roman Walk
March: Hereward Way; Woodman's Way
Peterborough: Circular Walks; Nene Way; Torpel Way
St Neots: River Walk

ESSEX

Basildon: Basildon Greenway; Basildon Nature Trail; Crays Hill Circular Walk
Chelmsford: Backwarden Nature Reserve; Hanningfield Reservoir
Chipping Ongar: St Peter's Way
Clare: St Peter's Way
Colchester: Essex Area Hundred Mile Walk; Roman River Valley Conservation Zone
Dedham: Constable Trail; Painters Way
Epping: Epping Forest Centenary Walk; Epping Forest Conservation Centre; Essex Way; Hatfield Forest Nature Trail; Three Forests Way
Great Dunmow: Rayne to Dunmow Railway Walk
Harlow: Harcamlow Way
Maldon: Dengie Coastal Walks
Walton-on-the-Naze: Naze Nature Trail

NORFOLK

Aylsham: Weavers Way
Cromer: Norfolk Coast Path; Weavers Way
Diss: Circular Walk
Great Yarmouth: Around Norfolk Walk; Peddars Way
Hunstanton: Peddars Way
Kings Lynn: Wash Coast Path
North Walsham: Bacton Wood Forest Walks
Norwich: Marriott's Way; Norfolk's Changing Heritage
Saxthorpe: Mannington Walks
Sheringham: Kelling Heath Nature Trail; Pretty Corner Walks
Thetford: King's Forest Trail; Santon Downham Forest Trail

SUFFOLK

Bungay: The Bigod Way
Hadleigh: Railway Walk
Halesworth: St Cross Farm Walks
Ipswich: Gipping Valley Walks; Shotley Peninsula
Kessingland: Suffolk Coast Path
Lavenham: Railway Walk
Long Melford: Railway Walk
Needham Market: Gipping Valley Walks
Lowestoft: Angles Way; Waveney District Walks
Orford: Orford Walks
Stowmarket: Gipping Valley Walks
Sudbury: Constable Trail; Painters Way; Sudbury Walk

Antiques

Paintings, furniture, porcelain, prints, decorative items, whatever you are particularly interested in from previous centuries – either as a serious collector or as an addicted browser – there are plenty of antique centres throughout the region. Many of them are housed in lovely buildings and situated in delightful, picturesque villages. For those who like the excitement of the auction room there are several auction rooms around the region where bargains might be found!

CAMBRIDGESHIRE

ART GALLERIES

Cambridge: Cambridge Darkroom; Gallery on the Cam; Holographic Exhibition; Kettles Yard
Peterborough: Peterborough Arts Centre

ESSEX

ANTIQUES

Coggeshall: Country Heritage Antiques
Colchester: Trinity Antiques Centre
Southend-on-Sea: Battlesbridge Antiques Centre

ART GALLERIES

Clacton-on-Sea: St Osyth's Priory
Colchester: The Minories; Vineyard Gallery
Harlow: The Playhouse
Southend-on-Sea: Beecroft Art Gallery; Delta Fine Arts Gallery; Leigh Heritage Centre

NORFOLK

ANTIQUES

Aylsham: Weekly Auction
Fakenham: Flea Market; Auction

ART GALLERIES

Great Yarmouth: Great Yarmouth Museum Exhibition Galleries
Norwich: Norwich Gallery; Sainsbury Centre for Visual Arts
Thetford: The Art Gallery

SUFFOLK

ANTIQUES

Beccles: Weekly Auction
Saxmundham: Auctions

ART GALLERIES

Aldeburgh: Snape Maltings
Bury St Edmunds: Market Cross
Halesworth: Halesworth Gallery
Ipswich: John Russell Gallery; Wolsey Art Gallery
Sudbury: Gainsborough's House; Laurimore Gallery

St Osyth's Priory, Clacton-on-Sea

Gainsborough's House, Sudbury

Aquariums

For the lovers of the 'deep' there are sea-life centres where it is possible to experience the unique magic of the underwater world with deep sea creatures only inches away. A new centre opened at Great Yarmouth in July, 1990, and at Hunstanton you can walk under water through an ocean tunnel to explore over twenty natural underwater settings.

ESSEX

Clacton-on-Sea: Pier

NORFOLK

Diss: Waveney Fish Farm
Great Yarmouth: Sea Life Centre
Hunstanton: Sea Life Centre

Arts & Crafts

Arts and crafts are richly represented in the eastern counties from dolls houses to crystal glass, stained glass to designer printed textiles, black sheep knitwear to fine needlework, exhibitions of local artists to local potters seen at work. There are craft societies such as the renowned Suffolk Craft Society, their annual exhibition draws shoppers from America and their produce, it is thought, will become 'the antiques of the future'.

CAMBRIDGESHIRE

Cambridge: Black Sheep Shop; Cambridge Brass Rubbing Centre; Eastern Counties Sheepskin Tannery Shop
Ely: Steeplegate Ltd

ESSEX

Coggeshall: Colne Valley Arts
Colchester: The Minories; Vineyard Gallery
Dedham: Dedham Art and Craft Centre
Maldon: The Friary Arts Centre

NORFOLK

Aylsham: Black Sheep Ltd
Blakeney: Made in Cley
Cromer: Alby Crafts; Old Forge Craft Gallery
Diss: The Particular Pottery
Holt: The Handworkers' Market; Wansbeck Dolls Houses
Hunstanton: Norfolk Lavender Ltd.
North Walsham: Cat Pottery

Norwich: The Dolls' House; Towerham Craft Centre; Wensom Lodge
Thetford: The Art Gallery
Walsingham: The Textile Centre
Wroxham: Willow Farm Dried Flowers

SUFFOLK

Aldeburgh: Snape Maltings; Suffolk Craft Society Exhibition
Bury St Edmunds: Craft at the Suffolk Barn
Hadleigh: Playthings of the Past
Leiston: Aldringham Craft Market
Southwold: The Parish Lantern
Stowmarket: Ascot House Crafts

Country Parks

Clare Country Park

There has been a steadily growing awareness of the importance of retaining areas of countryside for recreational use and this has led to the designation of many areas of ancient and new woodland, downland, lakes, parkland and heathland as country parks. Ranging in size from four to nine hundred acres, they offer country walks, fishing, horse rides, sailing, water sports, picnicking and nature reserves – plenty for everyone to enjoy.

CAMBRIDGESHIRE

Cambridge: Wandlebury
Huntingdon: Grafham Water; Hinchingbrooke Country Park
Peterborough: Ferry Meadows

ESSEX

Basildon: Langdon Hills; Wat Tyler Country Park
Brentwood: Thorndon Park; Weald
Chelmsford: Danbury; Marsh Farm
Coggeshall: Chalkney Woods
Epping: Epping Forest
Halstead: Gosfield Park
Great Dunmow: Garnetts Wood
Halstead: Gosfield park
Manningtree: Mistley Environmental Centre

Southend-on-Sea: Belfairs Park; Grove Woods; Hadleigh Castle; Hockley Woods

NORFOLK

Cromer: The Norfolk Shire Horse Centre
Great Yarmouth: Fritton Lake Country Park
Holt: Holt Country Park
King's Lynn: Sandringham Country Park

SUFFOLK

Brandon: Brandon Country Park
Bury St Edmunds: Nowton Park; West Stow Country Park
Clare: Clare Country Park

Factory Tours

The processes involved in the production of many well-known objects, both large and small, are fascinating to see. Some factories allow visitors to tour and see the stages involved in the manufacture of the finished item. In the eastern region there are opportunities to see the manufacture of cars at opposite ends of the market – the sporty Lotus or the fleet Ford motor car. Glass-blowing and crystal making can be seen at close quarters, a brewery will reveal a secret or two and allow you to taste the brew and there is even a rake factory to tour – a must for the avid gardener!

ESSEX

Brentwood: Ford Motor Company
Maldon: Bradwell Power Station;
   Malden Crystal Salt Co

NORFOLK

Holt: Langham Glass
Kings Lynn: Caithness Crystal
Norwich: Lotus Cars

SUFFOLK

Bury St Edmunds: Rake Factory
Leiston: Sizewell Power Station
Lowestoft: Lowestoft Fishing Industry
   and Harbour Tour; Oulton Road
   Brewery; Raglan Smokehouse
Woodbridge: RAF Bentwaters

Farm Parks

Farm Parks will allow you to spend 'a day down on the farm' and see the farm at work. You can watch the cows being milked and the milk being pasteurised and bottled, see the calves, pigs and chickens, watch the magnificent, gentle Suffolk Punch Shire horses working, see a rare Red Poll cow and other rare breeds or wander around collections of farm machinery and horse-drawn waggons – a wonderful way to see the countryside in action.

CAMBRIDGESHIRE

Cambridge: Wimpole Home Farm
March: Stags Holt Farm Park
Peterborough: Sacrewell Farm and
   Country Centre

ESSEX

Castle Hedingham: Fullers Dairy Farm
Epping: Hobbs Cross Dairy
Waltham Abbey: Hayes Hill Farm;
   Holyfield Hall Farm

NORFOLK

Hunstanton: Park Farm
Sheringham: Norfolk Shire Horse
   Centre

SUFFOLK

Halesworth: South Elmham Hall
Wickham Market: Easton Farm Park

Festivals & Fairs

The customs, traditions and history of the area live through the festivals and fairs that make the whole region a colourful, lively and fascinating world through the seasons. Everywhere are agricultural shows, county shows, flower festivals, fairs, traction-engine rallies, air displays, regattas, boat shows and music festivals. Many of the smaller events are more than worth a detour and a visit, they reveal much about the villages and towns that foster them and there are several events in this region, the Aldeburgh Music Festival, for example, that draw international support and acclaim.

CAMBRIDGESHIRE

Cambridge: May Week; Footlights Revue; May Bumps; Midsummer Fair; Cambridge Festival; Folk Festival; Bonfire and fireworks; Festival of Nine Lessons and Carols
Duxford: Air Show
Ely: Choral Society Concert; Folk Weekend
Huntingdon: Huntingdon Carnival; Shakespeare at the George
Kimbolton: Firework display
Peterborough: Straw Bear Festival; Shire Horse Show; Stilton Cheese Rolling; Truckfest; East of England Show
St Neots: Carnival; Arts Festival
Wisbech: Rose Fair

ESSEX

Brentwood: North Weald Fighter Meet
Burnham on Crouch: Burnham Week; Carnival Week
Chelmsford: Cathedral Festival
Chipping Ongar: Herb Festival
Colchester: Summer Show; Enterprise Exhibition; Essex History Fair; Military Tattoo; Oyster Feast
Great Dunmow: Dunmow Flitch
Maldon: Barge Match; Heybridge Basin Regatta; Christmas Victorian Evenings
Southend-on-Sea: Festival of Flowers and Craft; Air Show; Historic Transport Rally; Punch and Judy Festival; Raft Race; Carnival; Thames Barge Race; Whitebait Festival; Old Leigh Regatta
Thaxted: Morris Men Weekend
West Mersea: Mersea Regatta

NORFOLK

Cromer: Cromer Carnival
Fakenham: Fakenham Carnival
Kings Lynn: Craft and Art Fair; Festival of Music and the Arts; Norwich Union Carriage Driving Trials; Sandringham Flower Show
Thaxted: Morris Weekend

SUFFOLK

Aldeburgh: Aldeburgh Music Festival; Maltings Proms
Brandon: Forest Heath Arts Festival
Bury St Edmunds: Bury St Edmunds Festival; Cake and Ale Ceremony
Felixstowe: Folk Festival; Deben Week Regatta; Carnival
Hadleigh: Hadleigh Show; Millfield Fete; Deanery Show
Ipswich: East Coast Boat Show; Suffolk Show
Long Melford: Kentwell Hall Tudor Event
Lowestoft: Regatta; Carnival; Sea-Angling Festival
Mildenhall: Forest Heath Arts Festival; Mildenhall Air Fete

Food & Drink

The long farming tradition in East Anglia with its rich soils and long growing season has given it several regional delicacies. There are vineyards with award-winning vintages to try, herbal health drinks and some very fine beers, working mills that produce fresh ground flours, sea-food delicacies such as oysters, whelks, cockles and lobsters, dairy producers with delicious products including ice creams, mustards that are unavailable elsewhere can be found in Norwich, the home of Colmans.

CAMBRIDGESHIRE

Cambridge: Culpepers the Herbalists
Chatteris: Gray's Honey Farm
Linton: Chilford Hundred Vineyard; Culpepers
Wisbech: Elgoods Brewery

ESSEX

Burnham-on-Crouch: Mustard
Colchester: Oysters
Maldon: New Hall Vineyards
Southend-on-Sea: Cockles and whelks; Whitebait
West Mersea: Colchester Oyster Fisheries

NORFOLK

Cromer: Crabs

Diss: Pulham Vineyards
Downham Market: Norfolk Punch
Norwich: Colmans Mustard; Pickering and Son; Samphire
Sheringham: Lobsters
Swaffham: The Norfolk Pickling Centre

SUFFOLK

Clare: Boyton Vineyard; Cavendish Manor Vineyard
Framlingham: Shawsgate Vineyard
Lowestoft: Herrings
Saxmundham: Bruisyard Vineyard and Herb Gardens
Southwold: Adnams and Co
Stowmarket: Aspall Cider
Sudbury: Mauldons Brewery
Woodbridge: Suffolk Cider Company Ltd

Fun Parks

Whether it's waltzers, roller coasters, dodgems or big wheels, the coastal resorts offer all the fun of the fair at their permanent fun park sites. There are rides for the very young and amusements for the not-so-young too – entertainment for all the family.

ESSEX

Clacton-on-Sea: Pier
Southend-on-Sea: Peter Pan's Playground

NORFOLK

Great Yarmouth: Great Yarmouth Pleasure Beach, House of Wax; World of Wax

SUFFOLK

Felixstowe: Charles Manning's Amusement Park

Gardens

Whether on a grand scale and landscaped by Capability Brown or tiny cottage gardens created by the love of successive inhabitants over the years, gardens are always places to inspire and revive the most weary of spirits. A constant tribute to the co-operation of man and nature, a natural painting using the richest possible palette, one that changes with the seasons, gardens satisfy all the senses whilst also harbouring a glorious array of wildlife. The eastern counties have many beautiful gardens, formal and grand, intricate and herbal, rambling and fragrant open for you to explore.

CAMBRIDGESHIRE

Cambridge: Anglesey Abbey; Cambridge University Botanic Garden; Crossing House
Ely: Herb Garden
Huntingdon: Abbots Ripton Hall

ESSEX

Braintree: Saling Hall Garden
Chelmsford: Hyde Hall Garden
Chipping Ongar: Blake Hall Gardens
Colchester: By-Pass Nurseries
Dedham: East Bergholt Lodge
Finchingfield: Spains Hall
Harlow: Mark Hall Gardens
Manningtree: East Bergholt Lodge; The Fens
Saffron Walden: Bridge End Gardens
Southend-on-Sea: Churchill Gardens; Cliff Gardens; Library Gardens; Old World Garden; Warrior Square Garden

NORFOLK

Cromer: Alby Gardens: The Pleasaunce; Wolterton Hall Gardens
Diss: Bressingham Gardens
Great Yarmouth: Fritton lake

Holt: Glavenside Gardens
Kings Lynn: Congham Hall Gardens; Gooderstone Water Gardens; Wellbank's Orchid World
Ludham: How Hill Trust Garden
North Walsham: Rose World
Norwich: Rainthorpe Hall Gardens
Saxthorpe: Mannington Hall Gardens
Sheringham: Sheringham Park
Wells-next-the-Sea: Holkham Park Gardens

SUFFOLK

Bury St Edmunds: Abbey Gardens; The Appleby Rose Garden; Giffords Hall
Felixstowe: Cliff Gardens
Ipswich: Helmingham Hall; Thomson and Morgan Seed Trials
Lavenham: The Priory
Long Melford: Kentwell Hall
Lowestoft: Somerleyton Hall Maze
Needham Market: Blakenham Woodland Garden
Saxmundham: Bruisyard Herb Gardens
Stowmarket: Mickfield Fish and Water Garden Centre
Woodbridge: Letheringham Watermill Gardens

Ornamental gardens at Great Yarmouth

Sheringham Park

Guided Tours

There are many experts to show you the delights of the eastern region. The major cities and towns in East Anglia support Registered Guides who will have attended a training course sponsored by the East Anglia Tourist Board, they can be identified by the 'Blue Badge' they wear. Some of these regional guides also have a regional endorsement, enquire when you are making your booking. Several of the individual historic houses, churches and museums offer their own guided tours, they will give full details of times and duration of tours on application. The East Anglia Tourist Board will provide an information sheet on guiding activities, it is available from the address given below.

East Anglia Tourist Board
Toppesfield Hall
Hadleigh
Ipswich
☎ 0473 822922

CAMBRIDGESHIRE

Cambridge: Cathedral and City Tours; Fitzwilliam Museum; Good Friday Ltd
Ely: Cathedral and City Tours

ESSEX

Colchester: Town Tours
Saffron Walden: Walking Tours

NORFOLK

Kings Lynn: Town Tours
Norwich: City Tours; Dragon Hall Tours

SUFFOLK

Bury St Edmunds: Town Tours; Tours for Groups
Newmarket: Newmarket Equine Tours
Ipswich: Town Tours

King's College, Cambridge

Heritage

Over the years the impregnable forest that bounded the eastern counties was cut and cleared, the fens were drained and successive waves of invaders swept in from land and sea. The Angles and Vikings left their mark as did the Romans and Saxons – there are Roman remains and Saxon burial grounds. There are the keeps and walls of various castles that provide a reminder of the intrigue, rebellion and violence that occurred during different times in the region's past. The region's ecclesiastical past can be seen in the magnificent cathedrals at Ely, Peterborough and Norwich, in the grand abbeys that bear witness to the great power wielded by the abbots for centuries and in the priories where there is often a more romantic story connected with their founding.

CAMBRIDGESHIRE

Cambridge: Castle Mound; Gog Magog Hills and Wandlebury Ring
Duxford: Chapel
Ely: Ely Cathedral
Kimbolton: Kimbolton Castle
Peterborough: Flag Fen; Longthorpe Tower; Peterborough Cathedral; Thorney Abbey Church
Waterbeach: Denny Abbey

ESSEX

Castle Hedingham: Hedingham Castle
Chelmsford: Chelmsford Cathedral
Clacton-on-Sea: St Osyth's Priory
Coggeshall: Abbey; Grange Barn
Colchester: Balkerne Gate; Castle; Roman Walls; St John's Abbey Gateway
Harlow: Harlow Study and Visitors' Centre
Maldon: St Peter's on the Wall
Manningtree: Mistley Towers
Saffron Walden: Priors Hall Barn; The Maze
Southend-on-Sea: Hadleigh Castle
Stansted Mountfichet: Mountfichet Castle
Witham: Cressing Barns

NORFOLK

Blakeney: Guildhall
Cromer: Baconsthorpe Castle
East Dereham: North Elmham Saxon Cathedral and Bishop's Castle
Great Yarmouth: Burgh Castle; Nelson's Monument; St Olave's Priory
King's Lynn: Castle Rising
Ludham: St Benet's Abbey

Norwich: Norwich Castle; Norwich Cathedral; St John's Cathedral; St Peter Mancroft Church
Swaffham: Castle Acre Priory; Castle Acre Village; Cockley Cley Iceni Village
Thetford: Castle; Priory; Thetford Warren Lodge
Walsingham: Shrine of Our Lady of Walsingham; Slipper Chapel; Abbey Grounds
Wells-next-the-Sea: Binham Priory

SUFFOLK

Brandon: Grimes Graves; Heritage Centre; Weeting Castle
Bungay: Castle Ruins
Bury St Edmunds: Abbey; West Stow Anglo-Saxon village

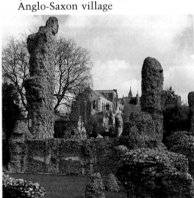

Abbey ruins, Bury St Edmunds

Caister-on-Sea: Roman Town
Clare: Clare Castle; Priory
Framlingham: Castle
Halesworth: South Elmham Minster
Leiston: Abbey
Orford: Butley Priory; Orford Castle
Woodbridge: Sutton Hoo

Historic Buildings

The buildings of the region relect the different influences that have affected the area over the centuries. Mediaeval times saw a proliferation of churches built through the region, financed by the rents, tithes and incomes from first wool and then corn that flowed into the clergy's coffers. Some of these churches are like small-scale cathedrals and many have exquisite features that make each one worth a visit.

CAMBRIDGESHIRE

Cambridge: Anglesey Abbey; College buildings; Great Gransden Post Mill; Great St Mary's Church; King's College Chapel; Lode Watermill; The Round Church; Trumpington Church
Ely: Downfield Windmill
Huntingdon: Houghton Mill
March: St Wendreda's Church
Peterborough: Sacrewell Farm and Country Centre
Ramsey: Ramsey Abbey; Ramsey Abbey Gatehouse
St Ives: Bridge Chapel

ESSEX

Brentwood: Mountnessing Windmill
Brightlingsea: All Saints Church
Chipping Ongar: Greensted Church
Coggeshall: St Peter ad Vincula; White Hart Hotel
Colchester: Bourne Mill; Dutch Quarter; Marquis of Granby; Siege House
Dedham: Bridge Cottage; Flatford Mill; Willie Lott's Cottage
Great Dunmow: Aythorpe Roding Post Mill; Little Easton Church
Harwich: Electric Palace Cinema; Harwich Redoubt
Maldon: All Saints Church; Moot Hall; St Giles Leper Hospital
Manningtree: The Wooden Fender Public House
Saffron Walden: The Eight Bells; The Sun Inn
Southend-on-Sea: Rayleigh Windmill
Stansted Mountfichet: Windmill
Thaxted: John Webb's Windmill; Guildhall
Tilbury: Fort
Waltham Abbey: Abbey Church

NORFOLK

Blakeney: Cley Mill
Diss: Thelnetham Windmill

Downham Market: Denver Windmill
East Dereham: Dereham Windmill; St Nicholas's Church
Great Yarmouth: St Olave's Windpump
Holt: Letheringsett Windmill
Hunstanton: Great Bircham Mill; Snettisham Watermill
Kings Lynn: St Margaret's Church
Ludham: Boardman's Mill; Thurne Dyke Windpump
Mundesley: Stow Mill
Norwich: Dragon Hall; The Guildhall
Wells-next-the-Sea: Holkham Hall
Wymondham: Abbey Church

SUFFOLK

Beccles: St Michael's Church
Bury St Edmunds: Bardwell Windmill; Pakenham Watermill
Framlingham: Saxstead Green Windmill
Hadleigh: The Deanery Tower; The Guildhall; St Mary's Church; Topplesfield Hall
Ipswich: Ancient House Bookshop
Lavenham: Guildhall; Little Hall; The Priory
Long Melford: Holy Trinity Church
Lowestoft: Herringfleet Marsh Mill
Mildenhall: St Mary's Church
Newmarket: Stevens Mill
Sudbury: St Peter's Church
Woodbridge: Buttrums Mill; Woodbridge Tide Mill

Colchester Old Siege House

Historic Houses

Over the centuries the fortunes of the country affected those of the regions and in turn were reflected in the style and grandeur of the houses built. Some included in this guide were the site of an historic event or the dwelling of a famous figure, others represent a family's prestige and a style of architecture. Most exhibit levels of workmanship and decoration that can be marvelled at and appreciated by all who see them.

CAMBRIDGESHIRE

Cambridge: Anglesey Abbey; Wimpole Hall
Godmanchester: Buckden Palace; Island Hall
Huntingdon: Hinchingbrooke House
Peterborough: Elton Hall
Wisbech: Peckover House

ESSEX

Coggeshall: Paycockes; The Fleece
Colchester: Layer Marney Tower
Halstead: Gosfield Hall
Saffron Walden: Audley End House
Southend-on-Sea: The Old House

NORFOLK

Aylsham: Blickling Hall
Cromer: Felbrigg Hall
Downham Market: Welle Manor Hall
East Dereham: Bishop Bonner's Cottage

King's Lynn: Houghton Hall; Sandringham House; Trinity Hospital
Norwich: Rainthorpe Hall
Swaffham: Oxburgh Hall
Wroxham: Beeston Hall

SUFFOLK

Brandon: Elveden Hall
Bury St Edmunds: Hengrave Hall; Ickworth
Halesworth: South Elmham Hall
Ipswich: Christchurch Mansion; Otley Hall
Lavenham: Little Hall
Long Melford: Kentwell Hall; Melford Hall
Lowestoft: Somerleyton Hall
Saxthorpe: Mannington Hall
Stowmarket: Haughley Park
Sudbury: Gainsborough's House

Hinchingbrooke House, Huntingdon

Museums

There are museums covering such diverse interests as polar research, lace, horseracing or mechanical music, some record purely local history whilst others such as the Fitzwilliam in Cambridge are internationally famous. Whatever subject you might have a particular fascination for, there is probably a museum somewere in the eastern counties to broaden your knowledge and feed your interest in the subject.

CAMBRIDGESHIRE

Cambridge: Cambridge and County Folk Museum; Fitzwilliam Museum; Museum of Technology; Scott Polar Research Institute; Sedgwick Museum of Geology; University Museum of Archaeology and Anthropology; University Museum of Classical Archaeology; University Museum of Zoology; Whipple Museum of the History of Science
Chatteris: Chatteris Museum
Duxford: Imperial War Museum
Ely: Ely Museum; Haddenham Farmland Museum; Oliver Cromwell Museum; Prickwillow Engine Museum; Stained Glass Museum; Stretham Beam Engine
Huntingdon: Cromwell Museum
March: March and District Museum
Peterborough: City Museum and Art Gallery
Ramsey: Ramsey Rural Museum
St Ives: Norris Library and Museum
St Neots: Longsands Museum
Wisbech: Fenland Aviation Museum; Wisbech and Fenland Museum

ESSEX

Basildon: National Motorboat Museum; Plotland Trail and Museum
Billericay: Barleylands Farm Museum; Cater Museum
Braintree: Heritage Centre
Burnham-on-Crouch: Burnham-on-Crouch Museum, Mangapps Farm Railway Museum
Canvey Island: Castle Point Transport Museum; Dutch Cottage Museum
Castle Hedingham: Essex Police Collection; Hedingham Castle
Chelmsford: Chelmsford and Essex Musnem
Colchester: Colchester and Essex Museum; Hollytrees; Museum of Natural History; Social History Museum; Tymperleys Clock Museum

Dedham: Sir Alfred Munnings Art Museum; Toy Museum
Epping: Queen Elizabeth's Hunting Lodge
Finchingfield: Guildhall
Grays: Thurrock Local History Museum
Halstead: Brewery Chapel Musem
Harlow: Harlow Museum; Mark Hall Cycle Museum
Harwich: Maritime Museum
Maldon: Agricultural Museum; Jaguar Motor Museum; Maldon Museum; Maritime Centre; Plume Library
Saffron Walden: Audley End House; Saffron Walden Museum
Southend-on-Sea: Battlesbridge Motor Cycle Museum; Central Museum; Leigh Heritage Centre; Prittlewell Priory Museum
Stansted Mountfitchet: Aklowa African Traditional Heritage Village
Thaxted: John Webb's Windmill; Thaxted Guildhall
Tilbury: Coalhouse Fort; Thurrock Riverside Museum
Waltham Abbey: Epping Forest District Museum
Walton-on-the-Naze: Walton Heritage Centre
West Mersea: Mersea Island Museum
Witham: Fossil Hall; Feering and Kelvedon Local History Museum

NORFOLK

Blakeney: Glandford Shell Museum
Caister-on-Sea: Caister Castle Car Collection
Cromer: Alby Lace Museum and Study Centre; Cromer Museum; Lifeboat Musem
Diss: Bressingham Steam Museum; Diss Museum; Strike School
East Dereham: Bishop Bonner's Cottage; Norfolk Rural Life Museum
Fakenham: Museum of Gas and Local History; The Thursford Colleciton; The Forge Museum

Great Yarmouth: Broadland Tractor Museum; Elizabethan House Museum; Maritime Museum for East Anglia; Old Merchant's House; Tolhouse Museum
Kings Lynn: Guildhall of St George; Lynn Museum; Museum of Social History; Regalia Rooms; Wolferton Station
Ludham: Toad Hall Cottage
Norwich: Bridewell Museum; City of Norwich Aviation Museum; Forncett Industrial Steam Museum; John Jarrold Printing Museum; Norwich Castle Museum; Royal Norfolk Regiment Museum; Sainsbury Centre for Visual Arts; St Peter Hungate Church Museum; Station 146 Seeting Airfield Control Tower; Strangers Hall Museum of Domestic Life; Strumpshaw Hall Steam Museum
Sheringham: The Muckleborough Collection
Swaffham: Cockley Cley; Dunham Museum; Swaffham Museum
Thetford: Ancient House Museum

Walsingham: Shirehall Museum
Wells-next-the-Sea: Bygones collection
Wymondham: Heritage Musem

SUFFOLK

Aldeburgh: Moot Hall
Beccles: Beccles and District Museum; William Clowes Print Museum
Bungay: Bungay Museum; Norfolk and Suffolk Aviation Museum
Bury St Edmunds: The Clock Museum; Moyses Hall Museum; Suffolk Regiment Museum
Clare: Ancient House Museum; Sue Ryder Foundation Museum
Dedham: Bridge Cottage; Granary Bygones
Felixstowe: Landguard Fort
Framlingham: 390th Bomb Group Memorial Air Museum; Lanman Museum; Laxfield and District Mueum
Halesworth: Halesworth and District Museum
Haverhill: Haverhill and District Local History Centre
Ipswich: Ipswich Museum
Leiston: The Long Shop
Lowestoft: East Anglia Transport Museum; Lowestoft and East Suffolk Maritime Museum; Lowestoft Museum; Royal Naval Patrol Service Museum
Mildenhall: Mildenhall and District Museum
Newmarket: National Horse Racing Museum
Orford: Dunwich Underwater Exploration Museum
Southwold: Dunwich Museum; Southwold Lifeboat Museum; Southwold Sailors Reading Room
Stowmarket: Cotton Mechanical Music Museum; Museum of East Anglian Life
Sudbury: Gainsborough's House
Wickham Market: Easton Farm Park; Museum of Grocery Shop Bygones
Woodbridge: Woodbridge Museum

Tolhouse Museum, Great Yarmouth

Natural History

The eastern counties are blessed with extensive stretches of wilderness where it is possible to see many rare animals, plants and birds if you can watch quietly. The north Norfolk coast with its extensive salt marshes and sand dunes has a rich variety of coastal plants and birds, the Broads are home to some of Britain's rarest wildlife including the bittern, the rare swallowtail butterfly, and the Norfolk hawker dragonfly whilst the Fens are home to many varieties of wetland plants and insects.

The region is scattered with nature reserves that often have trails, hides and information centres, some also have guides. There are several animal sanctuaries, unusual animal collections in natural surroundings and conservation centres that are fascinating to visit.

CAMBRIDGESHIRE

Cambridge: Coe Fen and Paradise Nature Trails
Ely: Roswell Pits; Wicken Fen
Godmanchester: Wood Green Animal Shelter
Huntingdon: Aversley Wood; Holme Fen; Monks Wood and Woodwalton Fen
March: Welney Wildfowl Refuge
Peterborough: Nene Washes
St Neots: Little Paxton
Wisbech: Wildfowl and Wetland Trust

ESSEX

Basildon: Nature Trail
Billericay: Norsey Wood
Brentwood: Norsey Wood Trail
Burnham-on-Crouch: Bradwell Field Studies and Sailing Centre
Chelmsford: Backwarden Nature Reserve Trail
Colchester: Abberton Reservoir; Fingringhoewick Naure Reserve; Roman River Valley Reserve
Harlow: Maymeads Marsh Conservation Area; Parndon Wood Nature Reserve
Harwich: Stour Wood and Copperas Bay
Maldon: Northey Island
Southend-on-Sea: Leigh Mudflats
Stansted Mountfitchet: Hatfield Forest
Walton on the Naze: John Weston Reserve; Naze Nature Trail
West Mersea: Colne Estuary

NORFOLK

Blakeney: Blakeney Point Nature Reserve; Cley Marshes
Brancaster: Titchwell
Holt: Holt Lowes
Kings Lynn: Sandringham Nature Trail

Ludham: Broadland Conservation Centre; Hickling Broad; How Hill Nature Reserve
Norwich: Redwings Horse Sanctuary; Stumpshaw Fen; Surlingham and Rockland Marshes
Thetford: Thetford Forest

SUFFOLK

Aldeburgh: North Warren
Brandon: Thetford Chase
Bungay: The Otter Trust
Clare: Clare Country Park
Lowestoft: Carlton Marshes
Saxmundham: Suffolk Wildlife Trust
Southwold: Dunwich Heath; Minsmere

Ornamental Parks

Ornamental parks provide colourful, fragrant recreational areas where you can take a stroll or take a seat and watch the world go by. They vary in size, elaboration and theme from town to town but always provide pleasure to those passing through them and to the wildlife who make them their habitat.

ESSEX

Chelmsford: Hylands Park
Colchester: Castle Park
Great Dunmow: Garnetts Wood
Harlow: Harlow Town Park; Latton Bush Park and Woods; Mulberry Green Nursery; Peldon Road Park; The Moorhen
Maldon: Promenade

Southend-on-Sea: Blenheim Park; Chalkwell Park; Priory Park

SUFFOLK

Bury St Edmunds: Ickworth Park
Ipswich: Suffolk Water Park
Saxmundham: Lakeside Common Park

Piers & Promenades

Piers and promenades are a feature of the seaside towns that grew into popular resorts during the Victorian and Edwardian eras. The piers offer traditional seaside amusements, miniature railways, fun fairs for the children and some have theatres that open for the summer season. The promenades along the seafronts often have delightful flower displays, they offer perfect vantage points to sit and watch the world go by.

ESSEX

Clacton-on-Sea: Clacton Pier
Southend-on-Sea: Southend Pier
Walton-on-the-Naze: Walton Pier

NORFOLK

Cromer: Cromer Pier

Clacton Pier, Clacton-on-Sea

Railways

Very few of us fail to respond to the delights of steam railways, entwined as they are with tales of our childhood. The heartening hoots they make as they puff by bring storybook pictures alive and for those enthralled by Thomas the Tank Engine he is chugging round the Nene Valley at Easter to take you for a ride.

CAMBRIDGESHIRE

Peterborough: Nene Valley Railway

ESSEX

Burnham-on-Crouch: Mangapps Farm Railway Museum
Castle Hedingham: Colne Valley Railway
Colchester: East Anglian Railway Museum
Maldon: Promenade Park Railway
Saffron Walden: Audley End Miniature Railway

NORFOLK

Aylsham: Bure Valley Railway
Diss: Bressingham Narrow Gauge Railway

Holt: North Norfolk Railway
Norwich: Norfolk Wildlife Park Railway
Sheringham: North Norfolk Railway
Walsingham: Wells and Walsingham Light Railway
Wells-next-the-Sea: Wells and Walsingham Light Railway
Wroxham: Barton House Railway

SUFFOLK

Kessingland: Suffolk Wildlife and Rare Breeds Park Railway
Lowestoft: East Anglia Transport Museum; Somerleyton Hall Railway

Colne Valley Railway, Castle Hedingham

43

Theatres

The eastern counties are well supplied with theatres; the coastal resorts have a wide range of summer season shows and the major towns of the region produce many innovative and acclaimed productions as well as the more familiar and much loved classics.

CAMBRIDGESHIRE

Cambridge: ADC Theatre; Arts Theatre; The Cambridge Playroom; Mumford Theatre
Peterborough: Cresset Theatre; Key Theatre
Wisbech: Angles Theatre

ESSEX

Basildon: Towngate Theatre
Chelmsford: Civic Theatre; Cramphorn Theatre
Clacton-on-Sea: Prince's Theatre; West Cliff Theatre
Colchester: Arts Centre; Mercury Theatre; University Theatre
Grays: Thameside Theatre
Halstead: Halstead Empire
Harlow: The Playhouse
Southend-on-Sea: Cliffs Pavilion; Palace Theatre

NORFOLK

Cromer: The Pier Pavilion
Great Yarmouth: Brittania Theatre; Hippodrome; Royalty Theatre; St George's Theatre; Wally Windmill's Playhouse; Wellington Pier Theatre; Winter Garden Theatre
Hunstanton: The Princess Theatre
Kings Lynn: Fermoy Centre
Norwich: Arts Centre; Maddermarket Theatre; Puppet Theatre; Theatre Royal
Sheringham: The Little Theatre

SUFFOLK

Bury St Edmunds: Theatre Royal
Felixstowe: Spa Pavilion Theatre
Ipswich: Wolsey Theatre
Lowestoft: Marina Theatre
Southwold: Southwold Summer Theatre
Sudbury: The Quay Theatre

Theme Parks

American-style magic where there is everything you can ride or climb on, scary rides and all the shows at Lowestoft or animated reality in an original children's adventure park that includes Badger's house from 'Wind in the Willows' and futuristic themes from 'Masters of the Universe' at Southend-on-Sea – unforgettable days out for children and many adults too!

ESSEX

Southend-on-Sea: Never Never Land

NORFOLK

Great Yarmouth: Merrivale Model Village; The Venetian Waterways

SUFFOLK

Lowestoft: Pleasurewood Hills

Never Never Land, Southend-on-Sea

Wildlife Parks

Many people have directed their love of animals and wildlife into the collection and breeding of often rare and exotic species. This has over recent years led to the opening of their collections to the public.

CAMBRIDGESHIRE

Huntingdon: Hamerton Wildlife Park

Hamerton Wildlife Park, Huntingdon

ESSEX

Saffron Walden: Mole Hall Wildlife Park

NORFOLK

East Dereham: Badley Moor Fish, Bird and Butterfly Centre
Great Yarmouth: Butterflies and Tropical Gardens
Holt: Kelly's Birds and Aviaries
Norwich: Norfolk Wildlife Park
Thetford: Kilverstone Wildlife Park

SUFFOLK

Bury St Edmunds: Butterfly Garden; Norton Tropical Bird Gardens
Kessingland: Suffolk Wildlife and Rare Breeds Park

Zoos

Tigers, lions, leopards, elephants, monkeys, bears even snakes and insects are a source of continual fascination to all ages, so what better way to spend a day than wandering round the zoo reminding oneself of the other inhabitants of our world and enjoying their interesting and often funny habits.

CAMBRIDGESHIRE

Linton: Linton Zoo
Peterborough: Peakirk Wildfowl Trust

ESSEX

Basildon: Basildon Zoo
Colchester: Colchester Zoo

NORFOLK

Diss: Banham Zoo and Monkey Sanctuary

Colchester Zoo

45

Boat Hire

Explore the countryside from the water, discover remote backwaters, enjoy the wildlife of the river-banks and marshes, cruise gently along, stop at some of the riverside pubs – the eastern counties with their miles of winding rivers and the Broads offer a vast water landscape for the floating visitor to experience. Boats can be hired from many centres around the region and, as with many of the facilities included in this guide, it is wise to telephone for information about the vessels available and the terms and conditions of hire. Everyone interested can try 'messing about on the river' in a wide selection of craft ranging from small motor cabin cruisers to barges, all-weather day launches to rowing boats.

CAMBRIDGESHIRE

Cambridge: Scudamore's; Two Tees Boat Yard; Tyrell's Marine Ltd
Huntingdon: Huntingdon Marine and Leisure Ltd; Purvis Marine Boatyard
March: Fox's Boats
St Ives: Tourist Information Centre; Westover Boat Company

NORFOLK

Great Yarmouth: Johnson's Yacht Station
Ludham: Pennant Holidays; Maycraft Ltd; Stalham Yacht Services Ltd
Norwich: Harbour Cruisers; Highcraft
Wroxham: Ferry Boatyard Ltd; Moore and Co

ESSEX

Chelmsford: Chelmer and Blackwater Navigation Ltd
Dedham: D E Smeeth
Halstead: Gosfield Lake and Leisure Park
Harwich: Orwell and Harwich Navigation Ltd

SUFFOLK

Brandon: Bridge House
Ipswich: Suffolk Water Park
Lowestoft: Waveney River Tours Ltd
Woodbridge: Waldringfield Boatyard Ltd

Boating on the River Ouse in Cambridgeshire

Boat Trips

For those who have no wish to captain their own vessel there are several organised boat trips to enjoy. There is a craft to suit everyone, steamer, pleasure barge, motor launch or historic wherry yacht – whatever appeals to take you up rivers, along the coast or out into the Wash to watch the seals.

CAMBRIDGESHRE

Cambridge: *The Marchioness*

ESSEX

Chelmsford: Chelmer and Blackwater Navigation Ltd
Harwich: Orwell and Harwich Navigation Co Ltd
Maldon: *Ostrea-Rose*

NORFOLK

Great Yarmouth: Norfolk Yacht Tours

Fakenham: William Scoles
Hunstanton: Searle's Hire Boats
Norwich: Southern River Steamers
Ludham: Mississippi River Boats; Pennant Cruises; Stalham Water Tours
Wroxham: Broads Tours Ltd; Faircraft Loynes; Tom Phillips

SUFFOLK

Aldeburgh: Snape Maltings
Lowestoft: Hoseasons Holidays Ltd; Waveney River Tours Ltd
Orford: *Lady Florence*
Woodbridge: Waldringfield Boat Yard

Canoeing

Canoeing appeals to a wide cross-section of people as you can choose between expeditions on calm waters or the challenge of pitting yourself against the wilder waters found in rivers with rapids and in the sea. Types of water are classified by the British Canoe Union and they range from placid water, white water Grades I to III and over, estuary, harbour through to sea and surf. To begin canoeing it is wise to seek expert guidance to learn the simple techniques and safety measures. There are many approved centres and the Canoe Union will supply a list on request from the address given below. Interestingly very few people learn to 'canoe' as canoes are open boats propelled by a single-bladed paddle whereas most people learn to 'kayak' in kayaks where they sit right inside propelled by a doubled-bladed paddle.

British Canoe Union
Mapperley Hall
Lucknow Avenue
Nottingham
☎ 0602 821100

CAMBRIDGESHIRE

Cambridge: Cambridge Canoe Club
Huntingdon: Purvis Marine Boatyard

ESSEX

Burnham-on-Crouch: Bradwell Field Studies and Sailing Centre

Harlow: Harlow Outdoor Pursuits Centre

SUFFOLK

Bury St Edmunds: St Edmundsbury Sailing and Canoeing Association
Bungay: Outney Meadow Caravan Park
Ipswich: Suffolk Water Park
Lowestoft: East Coast Canoes; Oulton Broad Canadian Canoe Centre.

Dinghy Sailing

Walking on water is not possible for most of us but sailing on it certainly is. Young and old, individuals and families have found great enjoyment in sailing over the years and continue to do so. Family sailing holidays provide lots of fun and there are many centres and schools recommended by the Royal Yachting Association (RYA) where it is possible to learn to sail and follow their Dinghy Sailing Scheme. Dinghy sailing can be enjoyed far from the sea anywhere there are stretches of water and seasonal or residential courses are available at many of the centres listed. For more information contact the RYA at the address below.

Royal Yachting Association
Romsey Road
Eastleigh
Hampshire
☎ 0703 629962

CAMBRIDGESHIRE

Cambridge: Cam Sailing Club;
Cambridge Sailing Club
St Ives: Meadow Lane Pits

Huntingdon: Grafham Water Sailing
Club

ESSEX

Burnham-on-Crouch: Bradwell Field
Studies and Sailing Centre ·
Chelmsford: Long Reach Dinghy and
Boardsailing Club
Harlow: The Moorhen

Sailing on the Norfolk Broads

Diving

Treasure troves beneath the sea whether old galleons or brilliant and bizarre underwater sea creatures attract many people to take up diving. Modern equipment is extremely light compared with the diving suits once worn so anyone who can swim and who is reasonably fit can try out an introductory diving course. The British Sub-Aqua Club (BSAC), the governing body of the sport, are known for the high standards they set and by following a course at a diving school or by joining one of the BSAC clubs it should be possible to attain their Novice Diver standard over three to six months. Continuing on to obtain their Sport Diver status will equip a diver to dive anywhere in the world in the company of other qualified divers. Underwater photography in tropical waters or exploring wrecks can begin with trying out an aqualung in a swimming pool. For more information contact the BSAC at the address given.

British Sub-Aqua Club (BSAC)
16 Upper Woburn Place
London
☎ 071 387 9302

CAMBRIDGESHIRE

Peterborough: Gildenburgh Water

Inland Waterways

What better way to discover a different aspect of the countryside than to glide peacefully though its waterways. British Waterways were built during the Industrial Revolution to transport goods between cities and now they are owned or managed by the British Waterways Board and nearly all are open to leisure cruising. Peaceful relaxed cruising, exploring the backwaters, enjoying the waterside pubs, meeting new people and observing the wildlife in the hedgerows and banks – what better way to spend some time.

The Norfolk Broads are ideal for those new to cruising holidays, lock-free and flat as are many of the 150 miles of Cambridgeshire Fen waterways. Modern narrow boats are fully equipped and there are many options for hire. For some help in making your decision about which way to go, the Inland Waterways Association might be able to help, they will provide information and have produced a guide to the inland waterways that could prove very useful, contact them at the address given here.

The Inland Waterways Association
114 Regents Park Road
London
☎ 071 586 2556

NORFOLK

Wroxham: Blakes Holidays Ltd

SUFFOLK

Lowestoft: Hoseasons Boating Holidays

Jet-Skiing

Jet-skiing is another exciting watersport for the adventure seeking water lover. There are only a few places that offer opportunities to pursue this sport in the eastern region at present but many of the numerous watersports centres will no doubt be including it in the near future.

CAMBRIDGESHIRE

Peterborough: Tallington Lakes Leisure Park

ESSEX

West Mersea

Punting

Punts seem to effortlessly glide along, no intrusive noise of an engine to disturb enjoyment of the river, no complicated controls to master, but anyone who has tried to punt will know that punting is a skill and one that can give rise to much hilarity in the learning. If you feel like the challenge then there are punts to hire but if you wish to enjoy the river then you can choose to be only a passenger. The venues for punting include the delightful willow-lined waters of the Cam from which you can enjoy the architecture and atmosphere provided by the colleges of Cambridge University.

Punting on the River Cam, Cambridgeshire

CAMBRIDGESHIRE

Cambridge: Scudamore's; Tyrells

NORFOLK

Wroxham: Norfolk Punt Club

Swimming

Swimming remains one of the most enjoyable and therapeutic of the watersports. The leisure centres throughout the region often have very exotic pool surrounds and include aquaslides, whirlpools and inflatables to provide extra fun in the water.

CAMBRIDGESHIRE

Cambridge: Abbey Sports Centre; Jesus Green Outdoor Swimming Pool; Kings Hedges Pool; Parkside Swimming Pool
Ely: Paradise Pool
Huntingdon: Huntingdon Recreation Centre
March: George Campbell Pool
Peterborough: Embankment Sports Complex; Jack Hunt Swimming Pool; Manor Leisure Centre; Orton Longueville Swimming Pool; Regional Swimming Pool
Ramsey: Ailwyn School Pool
St Ives: St Ivo Recreation Centre
St Neots: St Neots Sports Centre
Wisbech: Hudson Sports Centre

St Neots Sports Centre

ESSEX

Basildon: Gloucester Park Swimming Pool; Pitsea Swimming Pool; Wickford Swimming Pool
Billericay: Billericay Swimming Pool
Braintree: Riverside Pool
Brentwood: Brentwood Centre
Canvey Island: Runnymede Sports Hall; Waterside Farm Sports Centre
Chelmsford: Riverside Ice and Leisure Centre
Chipping Ongar: Ongar Sports Centre
Clacton: Clacton Leisure Centre

Colchester: Colchester Sports Centre
Epping: Loughton Pool
Grays: Blackshots Swim and Leisure Complex
Great Dunmow: Helena Romanes School
Harlow: Harlow Pool; Stewards School Pool
Harwich: Dovercourt Swimming Pool
Saffron Walden: Lord Butler Leisure Centre
Southend-on-Sea: Belfairs Swimming Pool; Clements Hall Leisure Centre; Shoeburyness Swimming Pool; Westcliff Leisure Centre
Waltham Abbey: Waltham Abbey Pool
Witham: Bramston Sports Centre

NORFOLK

Diss: Diss Swimming Pool
Downham Market: Downham Market Swimming Pool
East Dereham: East Dereham Swimming Pool
Great Yarmouth: Great Yarmouth Marina Leisure Centre; Phoenix Pool
Hunstanton: Oasis Leisure Centre
Kings Lynn: St James Swimming Pool
Norwich: Norwich City Baths
Sheringham: The Splash
Thetford: Breckland Sports Centre

SUFFOLK

Bury St Edmunds: Bury St Edmunds Sports and Leisure Centre
Felixstowe: Felixstowe Leisure Centre
Hadleigh: Hadleigh Swimming Pool
Haverhill: Haverhill Sports Centre
Ipswich: Crown Pools; Fore Street Baths
Lowestoft: Waveney Sports and Leisure Centre
Mildenhall: Mildenhall and District Swimming Pool
Newmarket: Newmarket Swimming Pool
Stowmarket: Mid Suffolk Leisure Centre
Sudbury: Kingfisher Leisure Pool
Woodbridge: Deben Swimming Pool

Water-Skiing

Much of this corner of the country was immersed in water until being drained over the last two centuries, not surprisingly it now offers a rich variety of venues for watersports. There are several clubs affiliated to the British Water Ski Federation where a safe pursuit of this exhilarating sport is encouraged. Basic equipment is usually provided and there are opportunities to develop the skill and confidence necessary to progress to jumps and competitions. For information and a list of clubs with details of their facilities contact the British Water Ski Federation at the address given.

British Water Ski Federation
390 City Road
London
☎ 071 833 2855/6

Colchester: Colchester Water Ski Club ·
Halstead: Halstead Water Ski Club
Maldon: Stone Watersports Club Ltd
Southend-on-Sea: Southend Water
  Sports Club
West Mersea

CAMBRIDGESHIRE

Godmanchester: Buckden Marina and
  Leisure Club
Peterborough: Kings Water Ski Club;
Tallington Lakes Leisure Park
St Neots: Boughton Lodge Water Sports
Club

ESSEX

Basildon: Castle View Water Ski Club;
  Wat Tyler Water Ski Club
Brentwood: Brentwood Windsurfing;
  Stubbers Outdoor Pursuits Centre
Clacton-on-Sea: Lakeside Watersports

NORFOLK

Hunstanton: Heacham Boat Owners
  Association; Hunstanton and
  District Water Ski Club
Kings Lynn: Pentney Water Sports Club
Norwich: Bluebird Deaf Water Ski
  Club; Buckenham Ferry Water Ski
  Club; Norwich and District Water
  Ski Club
Wells-next-the-Sea: Wells and District
  Ski Club

SUFFOLK

Felixstowe: Suffolk Water Sports Club

Windsurfing

Windsurfing or boardsailing as it is also known has become very popular and the colourful sails and characteristic silhouettes of the windsurfers are a familiar sight on many lakes and off many beaches. The relative ease with which windsurfers can be transported makes it a fairly flexible sport to pursue. To learn to windsurf it is advisable to approach a school approved by the Royal Yachting Association, most will supply boards, sails and wetsuits. You will be taken through the techniques involved on dry land before taking to the water and then over a couple of days you will learn how to sail a course, how to rig a board and how to observe the rules of safety for yourself and other water users. A beginners course does not involve a huge outlay and it might introduce you to an exciting new sport. Contact the Windsurfing Information Centre at the Royal Yachting Association for more details.

The Windsurfing Information Centre
Royal Yachting Association
Romsey Road
Eastleigh
Hampshire
☎ 0703 629962

CAMBRIDGESHIRE

Chatteris: Mepal Outdoor Centre
Huntingdon: Grafham Water
    Residential Centre; Jonti Sailboards

Peterborough: Surface Watersports;
    Tallington Windsurfing Club
St Ives: Meadow Lane Pits

ESSEX

Billericay: Harold Park
Brentwood: Brentwood Windsurfing;
    Stubbers Outdoor Pursuits Centre
Burnham-on-Crouch: Bradwell Field
    Studies and Sailing Centre; Town
    Playing Fields
Chelmsford: Channels Windsurfing
    Centre; Hanningfield Reservoir;
    Long Reach Dinghy and Boardsailing
    Club; South Woodham Ferrers Yacht
    Club
Clacton-on-Sea: Nucleus Sailboard and
    Leisure; Point Clear Windsurfing;
    Sailboard School
Southend-on-Sea: Chalkwell
    Windsurfing Club; Channels SOS;
    Thorpe Bay
West Mersea

NORFOLK

Great Yarmouth: Fritton Lake and
    Country Park

SUFFOLK

Felixstowe: Beach; Windsurfing
    Seasports
Ipswich: Oysterworld Sailboard School;
    Surf-Ace
Lowestoft: Watersports East Anglia Ltd

Yacht Charter

Yacht charter provides the opportunity to enjoy sailing holidays on a variety of boats that you do not have to maintain all the year round or indeed invest in in the first place. Skippered charter is relatively risk-free as the skipper usually knows his boat. For self-sail charter it is advisable to charter the boat from a company who will give you an introduction into handling the craft. For advice and information to help you select your charter contact the Yacht Charter Association at the address below.

Yacht Charter Association
60 Silverdale
New Milton
Hants
☎ 0425 619004

ESSEX

Maldon: Anglian Yacht Services;
 Ostrea Rose

NORFOLK

Great Yarmouth: Norfolk Yacht Tours
Norwich: Norfolk Wherry *Albion*;
 Wherry Yacht Charter

SUFFOLK

Ipswich: *Marjie*

Yachting

Yachting and yacht cruising are enjoyable to people of all ages and the eastern counties provide some excellent sailing opportunities. There are many yacht clubs, some of which will offer cruising courses for those interested in learning to sail or for those who wish to broaden their experience. For details and information about yachting and courses contact the Royal Yachting Association at the address below.

Royal Yachting Association
Romsey Road
Eastleigh
Hampshire
☎ 0703 629962

CAMBRIDGESHIRE

Ely: Ely Sailing Club
Kimbolton: Kimbolton School Sailing
 Club
Peterborough: Fenland Sailing Club

ESSEX

Brightlingsea: Brightlingsea Sailing Club; Colne Yacht Club
Burnham-on-Crouch: Burnham-on-Crouch Sailing Club; Creeksea Sailing Club; Crouch Yacht Club; East Anglian Offshore Racing Association; Royal Burnham Yacht Club; Royal Corinthian Yacht Club
Canvey Island: Benfleet Yacht Club; Halcon Boating Club; Island Yacht Club; Pitsea Motor Boat and Yacht Club
Clacton-on-Sea: Clacton Sailing Club
Colchester: Ardleigh Sailing Club; University of Essex Sailing Association; Wivenhoe Sailing Club
Harlow: Harlow (Blackwater) Sailing Club
Harwich: Harwich and Dovercourt Sailing Club; Harwich Town Sailing Club
Maldon: Lawling Sailing Association; Maldon Little Ship Club; Maldon Yacht Club; Stone Sailing Club
Manningtree: Stour Sailing Club
Southend-on-Sea: Alexandra Yacht Club; Thorpe Bay Yacht Club; Up River Yacht Club; Wakening Yacht Club
Walton-on-the-Naze: Walton and Frinton Yacht Club
West Mersea: Dabchicks Sailing Club

NORFOLK

Great Yarmouth: Blakeney Sailing Club; Great Yarmouth and Gorleston Sailing Club; Rollesby Broad Sailing Club
Kings Lynn: Ouse Amateur Sailing Club
Norwich: Brundall Motor Yacht Club; Buckenham Sailing Club; Coldham Hall Sailing Club; Norfolk Broads Yacht Club; Tama Sailing; Yare Sailing Club
Wells-next-the-Sea: Wells Sailing Club

SUFFOLK

Aldeburgh: Aldeburgh Yacht Club
Beccles: Beccles Amateur Sailing Club
Bury St Edmunds: St Edmundsbury Sailing and Canoeing Association; St Edmundsbury Yachting Association
Ipswich: East Anglian School of Sailing; Orwell Yacht Club; Oysterworld Nautical Training Centre; P & Q Sailing Centre; Pin Mill Sailing Club; Shotley Sailing Club
Lowestoft: *Excelsior*; Lowestoft Cruising Club; Waveney and Oulton Broad Yacht Club
Southwold: Southwold Sailing Club
Woodbridge: Deben Yacht Club; Orford Sailing Club; Woodbridge Cruising Club

Winter Sports

Skiing

The eastern counties are not noted for their snow-capped mountain slopes but lovers of skiing can still enjoy their sport on any of the dry slopes in the region. For more information about skiing in Britain contact the British Ski Federation at the address below.

British Ski Federation
8 Pyrford Road
West Byfleet
Surrey
☎ 0506 884343

CAMBRIDGESHIRE

Peterborough: Tallington Lakes Leisure Park

ESSEX

Brentwood: The Ski Centre
Harlow: Harlow Sportcentre

NORFOLK

Aylsham: The Ski Barn
Norwich: Norwich Ski Club

SUFFOLK

Ipswich: Suffolk Ski Centre; Suffolk Ski Club

Introduction to
Places

Discover the eastern counties of Cambridgeshire, Essex, Norfolk and Suffolk. Despite being close to London and easily accessible from the Midlands it still remains peaceful and its rich diversity of landscapes, sports and activities is relatively unexplored. There are pretty villages with half-timbered, pink washed or flint cottages, endless horizons broken by church towers and spires, cathedral cities with their many treasures, remote stretches of shoreline as well as golden sands and lively resorts. There is much to do and plenty to see.

Select the city, town or village you wish to visit, they are arranged alphabetically, and you will find a description, local information including population figures where available, and a detailed list of leisure activities with the telephone number, address or access information and any other interesting details. If you want to know more about a particular activity look it up in the activities section where you will find general information about it, the name and address of the governing body plus a list of all the places in the region where you can enjoy the activity. You might find a familiar place has unexpected opportunities to enjoy a favourite pursuit or an unfamiliar place is much more exciting than you expected!

Guide to map symbols

☎	telephone
_i_	tourist information centre
⛳₁₈	18-hole golf course
⛳₉	9-hole golf course
P	car parking
✝	abbey, cathedral, church of interest
⌂	historic building, historic house, historic property
⬜	museum, art gallery
⇌	BR station
⊗	leisure centre, sports centre, swimming pool
→	one-way streets

Cromer Carnival Procession

Aldeburgh beach

Halesworth

56

Aldeburgh is a coastal fishing town and flourishing seaside resort with good hotels and a mixture of architectural styles. The sea has eroded the shoreline over the centuries so that the Tudor town centre including the 16th century Moat Hall now stand on the shingle beach only yards from the sea.

Aldeburgh's world-famous music festival is held every June. It was begun by Benjamin Britten and Peter Pears in 1948 and has developed into a year-round programme of music shared between Aldeburgh and Snape Maltings where the old maltings have been converted into a complex for the arts. The River Alde provides good sailing and fishing whilst the surrounding area is ideal for birdwatching and rambling.

i The Cinema
High Street
☎ 0728 453637
Market day Monday
Early closing Wednesday
Population 2918

Multi-Activity Holidays

SPECIAL INTEREST CENTRES

Snape Maltings
Near Saxmundham
Programme of painting, craft and special interest weekends, unusual self-catering accommodation.
☎ 072 888 303/5

Outdoor Leisure

FISHING

Sea Fishing
Estuary of the River Alde, from the jetty or the beach – October and November are the best months.

GOLF

Aldeburgh Golf Course 🏌
Saxmundham Road
1 mile west of Aldeburgh on the A1094
☎ 0728 452890

Special Interests

ART GALLERIES

Snape Maltings
Near Saxmundham
Collection of old Maltings buildings converted into a complex for the arts including galleries and a concert hall famous for hosting the Aldeburgh Festival.
☎ 072 888 303/5

FESTIVALS AND FAIRS

June
Aldeburgh Music Festival

August
Maltings Proms
Venues at Snape Maltings and Aldeburgh
Contact the Aldeburgh Foundation
FREEPOST, Aldeburgh, Suffolk
☎ 0728 452935

MUSEUMS

Moot Hall
High Street
16th century listed building, museum with items of local interest.

Moot Hall

NATURAL HISTORY

North Warren (RSPB)
Access via a car park off the B1122
Aldeburgh to Leiston road
Heathland and reed bed.
☎ 072 873 281 for enquiries

Water Sports

BOAT TRIPS

Snape Maltings
1 hour trips on the River Alde from Snape Maltings on the *Lady Moyra*.
☎ 072 888 303

Aylsham is an historic old market town situated between Norwich and Cromer. The attractive central market place is surrounded by interesting buildings many of which display the distinctive Dutch influence common to this area. There is a twice-weekly market and a weekly auction of books, antiques and fine arts. Aylsham is a good centre from which to explore the surrounding area, some of Norfolk's most beautiful countryside, either on foot or by the newly opened Bure Valley Railway.

i The Bure Valley Railway Ltd
Aylsham Station
☎ 0263 733903

Market days Monday, Saturday
Early closing Wednesday
Population 5421

Outdoor Leisure

FISHING

Coarse Fishing
For information and permits contact the National Rivers Authority: Anglian Region, Kingfisher House, Goldhay Way, Orton Goldhay, Peterborough
☎ 0733 371811
Eastern Region, 79 Thorpe Road, Norwich
☎ 0603 662800

Bure Valley Lakes
12 acres with brown and rainbow trout.
☎ 026387 666

HORSE RIDING

Rectory Road Riding School
Off the A145 between North Walsham and Aylsham at Suffield
Children's riding holidays. BHS approved.
☎ 0263 761367

WALKING AND RAMBLING

Weavers Way
This route links the Norfolk Coast Path at Cromer with Great Yarmouth, it passes through and near some of the Norfolk Broads. Details are available from the Norfolk County Council.
☎ 0603 622233

Special Interests

Blickling Hall

HISTORIC HOUSES

Blickling Hall
North-west of Aylsham on the B1354
Jacobean mansion with gardens, orangery and parkland.
☎ 0263 733084

RAILWAYS

Bure Valley Railway
Aylsham Station
Newly opened 9-mile narrow gauge steam railway from Aylsham to Wroxham.
☎ 0263 722903

Winter Sports

SKIING

Aylsham Ski Barn
Banningham Road
Indoor beginners slope, tuition, open by appointment.
☎ 0263 733893

Basildon

Basildon is a large town situated within easy reach of the south Essex coastal resorts. A London overspill town, it has increased in size rapidly in recent years, many major companies are now based here. This rapid development has brought an associated increase of opportunities for sport, leisure and entertainment, the Towngate development, for instance, includes a fine theatre and an extensive shopping complex. The town is easily accessible from London by road and rail.

Market days Tuesday, Friday, Saturday
Early closing Wednesday
Population 152,301

Adventure Sports

CLIMBING

Terry Marsh Sports Centre
Eversley Park, Crest Avenue, Pitsea
☎ 0268 583076

Indoor Sports

LEISURE CENTRES

Basildon Sports Centre
Nethermayne
☎ 0268 533166

Bromford Sports Centre
Bromford School, Grange Avenue, Wickford
☎ 0268 769369

The Markhams Chase Sports Centre
Markhams Chase, Lee Chapel North
☎ 0268 410126

SQUASH

Basildon Sports
☎ 0268 533166

Bromford Sports Centre
☎ 0268 769369

The Markham Chase Sports Centre
☎ 0268 410126

Outdoor Leisure

FISHING

Coarse Fishing
For information and permits contact the National Rivers Authority, Kelvedon District Office
☎ 0376 72091

Berwick Ponds
Near Rainham

Cobblers Mead Lake
Corringham
☎ 0268 683946

Old Hall Lake
Ockenden

Stanford-le-Hope
Gravel pits.
Contact: Chertsey Angling Club
☎ 0932 564872

GOLF

Basildon Golf Club ⌕₁₈
Clay Hill Lane
Undulating course, restrictions on visitors at weekends and Bank Holidays.
☎ 0268 533 532

Basildon Golf Course ⌕₁₈
1 mile south of Basildon on the A176 at Kingswood
☎ 0268 3297

Aquatels ⌕₉
Cranes Farm Road
☎ 0268 27278

HORSE RIDING

Longwood Equestrian Centre
Dry Street
2 miles from Basildon off the A176
Residential instructional holidays. BHS approved.
☎ 0268 412184

WALKING AND RAMBLING

Basildon Greenway
Circular footpaths in and around Basildon.
☎ 0268 550088

Basildon Nature Trail
5-mile walk through woodland and country parks.
☎ 0268 419095

Crays Hill Circular Walk
5-mile circular walk.
☎ 0268 419095

Special Interests

COUNTRY PARKS

Langdon Hills Country Park
1 mile south-west of Basildon
Overlooks the Thames estuary, range of
scenery and woodland.
☎ 0268 42066

Wat Tyler Country Park
Pitsea
Newly created, focus on conservation
and natural history, two museums, craft
workshops and a marina.
☎ 0268 559833

MUSEUMS

National Motorboat Museum
Wat Tyler Country Park, Pitsea
Illustrated history of the motorboat over
the last century.
☎ 0268 550077

Plotland Trail and Museum
Dunton
Second World War lifestyles.
☎ 0268 419095

NATURAL HISTORY

Basildon Nature Trail
☎ 0268 419095

THEATRES

Towngate Theatre
☎ 0268 532632

ZOOS

Basildon Zoo
Animals and birds, children's zoo, café
and picnic area.
☎ 0268 553985

Water Sports

SWIMMING

Gloucester Park Swimming Pool
Broadmane
33-metre pool, learner pool, fitness
room.
☎ 0268 23588

Pitsea Swimming Pool
Rectory Park Drive, Pitsea
25-metre pool, sauna, solarium.
☎ 0268 556734

Wickford Swimming Pool
Market Avenue, Wickford
25-metre pool, solarium.
☎ 0268 765460

WATER SKIING

Castle View Water Ski Club
39 Jotmans Lane, Benfleet
☎ 070 255 1626

Wat Tyler Water Ski Club
Wat Tyler Park, Pitsea
☎ 027 765 3479

Beccles is an old market town and an ideal centre from which to explore and enjoy the Waveney valley. It has a fine quay and yacht station and is a major centre for holiday boating in the broads. Boat houses and landing stages are a common sight in this town where gardens run down to the water's edge. The town offers much to see and explore with several ancient buildings including the church of St Michael which has a 14th century detached bell tower that stands as a notable landmark in the area and two fascinating museums. There are plenty of sports facilities including a sports centre, a golf course and some excellent locations for a day's fishing.

i The Quay
Fen Lane
☎ 0502 713196

Market day Friday
Early closing Wednesday
Population 10,815

Indoor Sports

LEISURE CENTRES

Beccles Sports Centre
Ringsfield Road
☎ 0502 712039

SQUASH

Beccles Sports Centre
☎ 0502 712039

Outdoor Leisure

FISHING

Coarse Fishing
Good fishing on the River Waveney for pike, perch, roach, rudd, tench and bream. For information and permits contact the National Rivers Authority
☎ 0733 371811
☎ 0473 727712

GOLF

Wood Valley Golf Club
The Common
Restrictions at Bank Holidays and weekends.
☎ 0502 712244

HORSE RIDING

Barnby Training Centre
Church Farm, Beccles Road, Barnby
Instruction in riding and jumping.
Accommodation.
☎ 0502 76790

Special Interests

ANTIQUES

Auction
Gresham Road
Weekly auction on Fridays.
☎ 0502 712122

HISTORIC BUILDINGS

St Michael's Church
14th century detached bell tower, notable landmark, peal of ten bells.

MUSEUMS

Beccles and District Museum
Newgate
Local history, printing, agriculture and 19th century costume.
☎ 0502 712628

William Clowes Print Museum
Newgate
The history of printing from 1800; tours.
☎ 0502 712884

Water Sports

YACHTING

Beccles Amateur Sailing Club
On the south bank of the River Waveney. RYA affiliated.
☎ 0502 715026

61

Billcricay, tucked away in southern Essex, allows easy access to both the coast and central London. The town has two interesting museums one covers the history of the Fire Brigade and the other gives a window on farm life in days gone by. Riding, windsurfing, and walking can all be enjoyed in or around the town.

Early closing Thursday
Population 30,000

Outdoor Leisure

HORSE RIDING

Brook Farm Equestrian Centre
Stock Road, Stock
Non-residential children's riding holidays. BHS approved.
☎ 0277 840425

De Beauvoir Farm Livery Yard
Church Farm, Ramsden Heath
☎ 0268 710534/711302

Park Lane Riding and Livery Stables
Park Lane, Ramsden Heath
☎ 0268 710145

Special Interests

MUSEUMS

Barleylands Farm Museum
Wickford Road
Vintage farm machinery on a working farm.
☎ 0268 282090

Cater Museum
High Street
Victorian domestic settings and Fire Brigade history.
☎ 0277 622023

NATURAL HISTORY

Norsey Wood
Outwood Common Road
Mediaeval coppice woodland of archaeological and conservation importance.
☎ 0277 624553

Water Sports

SWIMMING

Billericay Swimming Pool
Lake Meadow Recreation Ground
25-metre pool.
☎ 0277 65711

WINDSURFING

Harold Park
South Hanningfield Reservoir
Tuition, board hire, shop and meals.
☎ 0708 856528

Barleylands Farm Museum

A small, quiet, coastal village Blakeney is well known for its important nature reserve where seals and a wide variety of seabirds can be seen, a boat service goes to the reserve. It's possible to see shells from around the world, watch pots and jewellery being made or explore some historic buildings in Blakeney and the surrounding area.

Early closing Wednesday
Population 1559

Outdoor Leisure

BIRDWATCHING

Cley Marshes
Fresh and saltwater marshes, excellent bird watching. Access by permit available from the visitor centre. Contact the Norfolk Naturalists' Trust for details.
☎ 0603 625540

Special Interests

ARTS AND CRAFTS

Made in Cley
High Street, Cley-next-the-Sea
Hand-thrown pottery, silver and gold jewellery housed in a historic building.
☎ 0263 740134

HERITAGE

Blakeney Guildhall
Remains of 14th century building.

HISTORIC BUILDINGS

Cley Mill
Cley-next-the-Sea
Well preserved tower mill, used as a flour mill until 1918.
☎ 0263 740209

MUSEUMS

Glandford Shell Museum
On the B1156 between Blakeney and Holt at Glandford. Shells from around the world. A tapestry of the North Norfolk Coast.
☎ 0263 740081

NATURAL HISTORY

Blakeney Point Nature Reserve
Access on foot along shingle spit or by boat from Morston or Blakeney quays. Wildfowl breeding ground, hides, seals. National Trust.

Blakeney Harbour

There is a Heritage Centre in Braintree Town Hall that depicts the town's importance in wool, silk and engineering. The old and the new have blended well, every street has ancient houses and tours of these attractive old buildings can be arranged. Braintree remains a busy market town.

i Town Hall Centre
Market Square
☎ 0376 550066

Market day Wednesday
Early closing Thursday
Population 31,139

Indoor Sports

SQUASH

Riverside Pool
St John Avenue
☎ 0376 23240

Outdoor Leisure

CYCLING

Routes designed by Braintree District Council Community and Leisure Services Department, starting at the youth hostel at Castle Hedingham. For details contact the Tourist Information Centre.

Route 1
Castle Hedingham to Clare and the Belchamps

Route 2
Castle Hedingham to Halstead and the Colne Valley

Route 3
Castle Hedingham to Finchingfield

FISHING

Coarse Fishing
Rivers Blackwater and Pant are well stocked with roach, perch, rudd, dace and chubb. For information and permits contact the National Rivers Authority
☎ 0733 371811
☎ 0473 727712

The Right Angle Tackle Shop
18 New Street
Tickets to fish on the rivers Blackwater and Pant.
☎ 0376 49550

64

GOLF

Braintree Golf Club ⌐₁₈
Kings Lane, Stisted
Parkland course, restrictions on visitors at weekends and Bank Holidays.
☎ 0376 24117
☎ 0376 43465 the pro shop

Towerlands Golf Club ⌐₁₈
Panfield Road
☎ 0376 26802

HORSE RIDING

Rayne Riding Centre
Fairy Hall Lane
General instruction, schooling for competition and livery.
☎ 0376 22231

Wethersfield Riding Stables
Hedingham Road, Wethersfield
☎ 0371 851089

Special Interests

GARDENS

Saling Hall Garden
Great Saling, near Braintree
Water gardens and a walled garden dating from 1698; unusual trees.

GUIDED TOURS

Contact the Tourist Information Centre
☎ 0376 550066

MUSEUMS

Heritage Centre
Town Hall, Market Square
Town's development from Stone Age; textiles, engineering, photographs.

Water Sports

SWIMMING

Riverside Pool
25-metre pool, learner pool, squash courts.
☎ 0376 23240

Brancaster is a small north-west Norfolk coastal village. It is separated from the sea, which is only a mile away, by saltings and reeds. The attractive sandy beach has strong tides making swimming dangerous. It is in an area of great interest to wildlife lovers and birdwatchers, the famous Titchwell Marsh reserve and Scolt Head Island are both nearby.

Outdoor Leisure

BIRDWATCHING

Scolt Head Island
1¹/₂ miles east from Brancaster Staithe, access by boat
Island bird sanctuary and nature study area. Nature Conservancy Council.

Titchwell Marsh (RSPB)
Access via the reserve car park off the A149 between Thornham and Titchwell villages.

A famous reserve of reed beds, salt marsh and sandy shores, where a wide variety of birds including ringed plovers, dunlin, ruffs and the more unusual curlew sandpipers, black-tailed godwits and kingfishers may be seen from hides.
☎ 0485 210799

GOLF

Royal West Norfolk Golf Club ⓒ₁₈
Links course approach road subject to tidal flooding. No visitors at Bank Holidays, or during July, August and September.
☎ 0485 210223

Brandon, a Suffolk market town, is situated amongst heathland, warrens and fir woods on the south bank of the Little Ouse. Flint has played a significant part in its history, now used in buildings it has been mined here since Neolithic times for arrowheads and implements. The headquarters of the Forestry Commission is in the area and the woodlands they care for have done much to bind the shifting Breckland sands. Thetford Chase is one of the largest man-made forests in the country.

Market days Thursday, Saturday
Early closing Wednesday

Multi-Activity Holidays

MULTI-ACTIVITY CENTRES

Centre Parcs
Sub-tropical pool complex; family breaks; villas; facilities for wide range of indoor and outdoor sports.
☎ 0933 401 401

Outdoor Leisure

ORIENTEERING

Brandon Country Park
Permanent course is laid out in the park.

Special Interests

Brandon Country Park
¹/₂ mile south on the B1106
30 acres of parkland and woodland, nature trails, forest walk, orienteering, park centre.

FESTIVALS AND FAIRS

June
Forest Heath Arts Festival

HERITAGE

Grimes Graves
1 mile north of Brandon on the B1108
Neolithic flint mines 4000 years old; excavated first in the 1870s; intricate network of over 300 pits and shafts; one pit open to the public. English Heritage.

Heritage Centre

Centre dedicated to the history of the Brandon district is to open in January 1991. For details contact Forest Heath District Council.
☎ 0638 716000

Weeting Castle

1 mile north of Brandon on the B1108 Remains of a moated castle. English Heritage.

HISTORIC HOUSES

Elveden Hall

On the A11 at Elveden
Modest Georgian House transformed into an oriental palace with a copper dome and tons of Italian carved marble by Majaraja Duleep Singh; bought later by a member of the Guinness brewing family and embellished.

NATURAL HISTORY

Thetford Chase

80 square miles of beeches, oak and other hardwoods with a wide range of wildlife including Muntjac deer, badgers, crossbilled goshawks and rare plants such as gentians, military orchids and maiden pinks.

ESSEX / Brentwood / ESSEX

Thorndon Park, Brentwood

Brentwood is an excellent centre for walks through parkland and unspoilt country even though it is so close to central London. There is plenty of scope to pursue many sporting and leisure activities including golf, riding, squash, windsurfing or even a quiet day's fishing either in Brentwood or the surrounding countryside.

Early closing Thursday
Population 51,643

Indoor Sports

LEISURE CENTRES

Brentwood Centre
Doddinghurst Road
☎ 0277 229621

The Courage Hall
☎ 0277 227522

SQUASH

Brentwood Centre
☎ 0277 229621

The Courage Hall
☎ 0277 227522

Outdoor Leisure

CARAVANNING AND CAMPING

Kelvedon Hatch Camping and Caravanning Site
Just north of Bentley, on the A128 from Brentwood
150 caravan and tent pitches (no singles).
☎ 0277 372773

FISHING

Coarse Fishing
For information and permits contact the National Rivers Authority, Kelvedon District Office
☎ 0376 72091

Moor Hall Farm
Herongate

South Weald Lakes
Weald Country Park, south-west of Brentwood

GOLF

Bentley Golf and Country Club
Ongar Road
3 miles north-west of Brentwood on the A128
☎ 0277 373179

Hartswood Golf Course ⛳
King George's Playing Fields
☎ 0277 218850

Orsett Park Golf Club ⛳
On the A128 between Brentwood and Orsett
☎ 0375 891226

Thorndon Park Golf Club ⛳
On the A128 Ingrave Road
☎ 0277 811666

Upminster Golf Course ⛳
114 Hall lane, Upminster
☎ 0402 222788

Warley Park Golf Club
Magpie Lane, Little Warley
☎ 0277 224891

HORSE RIDING

Folkes Farm Riding and Livery Stables
Folkes Lane, Upminster
Residential instructional holidays. BHS approved.
☎ 0277 212002

Foxhound Riding School Ltd
Baker Street, Orsett
Residential instructional holidays. BHS approved.
☎ 0375 891367

Lillyputts Equestrian Centre
272 Wingletye Lane, Hornchurch
Residential instructional holidays. BHS approved.
☎ 04024 53908

TENNIS

Clearview
Warley Hall Lane, Little Warley
☎ 0277 811569

Special Interests

COUNTRY PARKS

Thorndon Park
2 miles south of Brentwood
373 acres of woodland, lakes and walks.
☎ 0277 211250

Weald
1 mile north of Brentwood
428 acres of woodland, lakes and deer.
☎ 0277 216297

FACTORY VISITS

Ford Motor Company
Eagle Way, Warley
Open by appointment only.
☎ 081 526 2570

FESTIVALS AND FAIRS

May
North Weald Fighter Meet at North Weald Airfield. Annual air display of historic aircraft.
☎ 0378 560000

HISTORIC BUILDINGS

Mountnessing Windmill
Mountnessing
19th century post mill restored to
working order.
☎ 0245 352237 extn 293

NATURAL HISTORY

Norsey Wood Trail
Nature reserve.
☎ 0277 624553

Water Sports

SWIMMING

Brentwood Centre
☎ 0277 229621

WINDSURFING

Brentwood Windsurfing
2 The Parade, Colchester Road
☎ 0268 711350

Stubbers Outdoor Pursuits Centre
Ockenden Road, Upminster
Tuition, residential courses, video
coaching; showers, shop.
☎ 0402 224753

Winter Sports

SKIING

The Ski Centre
Brentwood Park, Warley Gap
☎ 0277 211994

/ ESSEX / **Brightlingsea** / ESSEX /

Brightlingsea is an old fishing and yachting port situated at the mouth of the Colne estuary. It offers some of the best sailing available along the east coast as well as some interesting walks along the banks of Brightlingsea Creek and the River Colne where the saltings are home to a wealth of birdlife.

Early closing Thursday
Population 7297

Outdoor Leisure

BIRDWATCHING

Birdwatching on the saltings of
Brightlingsea Creek and the River Colne.

CAMPING AND CARAVANNING

Caravan Club
Lower Park Road
30 caravan and 30 tent pitches. Showers.
☎ 0206 304080

Special Interests

HISTORIC BUILDINGS

All Saints Church
Perpendicular church with fine 94-foot
tower.

Water Sports

YACHTING

Brightlingsea Sailing Club
Waterside
☎ 0206 3275

Colne Yacht Club
Yachting facilities available.
☎ 0206 303275

/ SUFFOLK / **Bungay** / SUFFOLK /

Bungay, an ancient market town, stands on Suffolk's borders with Norfolk. The town is noted for its varied architecture - mediaeval, ecclesiastical, military and domestic Georgian styles intermingle. The Castle, rebuilt by the last Bigod earl in the 14th century and later handed on to Edward the Confessor, remains as ruins that thread their way through part of the town as alley walls and masonry fragments. The remaining twin towers of the castle and the Castle Meadow provide an excellent vantage point over the water meadows to the west of the town.

Bungay has much to offer the visitor both within the town and in the surrounding countryside – it is an excellent centre from which to explore the Waveney Valley, the Broads and the Suffolk coast.

Market day Thursday
Early closing Wednesday
Population 4116

Indoor Sports

LEISURE CENTRES

Bungay Sports Hall
Queens Road
☎ 0986 4515

SQUASH

Bungay Sports Hall
☎ 0986 4515

Outdoor Leisure

FISHING

Coarse Fishing
Good coarse fishing on the River Waveney. For information and permits contact the National Rivers Authority
☎ 0733 371811

Broome Pits
Yarmouth Road, Broome
25 acres, roach. Details available from the Bungay Angling Centre
☎ 0986 38432

Bungay Cherry Tree Angling Club
Mr I Gosling, 37 St Mary's Terrace
☎ 0986 3982

Game Fishing
Fishing for brown and rainbow trout at a local fishery.

Halcyon Lake Fishery
Waveney Valley, near Bungay
5 acres, season tickets only.
☎ 0986 86517

GOLF

Bungay and Waveney Valley Golf Club ♦₁₈
½ mile north-west of Bungay on the A143 at Outney Common
Links type course, natural features.
☎ 0986 892337

WALKING AND RAMBLING

The Bigod Way
A well signposted footpath walk through a range of countryside, from 2 to 10 miles. A guide is available at the local Council office, shops and hotels.

Special Interests

HERITAGE

Bungay Castle Ruins
Town centre
Twin towers of Norman castle; Saxon mounds. Keyholders listed on site.

MUSEUMS

Bungay Museum
Waveney District Council Offices, Broad Street
Local history.
☎ 0986 2548

Norfolk and Suffolk Aviation Museum
3 miles south-west of Bungay on the B1062 at Flixton
Historic aircraft, models and paintings on display.

NATURAL HISTORY

The Otter Trust
1 mile west of Bungay off the A143 at Earsham
World's largest collection of otters in natural enclosures; otters bred for re-introduction to the wild. Three lakes, large collection of European wildfowl, Chinese water-deer and Muntjac deer. Visitors centre, tea room and gift shop.
☎ 0986 893470

Water Sports

CANOEING

Outney Meadow Caravan Park
Canoes, rowing boats and skiffs for hourly or daily hire.
☎ 0986 2338

69

Burnham-on-Crouch

Burnham-on-Crouch is a small coastal town and sailing centre. It is home to many famous yacht clubs including the Royal Burnham Yacht Club where the Americans Cup winner, 'Victory', was registered. The Quay is a mixture of colour-washed houses and cottages. Where smells of the sea accompany the masts that bob on the tide. A modern marina and a number of specialist restaurants, pubs and antique shops offer the visitor much of interest to explore.

Early closing Wednesday
Population 6300

Indoor Sports

SQUASH

Royal Corinthian Yacht Club
The Quay
☎ 0602 782105

Multi-Activity Holidays

MULTI-ACTIVITY CENTRES

Bradwell Field Studies and Sailing Centre
Bradwell Waterside, near Southminster
Off shore cruising, dinghy sailing, canoeing, windsurfing, RYA centre. Birdwatching courses for groups and individuals.
☎ 0621 76256

Outdoor Leisure

BIRDWATCHING

Bradwell Field Studies Centre
☎ 0621 76256

CAMPING AND CARAVANNING

Creeksea Place Caravan Park
Ferry Road, Creeksea
Wooded park with lakes in manor grounds, near river and golf course. Many facilities.
☎ 0621 782675

Silver Road Caravan Park
5 Silver Road
Grass site with fifty caravan and tent pitches. Showers.
☎ 0621 782934

FISHING

Sea Fishing
1 mile west of Burnham-on-Crouch on the River Crouch at Creeksea

GOLF

Burnham-on-Crouch Golf Club ⛳
Ferry lane, Creeksea
1¼ miles west of Burnham-on-Crouch off the B1010
☎ 0621 782282

HORSE RIDING

Medway Riding Centre
Medway Farm, Southminster Road, Althorne
Non-resident instructional holidays.
BHS approved.
☎ 0621 740419

Elmwood Equestrian Centre
Elm Farm, Creeksea
☎ 0621 783216

Special Interests

FESTIVALS AND FAIRS

August
Burnham Week: important week in the yachting calendar. Racing on the River Crouch. Details available from any of the Burnham yacht clubs listed below.

September
Burnham-on-Crouch Carnival Week Culminates in grand carnival procession. (Last week of September.)

FOOD AND DRINK

Mustard
Many varieties of mustard from the Burnham Mustard Company available in local shops.

MUSEUMS

Burnham-on-Crouch Museum
Agricultural, maritime and local history displays.

Mangapps Farm Railway Museum
Mangapps Farm, Southminster Road
Steam and diesel locos under cover and
400-metre railway line. Steam days.
☎ 0621 784898

Mangapps Farm Railway Museum
☎ 0621 784898

Water Sports

CANOEING

**Bradwell Field Studies and Sailing
Centre**
☎ 0621 76256

WINDSURFING

**Bradwell Field Studies and Sailing
Centre**
☎ 0621 76256

Town Playing Fields
Board and suit hire available.

YACHTING

Burnham-on-Crouch Sailing Club
The Quay
RYA affiliated.
☎ 0621 782878

Creeksea Sailing Club
Creeksea
RYA affiliated.
☎ 0621 783241

Crouch Yacht Club
Coronation Road
RYA affiliated.
☎ 0621 782252

**East Anglian Offshore Racing
Association**
☎ 0621 783630

Royal Burnham Yacht Club
The Quay
RYA affiliated.
☎ 0621 782044

Royal Corinthian Yacht Club
The Quay
RYA affiliated.
☎ 0621 782105

Burnham Riverside

71

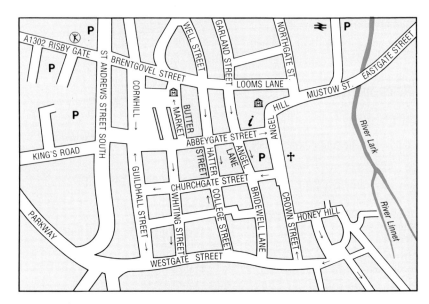

Bury St Edmunds is an ancient market town ideally situated for touring the eastern counties. It has played an important part in English history over the centuries. A shrine was built here in the 9th century for the corpse of St Edmund, he was the King of East Anglia and his burial place became known as St Edmundsbury. The magnificent abbey became a place of pilgrimage and the seat of the powerful abbots of St Edmundsbury. The west front of the Abbey, which is set in beautiful gardens beside the River lark, has Tudor, Georgian and Victorian houses built into its ruins.

The town and surrounding countryside have much to offer the vistor – Moyses Hall Museum, the Clock Museum, the Regency Theatre Royal, the lovely Ickworth House and park should not be missed – and there is also the recently opened Nowton Park, 172 acres of parkland and woods to walk and enjoy.

i 6 Angel Hill
☎ 0284 764667
Market days Wednesday, Saturday
Early closing Thursday
Population 33,500

Adventure Sports

CLIMBING

Bury St Edmunds Sports and Leisure Centre
Beetons Way
☎ 0284 753496

SHOOTING

Bury St Edmunds Sports and Leisure Centre
☎ 0284 753496

Aerial Sports

GLIDING

Rattlesden Gliding Club
The Airfield, Hightown Green
☎ 04493 7789

Indoor Sports

LEISURE CENTRES

Bury St Edmunds Sports and Leisure Centre
Facilities include badminton, basketball, volleyball, swimming pools, weight training, sauna, solarium, bar and cafeteria.
☎ 0284 753496

ROLLER SKATING

Rollerbury
Station Hill
National Roller Skating Centre for serious and fun skaters. Disco, sound and light, restaurant and bar; hire facilities, tuition.
☎ 0284 701215

SQUASH

Bury St Edmunds Sports and Leisure Centre
☎ 0284 753496

Outdoor Leisure

FISHING

Coarse Fishing
For details of fishing in the rivers Stour, Colne, Blackwater, Chelmer and Crouch, contact Ted Pearson.
☎ 0206 763344

GOLF

Bury St Edmunds Golf Club ⓘ₁₈
Tut Hill
Undulating, parkland course.
☎ 0284 755979

Flempton Golf Club ⓘ₉
Slightly undulating, well bunkered course.
☎ 0284 84291

Fornham Park Golf and Country Club ⓘ₁₈
Fornham All Saints
Flat parkland with rivers and lakes.
☎ 0284 706777

Royal Worlington Golf Club ⓘ₉
Links course.
☎ 0638 712216

Special Interests

ART AND CRAFTS

Craft at the Suffolk Barn
Franham Road, Great Barton
Restored barn. Plants, flowers, books and local crafts. Gardens.
☎ 0284 8731

ART GALLERIES

Market Cross
Designed in 1774 by Robert Adam as a theatre; converted in 1970 to gallery housed on upper floor.
☎ 0284 762081

COUNTRY PARKS

Nowton Park
Outskirts of town
New parkland – 172 acres of woods, copses, specimen trees, sheep pasture, hay meadows with Muntjac deer. Waymarked circular walks are planned for Spring 1991.

West Stow Country Park
On the A110 at West Stow
125-acre park, heaths, woods, river and a lake. Nature trail, nature reserve, wildfowl reserve overlooked by hide.
☎ 0284 728718

FACTORY VISITS

Rake Factory
3 miles south of Bury St Edmunds at Little Welnetham
19th century working factory making rakes and scythes. Shop. Tours by appointment.
☎ 0284 868176

FESTIVALS AND FAIRS

May
Bury St Edmunds Festival
Contact the Tourist Information Centre for details.
☎ 0284 764667

June
Cake and Ale Ceremony when cake, ale and money are distributed to the poor of the parish from St Mary's Church.

GARDENS

Abbey Gardens
Attractive gardens around the Abbey ruins, once botanic gardens belonging to the Marquis of Bristol.
☎ 0284 763233

The Appleby Rose Garden
Traditional rose garden. Details from the Tourist Information Centre.

Giffords Hall
Near Bury St Edmunds at Hartest
33-acre small country living with wild flowers, organic vegetables and wine. Bees, chickens and rare sheep.
☎ 0284 830464

GUIDED TOURS

Regular town tours and special tours for groups. Contact the Tourist Information Centre.
☎ 0284 764667

Tours for Groups
Arranged throughout the year
Contact Mrs A Fayers.
☎ 0284 752433

HERITAGE

Bury St Edmunds Abbey
Ruins of this large abbey featuring
preserved gateways. Gardens.
☎ 0284 763233

Bury St Edmunds Abbeygate

West Stow Anglo-Saxon Village
7 miles from Bury St Edmunds on the
A110 at West Stow
Anglo-Saxon site with reconstructed
buildings, information centre.
☎ 0284 728718 (from Spring 1991)

HISTORIC BUILDINGS

Bardwell Windmill
8 miles north-east of Bury St Edmunds
on the A143
Wind or steam powered mill with
traction engine; flours for sale.
☎ 0359 51331

Pakenham Watermill
5 miles north-east of Bury St Edmunds
18th century working mill on Domesday
site; flours for sale.
☎ 0359 70570

HISTORIC HOUSES

Hengrave Hall
3 miles north-west of the town
Early Tudor house, mediaeval church
with 11th century round tower in
grounds. Visits by appointment.
☎ 0248 701561

Ickworth

Ickworth
Palladian house with 106-ft Rotunda
housing Georgian silverware, Regency
and 18th century furniture and set in
Ickworth Park. National Trust.
☎ 028488 270

MUSEUMS

The Clock Museum
Angel Corner
Timepieces dating from the 16th century
to the present day; original collection
donated by the late Frederic Gershom
Parkington; exhibited in a Queen Anne
house.
☎ 0284 757071

The Clock Museum

Moyses Hall Museum
Norman building, local history,
archaeology, Red Barn murder relics.
☎ 0284 757488

Suffolk Regiment Museum
Gibraltar Barracks, Out Risbygate Street
Historical exhibits of Suffolk and
Cambridgeshire Regiments.
☎ 0284 752394

ORNAMENTAL PARKS

Ickworth Park
Woodland, park, orangery and formal
gardens landscaped by Capability Brown.
☎ 028488 270

THEATRES

Theatre Royal
Westgate Street
Small Regency theatre designed by
William Wilkins.
☎ 0284 755127

WILDLIFE PARKS

Butterfly Garden
Barrow
☎ 0284 810859

Norton Tropical Bird Gardens
7 miles east of Bury St Edmunds on the
A1088 at Pakenham
100 species in a 4-acre garden, children's
corner, refreshments.
☎ 0359 30957

Water Sports

CANOEING

**St Edmundsbury Sailing and Canoeing
Association**
Contact Mr M Pettit, 5 Barnfield,
Chebbington

SWIMMING

**Bury St Edmunds Sports and Leisure
Centre**
☎ 0284 753496

YACHTING

St Edmundsbury Yachting Association
RYA affiliated.
Contact Sue Flintham, 11 St Johns Place
☎ 0284 754916

Abbots Bridge, Abbey Gardens, Bury St Edmunds

A small attractive coastal town with a wide sandy beach and low sandy cliffs at the north end, Caister-on-Sea is a popular family resort. Originally it was a Roman port and Roman remains are still visible. The ruins of a 15th century moated castle now house a museum of vintage and veteran cars.

Caister offers opportunities for sailing, windsurfing, golf and some pleasant coastal walks. It is close to the busy resort of Great Yarmouth with its wide range of amusements and entertainment facilities.

i Marine Parade
Great Yarmouth
☎ 0493 84219

Outdoor Leisure

GOLF

Great Yarmouth and Caister Golf Club
Beach House, Caister Road
Natural links course by dunes.
Restrictions on visitors at weekends and Bank Holidays.
☎ 0493 728699/720421

Special Interest

HERITAGE

Caister Roman Town
Old-established Roman commercial port.

MUSEUMS

Caister Castle Car Collection
Britain's largest private collection of motor vehicles dating from 1893 to present day. Open from May to September.
☎ 057 284 251

Great Yarmouth Beach

Cambridge

Cambridge must be one of the loveliest cities in Britain – its wealth of architectural styles, the Colleges, the courtyards, King's College Chapel, the bridge and the famous 'Backs' along the River Cam continue to captivate countless visitors. An ancient city, its history dating back to Neolithic times, it was settled by the Romans, Saxons and later the Normans. It prospered as a trading centre during the 10th century developing as a teaching centre until, in the 13th century, the University was founded. Peterhouse, founded by the Bishop of Ely in 1284, is the oldest of the colleges, both it and many of the other oldest colleges and University buildings are all within walking distance of each other in the centre of the town. Many college courtyards, chapels and gardens are open to visitors. Some of the most beautiful are Clare, King's, Jesus, Emmanuel, Trinity and Magdalene.

Cambridge is a major cultural centre having an excellent selection of important museums that include the Fitzwilliam, the Folk Museum, the University Museum Archaeology and Anthropology and the Scott Polar Research Institute. The Arts Theatre presents a diverse programme including the well-known Footlights Revue in which many famous names in entertainment have made their debut. The Cambridge Festival and the Folk Festival are two popular international events and May Week is the University's event of the year.

Punts gliding between the willow branches overhanging the River Cam encapsulates one aspect of Cambridge – they are not as easy to manoeuvre as they look but great fun can be had trying! The Cam is also an ideal river for rowing and riverside picnics.

Cambridge incorporates excellent shopping and entertainment facilities amongst its ancient streets, it has a market everyday except Sunday in Market Square, and whether it is books (new, second-hand or antiquarian), antiques, fine art, clothes or good food and atmospheric pubs there is a wealth of choice among the main streets and passageways of the city. Cambridge is indeed a truly beautiful city with something for everyone to feast on and enjoy.

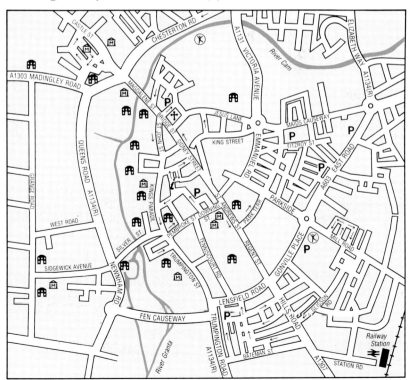

i Wheeler Street
☎ 0223 322640
Market days Monday to Saturday
Early closing Thursday
Population 102,000

Adventure Sports

CLIMBING

Kelsey Kerridge Sports hall
Queen Anne Terrace, Gonville Place
☎ 0223 207328

SHOOTING

Cambridge Shooting Association
☎ 0223 207328

Cambridge SG Ground
Off the A1303 at Madingley
☎ 0223 248468

Cambridge University CPSC Ground
Mill Road
☎ 045 284 264

Cottenham CPC Ground
Smithy Fen, Cottenham
☎ 0954 50061

Kelsey Kerridge Sports Hall
☎ 0223 207328

Aerial Sports

FLYING

Cambridge Aero Club
The Airport, Newmarket Road
☎ 0223 61133

GLIDING

Cambridge University Gliding Club
Duxford Airfield, Duxford
☎ 0223 832197/832068

Indoor Sports

LEISURE CENTRES

Kelsey Kerridge Sports Hall
☎ 0223 463210

ROLLER SKATING

Kelsey Kerridge Sports Hall
Saturday evening sessions.
☎ 0223 463210

SQUASH

Kelsey Kerridge Sports Hall
☎ 0223 463210

Multi-Activity Holidays

SPECIAL INTEREST CENTRES

The Windmill Stables
Shepreth Road, Barrington
Children's residential instructional
holidays. BHS approved.
☎ 0223 871487

Outdoor Leisure

CAMPING AND CARAVANNING

**Great Shelford Camping and
Caravanning Club Site**
19 Cabbage Moor, Great Shelford
Capacity for 100 tents and caravans with
extensive facilities
☎ 0223 841185

Highfield Farm Camping Site
Highfield Farm, Long Road, Comberton
Pitches for 60 tents and 120 caravans
with extensive facilities.
☎ 0223 262308

Roseberry Tourist Park
Pitches for 80 tents and caravans with
extensive facilities.
☎ 0954 60346

CYCLING

Armada Cycles
47 Suez Road
☎ 0223 210421
Town Centre
Much of Cambridge town centre has
been adapted for cyclists. For hire of
cycles, contact the Tourist Information
Centre.
☎ 0223 322640

FISHING

Coarse Fishing
For information and permits contact the
National Rivers Authority
☎ 0733 371811

**Cambridgeshire and Isle of Ely
Federation of Anglers**
☎ 0223 861748

FOOTBALL

Cambridge United Football Club
Newmarket Road
☎ 0223 241237

78

GOLF

Cambridgeshire Moat House Hotel Golf Club 🏌18
5 miles north-west of Cambridge on the A604 at Bar Hill
Equipment hire available but at least four own clubs per player essential. Wide wheel trolleys only in winter.
☎ 0954 780555

Girton Golf Club 🏌18
Dodford Lane, Girton
Non-members may play Monday to Friday. Club hire available. Wide wheel trolleys only. Advance booking required.
☎ 0223 276169

The Gog Magog Golf Club 🏌18 🏌9
4 miles south-east of Cambridge on the A605
Non-members may play Monday to Friday. A handicap of 18 or less and a certificate are required. Own clubs and wide wheel trolleys required. Advance booking essential.
☎ 0223 246058

HORSE RIDING

Broadway Farm
6 miles north-west of Cambridge at Lolworth
Facilities for the disabled.
☎ 0954 780159

Gransden Hall Riding School
12 miles south-west of Cambridge at Great Gransden
☎ 0767 7366

Haggis Farm Stables
Cambridge Road, Barton
Children's stable management courses.
☎ 0223 460353

New Farm Stables
8 miles west of Cambridge at Bourne
☎ 0954 4501

Park House Stables Ltd
5 miles south-west of Cambridge at Harston
All weather surface.
☎ 0223 870075

Sawston Riding School
Common Lane Farm, Common Lane, Sawston
☎ 0223 835198

The Windmill Stables
0223 8/1487

TENNIS

Cambridge Indoor Tennis Centre
Long Road Sixth Form College, Long Road
☎ 0223 411583

Cambridge Lawn Tennis Club
☎ 0223 355359

Christ's Pieces
Hard courts.

Jesus Green
Grass and hard courts. Contact the groundsman.

Lammas Land
Hard courts.

Queen Edith's Way
Hard courts.

WALKING AND RAMBLING

Coe Fen and Paradise Nature Trails
Nature trails on common land beside the River Cam. Details from the Cambridgeshire Wildlife Trust.
☎ 0223 880788

Devil's Dyke
$7^{1}/_{2}$ miles defensive fortification ditch dating from 500 AD running from north of Reach to south of Stetchworth.
☎ 0223 880788

Gog Magog Hills
$3^{3}/_{4}$ miles south-east of Cambridge on the A1307
Woods and open stretches of grass.

Roman Road Circular Walk
6-mile waymarked walk from Stapleford to Wandlebury along the River Granta. Contact the Cambridgeshire County Council.
☎ 0223 317404

Shepreth Riverside Walk
Tree-fringed meadows alongside the River Cam. Walking, picnics, nature study. Contact the Cambridgeshire County Council.
☎ 0223 317404

Wimpole Way
13 miles from Cambridge to Wimpole Hall
Contact the Cambridgeshire County Council.
☎ 0223 317404

Special Interests

ART GALLERIES

Cambridge Darkroom
Dales Brewery, Gwydir Street
Photographic gallery. Workshop available for children in the summer.
☎ 0223 350725

Gallery on the Cam
Near Jesus Lock
Floating art gallery.

Holographic Exhibition
Magdalene Street

Kettles Yard
Castle Street
20th century paintings and sculpture.
Art classes for children on Wednesday
afternoons.
☎ 0223 352124

ARTS AND CRAFTS

Black Sheep Shop
15 Green Street
Woollen, tweed and knitted clothing.
☎ 0223 327262

Cambridge Brass Rubbing Centre
St Giles Church, Castle Street
☎ 0223 464767

**Eastern Counties Sheepskin Tannery
Shop**
London Road, Sawston
Sheepskin and leather items.
☎ 0223 834757

COUNTRY PARKS

Wandlebury
5 miles south-east of Cambridge off the
A1307
Parkland, woodland, Iron Age hill fort
and nature trail.

FARM PARKS

Wimpole Home Farm
8 miles south-west of Cambridge off the
A603
Farm museum and rare breeds, film loft
and pets' corner, in park surrounding
Wimpole Hall. Horsedrawn cart rides.
☎ 0223 207257

May Week

FESTIVALS AND FAIRS

June
'May Week'
Celebrates the end of the University's
year; May Balls, boat races and open air
theatre.

Footlights Review
Annual student production at the Arts
Theatre.
☎ 0223 352000

'May Bumps'
University rowing races from Milton to
Cambridge on the River Cam.

Midsummer Fair
Midsummer Common
Funfair and trade stalls.

July
Cambridge Festival
Whole range of entertainment from art
exhibitions and drama to Elizabethan
banquets; the main attractions are the
concerts and recitals given in various
city and college buildings over the two
weeks of the festival.

Cambridge Folk Festival
Cherry Hinton Hall Grounds
☎ 0223 357851

November
Bonfire and fireworks on Midsummer
Common.

December
Festival of Nine Lessons and Carols
Kings College Chapel
World-famous Christmas Eve service by
Kings College Choir – queue early for
the afternoon start!

FOOD AND DRINK

Culpeper the Herbalists
25 Lion Yard
Herbal teas, honeys and fresh herb
jellies. Cosmetics and gifts.
☎ 0223 67370

GARDENS

Anglesey Abbey
6 miles north-east of Cambridge on the
B1101 at Lode
Outstanding 100-acre garden of lawns,
rare trees and flowers. Historic house.
☎ 0223 811200

Cambridge University Botanic Garden
Cory Lodge, Bateman Street
Arboretum; rock, scented and winter
gardens, fascinating variety of plants.
Guided tours can be arranged.
☎ 0223 336265

Crossing House
Meldreth Road, Shepreth
Cottage garden with many old-fashioned plants.
☎ 0763 261071

GUIDED TOURS

Cathedral and City Tours
Regular city and college tours. Guides available for groups. Contact the Tourist Information Centre for details.

Good Friday Ltd
Tourism Reception, Cambridge Railway Station
Open-top bus tours of Cambridge, leaving every 15 minutes daily.
☎ 0223 62444

HERITAGE

Castle Mound
Castle Street
Good viewpoint of the city.

Gog Magog Hills and Wandlebury Ring
3³/₄ miles south-east of Cambridge on the A1307
Iron age fort of Wandlebury.

HISTORIC BUILDINGS

Great Gransden Post Mill
10 miles west of Cambridge on the B1046
Well-preserved open-trestle post mill built in 1674, restored in 1984 – ask at the local Post Office for keyholders.

Great St Mary's Church
Kings Parade
The tower of this University church can be climbed between 10.30 and 4.00 pm.

King's College Chapel
King's Parade
Chapel with exhibition of why and how it was built.
☎ 0223 3504

Lode Watermill
6 miles north-east of Cambridge on the B1102 at Lode
Working watermill. National Trust.
☎ 0223 207257

The Round Church
Junction of St Johns Street and Bridge Street
The Church of the Holy Sepulchre is the oldest of the four remaining round churches in England; it was built around 1130 and restored in 1841.

Trumpington Church
2 miles south of Cambridge on the A1301
Mediaeval church containing the second oldest monumental brass in England depicting Sir Roger de Trumpington.

HISTORIC HOUSES

Anglesey Abbey
Lode
13th century Augustinian priory converted to a house in the 16th century. Outstanding art collection; superb gardens.
☎ 0223 811200

Wimpole Hall
6 miles south-west of Cambridge off the A603
Spectacular 18th century mansion, beautifully landscaped park and Chinese bridge.
☎ 0223 207257

MUSEUMS

Cambridge and County Folk Museum
2 – 3 Castle Street
Everyday life from 1650 to the present day displayed in early timber-framed building. Children's activity days; groups by appointment.
☎ 0223 355159

Fitzwilliam Museum
Trumpington Street
Museum and outstanding art gallery; extensive Egyptian, Greek and Roman collections, illuminated manuscripts, English pottery and porcelain, paintings include works by Titian, Gainsborough, Hogarth and Turner.
☎ 0223 332900

Museum of Technology
Riverside, off the Newmarket Road
Steam engines and printing machines housed in an old pumping station. Occasional steam days.
☎ 0223 68650

Scott Polar Research Institute
Lensfield Road
Displays on current exploration and some relics of earlier expeditions.
☎ 0223 336540

Sedgwick Museum of Geology
Downing Street
See the dinosaurs and fossils from all over the world.
☎ 0223 333456

University Museum of Archaeology and Anthropology
Downing Street
☎ 0223 333516

University Museum of Classical Archaeology
Sidgwick Avenue
☎ 0223 335152

University Museum of Zoology
Downing Street
Specimens used for teaching purposes, fossils and skeletons.
☎ 0223 336650

Whipple Museum of the History of Science
Free School Lane
Collection of historic scientific instruments.
☎ 0223 334540

NATURAL HISTORY

Coe Fen and Paradise Nature Trails
Natural trails on common land by the River Cam. Contact the Cambridgeshire Wildlife Trust.
☎ 0223 880788

THEATRES

ADC Theatre
Park Street
University and amateur groups.
☎ 0223 352001/359547

Arts Theatre
Peas Hill
Visiting professional companies.
☎ 0223 352000/355246

The Cambridge Playroom
10 St Edward's Passage
Student productions during term and the Cambridge Festival.

Mumford Theatre
Anglia Higher Educational College, East Road
Student productions.
☎ 0223 352932

Water Sports

BOAT HIRE

Scudamore's
Granta Place
Punts and rowing boats for hire. Start at Granta Place, near Silver Street Bridge or Magdalene Street.
☎ 0223 359750

Two Tees Boat Yard
70 Water Street, Chesterton
Weekly and part week hire for boating on the Cambridgeshire waterways and fens.
☎ 0223 65597

82

Tyrell's Marine Ltd
23-27 Bermuda Road
Punts, rowing boats and canoes for hire at Jesus Green
☎ 0223 352847/63080

BOAT TRIPS

The Marchioness
Jesus Lock
Summer trips on the River Cam.
☎ 0223 324325

CANOEING

Cambridge Canoe Club
☎ 0223 311715

PUNTING

Scudamore's
Start at Granta Place or Magdalene Street
☎ 0223 352847/63080

ROWING

Cambridge Veterans Rowing Club
☎ 0223 844166

City of Cambridge Rowing Club
☎ 0223 314984 evenings

SAILING

Cam Sailing Club
On the A10 north of Cambridge at Waterbeach
RYA affiliated.
☎ 0440 706697

Cambridge Sailing Club
☎ 0223 290420

SWIMMING

Abbey Sports Centre
Whitehill Road
16-metre pool.
☎ 0223 213352

Jesus Green Outdoor Swimming Pool
Open in summer only.

Kings Hedges Pool
Kings Hedges Road
16-metre pool.
☎ 0223 353248

Parkside Swimming Pool
☎ 0223 350008

Canvey Island is an industrial, residential and seaside island on the Thames Estuary. It is close to the major shopping and entertainment centres of Basildon and Southend-on-Sea. The island has two interesting museums and there are opportunities to pursue sailing and water sports as well as golf.

Market Days Tuesday, Friday, Saturday
Early closing Thursday
Population 35,500

Dutch Cottage Museum
17th century cottage built by marsh drainage workmen housing natural history exhibits.
☎ 0268 794005

Indoor Sports

LEISURE CENTRES

Runnymede Sports Hall
Runnymede Chase, Thundersley
☎ 0374 558717

Waterside Farm Sports Centre
Somnes Avenue
☎ 0268 696201

Outdoor Leisure

CAMPING AND CARAVANNING

Kings Holiday Park
4 miles from the A13
Overlooked by Hadleigh Castle Country Park. 150 pitches. Extensive facilities including bar, nightclub and restaurant.
☎ 0268 511555

GOLF

Boyce Hill Golf Club
Vicarage Hill, South Benfleet
☎ 0268 793625

Castle Point Golf Club
Canvey Road, Somnes Avenue
☎ 0268 510830

Special Interests

MUSEUMS

Castle Point Transport Museum
Canvey Bus Garage, Point Road
A collection of public service vehicles, either restored or undergoing restoration.
☎ 0268 684272

Water Sports

SWIMMING

Runnymede Sports Hall
Swimming and learner pools.
☎ 0374 558717

Waterside Farm Sports Centre
Swimming pool, learner pool, flume.
☎ 0268 696201

YACHTING

Benfleet Yacht Club
Canvey Road
☎ 0268 792278

Halcon Boating Club
Halcon Marina, The Point
☎ 0268 699537

Island Yacht Club
10 Wall Road
RYA affiliated.
☎ 0268 683948

Pitsea Motor Boat and Yacht Club
Hole Haven
RYA affiliated.
☎ 0268 287711

Castle Hedingham is a lovely old village near the Suffolk border. The town is dominated by a great Norman castle keep, a local landmark. This little mediaeval town has attractive small shops and is set in beautiful countryside.

Outdoor Leisure

CYCLING

Four Seasons Cycling Holidays
The Old School House, St James Street
Weekly tours; luggage porter.
☎ 0787 61370

Special Interests

FARM PARKS

Fullers Dairy Farm
Sible Hedingham
Working dairy farm. Full range of produce for sale.
☎ 0787 60329

HERITAGE

Hedingham Castle
One of the last Norman castles in Britain, built by the de Veres, Earls of Oxford in 1140, it retains a very fine Norman arch and is approached by a beautiful Tudor bridge that spans the dry moat.
☎ 0787 60261

MUSEUMS

Essex Police Collection
Police Station
Unique collection of over 3000 police-related items from around the world. Viewing by appointment only.
☎ 0787 472451

Hedingham Castle
Local history exhibits.
☎ 0787 60261

RAILWAYS

Colne Valley Railway
Castle Hedingham Station
Full size steam railway; museum; restaurant.
☎ 0787 61174

Chatteris is a small market town in the centre of an area of intensive arable farming where the rich black fenland soil has been drained by a succession of drainage schemes, the most spectacular being the Old and New Hundred Foot Rivers found to the south-east of the town. A museum in the High Street depicts the history of the town and there is a water-based recreation centre at Mepal nearby.

Market day Friday
Early closing Wednesday

Adventure Sports

SHOOTING

Fenland GC Ground
Washbrook Farm, Doddington
☎ 0354 53290

Aerial Sports

MICROLIGHT FLYING

Air School Instruction
☎ 0354 740953

Indoor Sports

LEISURE CENTRES

Cromwell Community College
Wenny Road
☎ 0354 32527

Multi-Activity Holidays

SPECIAL INTEREST CENTRES

Mepal Outdoor Centre
Chatteris Road, Mepal
Residential activity holidays at
watersports activity centre: canoeing,
fishing, windsurfing, sailing. RYA
recognised.
☎ 0354 32251

Outdoor Leisure

BIRDWATCHING

Ouse Washes Reserve
Welches Dam, Manea
11 hides overlooking washland pools,
wintering fowl especially widgeon,
migrant and breeding waders. RSPB and
the Cambridgeshire Wildlife Trust.
☎ 035 478 212

Special Interests

FOOD AND DRINK

Gray's Honey Farm
2 miles from Chatteris off the A141 at
Cross Drove
Shop, exhibition, refreshments, aviary
and picnic area.
☎ 0354 33798

MUSEUMS

Chatteris Museum
Grove House, High Street
Victorian and Edwardian clothes,
artefacts, documents, maps and local
history. Open Thursday afternoons and
by appointment.
☎ 0354 2414

ESSEX / Chelmsford ESSEX

Chelmsford, the county town of Essex, has lost much of its rural character as it has
developed. It has however retained several interesting buildings including the Church
of St Mary the Virgin which became a cathedral in the early part of this century.
There are beautiful and picturesque villages in the surrounding area as well as several
country parks and gardens. For the sports enthusiast there are many sporting options
including ice skating, fishing, golf or windsurfing.

Chelmsford Cathedral

i County Hall
Market Road
☎ 0245 283400

Market days Tuesday to Saturday
Early closing Wednesday
Population 151,000

Aerial Sports

MICROLIGHT FLYING

Micro-Air Flying Club
83a Mildmay Road
☎ 0245 490408

PARACHUTING

East Coast Parachute Centre
8 Burns Crescent
☎ 0245 268772

85

Indoor Sports

ICE SKATING

Riverside Ice and Leisure Centre
Victoria Road
☎ 0245 328535

LEISURE CENTRES

Riverside Ice and Leisure Centre
Sports hall, gym, snooker hall, leisure
suite, pools, ice rink and squash courts.
☎ 0245 492954

William de Ferrers Sports Centre
Trinity Square, South Woodham Ferrers
☎ 0245 328535

SQUASH

Dovedale Sports Centre
Vicarage Road
☎ 0245 269020

Riverside Ice and Leisure Centre
☎ 0245 269417

Outdoor Leisure

CRICKET

Essex County Cricket Ground
New Writtle Street
☎ 0245 252420

FISHING

Coarse Fishing
Fishing is free in many waters in and
around Chelmsford. For information and
permits contact the National Rivers
Authority.
☎ 0733 371811
☎ 0473 727712

Boreham
Contact the Chertsey Angling Club.
☎ 0932 564872

Danbury Park Lakes
5 miles east of Chelmsford
Warden on site.

Game Fishing
Hanningfield Reservoir is open to day
ticket and season ticket holders. Details
available from the Fishery Officer, Essex
Water Company.
☎ 0268 710101

GOLF

Channels Golf Club ⛳
Belstead, Farm Lane, Little Waltham
☎ 0245 440005

Three Rivers Golf Club ⛳ ⛳
Stow Road, Purleigh
Parkland course, restrictions on visitors
at weekends and Bank Holidays.
☎ 0621 828631

Widford Golf Course ⛳
1½ miles south of Chelmsford off the
A12
☎ 0245 50555

HORSE RIDING

Hill Farm
Pan Lane, East Hanningfield
Riding and jumping instruction.
☎ 0245 400115

WALKING AND RAMBLING

Backwarden Nature Reserve
1½ mile nature trail through heath and
woodland; pools, marsh and bogland.
Contact the Essex Naturalists' Trust.

Hanningfield Reservoir
Picnic area and nature trails. The access
will not permit coaches.
☎ 0268 710101

Special Interests

COUNTRY PARKS

Danbury Country Park
5 miles east of Chelmsford
39-acre country park with lakes and
woodland, exotic trees and shrubs.
☎ 0245 412350

Marsh Farm Country Park
Off the A130 at South Woodham Ferrers
Working farm centre (under cover),
nature reserve and adventure
playground.

FESTIVALS AND FAIRS

May
Chelmsford Cathedral Festival

GARDENS

Hyde Hall Garden
On the A130 Chelmsford to Southend
road
Garden and woodland.
☎ 0245 400256

HERITAGE

Chelmsford Cathedral
Town centre
15th century perpendicular church,
given cathedral status in 1914.

MUSEUMS

Chelmsford and Essex Museum
Oaklands Park, Moulsham Street
Social and natural history,
archaeological material, exhibitions.
☎ 0245 353066

ORNAMENTAL PARKS

Hylands Park
400-acre public park and woodland.
Local events.

THEATRES

Civic Theatre
Duke Street
☎ 0245 261659

Cramphorn Theatre
☎ 0245 495028

Water Sports

BOAT HIRE

Chelmer and Blackwater Navigation Ltd
Paper Mill Lock, Little Baddow
Modern pleasure barge, bar,
refreshments. Groups of up to 48.
☎ 0245 415520

SWIMMING

Riverside Ice and Leisure Centre
Swimming pool, learner pool, flume.
☎ 0245 269417

WINDSURFING

Channels Windsurfing Centre
Belstead Farm Lane, Little Waltham
RYA recognised. Instruction, video
tuition, board hire and showers. Shop;
meals.
☎ 0245 441000/442488

Hanningfield Reservoir
Equipment hire and tuition available.
☎ 0268 710101

**Long Reach Dinghy and Board Sailing
Club**
South Woodham Ferrers

South Woodham Ferrers Yacht Club
7 Leeward Road, South Woodham
Ferrers
RYA affiliated.
☎ 0245 321349 for the Commodore

Chipping Ongar is situated in farming country, 'ongar' is an Anglo-Saxon word
meaning 'grazing land'. An attractive village, there are houses dating from the 17th
century, a castle mound and a notable Saxon church at nearby Greensted. A sports
centre provides several sporting options and the large gardens at Bobbingworth will
please both the keen gardener and those who would like an aromatic walk.

Early closing Wednesday
Population 5993

Indoor Sports

LEISURE CENTRES

Ongar Sports Centre
Fyfield Road
☎ 0277 363969

SQUASH

Ongar Sports Centre
☎ 0277 363969

Outdoor Leisure

FISHING

Coarse Fishing
Fishing available at Raphael Park, Ongar.
For information and permits contact the
National Rivers Authority.
☎ 0733 371811
☎ 0473 727712

WALKING AND RAMBLING

St Peter's Way
45-mile walk from Chipping Ongar to
the ancient chapel of St Peter's on the
wall at Bradwell.
☎ 0223 317404

Special Interests

FESTIVALS AND FAIRS

June
Herb festival is held at Greensted
Church biannually.
☎ 0277 364694

GARDENS

Blake Hall Gardens
Bobbingworth
25 acres of gardens with tropical house.
RAF operations room.
☎ 0277 362502

HISTORIC BUILDINGS

Greensted Church
9th century church, the only surviving
Saxon church with a nave wall built of
logs.
☎ 0277 364694

Water Sports

SWIMMING

Ongar Sports Centre
☎ 0277 363969

ESSEX   **Clacton-on-Sea**   ESSEX

Clacton-on-Sea has a south facing, seven-mile stretch of sandy coastline. It became a popular seaside resort during the Victorian and Edwardian era. It has a pier, pavilion, promenade, tree-lined streets and colourful gardens. There are theatres, a range of amusement centres, a programme of holiday entertainments, all the facilities of a sports and leisure centre and opportunities for sailing and windsurfing.

St Osyth is nearby with its imposing and historic priory founded by St Osyth, wife of a 7th century East Anglian king who was beheaded by the Danes. It offers the visitor old-world village charm and rural beauty as well as a long uncrowded beach and a large shallow lake, created by the damming of St Osyth creek, perfect for waterskiing and other water sports.

Market days Tuesday, Saturday
Early closing Wednesday
Population 47,188

Aerial Sports

FLYING

Clacton Aero Club
Clacton Airfield
☎ 0255 424671

Indoor Sports

LEISURE CENTRES

Clacton Leisure Centre
Vista Recreation Ground
☎ 0255 429647

Outdoor Leisure

CAMPING AND CARAVANNING

Brook Farm Caravan Park
Off the A133, 1¹/₂ miles from the
seafront
Non-commercial park in farmland
setting. 18 caravan pitches and extensive
facilities.
☎ 0255 860218

Highfield Holiday Park
2 miles from the seafront, on the A133
English Tourist Board Rose Award park.
100 caravan pitches, caravans and
chalets for hire; extensive facilities, no
dogs allowed.
☎ 0255 424244

Hutleys Caravan Park
On the B1027 at St Osyth Beach
20 mobile caravan pitches, extensive
facilities, privately owned beach, no dogs
allowed.
☎ 0255 820712

Leisure Glades Touring Park
Pump Hill Garage, St Johns Road,
St Osyth
40 caravan pitches and 20 tent pitches,
facilities.
☎ 0255 821190

Point Clear Holiday Park
Point Clear, St Osyth
31 caravan pitches and 20 tent pitches,
facilities.
☎ 0255 820416

Seawick Holiday Lido Ltd
St Osyth Beach
110 caravans and 50 chalets for hire;
extensive facilities include heated
indoor pool, gym, sauna and bars.
☎ 0255 820416

Tower Caravan Park
3 miles from Clacton at Jaywick
100 caravan pitches, caravans for hire;
extensive facilities include licenced
club. No dogs allowed. Couples and
families only.
☎ 0255 820372

Valley Farm Caravan Park
On jctn of the B1033 and the B1042
30 caravan pitches, caravans for hire,
extensive facilities, couples and families
only.
☎ 0255 422484

FISHING

Coarse Fishing
For fishing at Lake Walk, weekly tickets
are available from the local tackle shop.

Brian Dean Tackle Shop
Pallister Road
☎ 0255 425992

Sea Fishing
Contact the Tourist Information Centre.
☎ 0255 423400

GOLF

Clacton-on-Sea Golf Club ⌐₁₈
West Road
Flat links course, restrictions on visitors
at weekends and Bank Holidays.
☎ 0255 421919

Special Interests

AQUARIUMS

Clacton Pier
Aquarium and sea lion show.
☎ 0255 421115

HERITAGE

St Osyth's Priory
12th century abbey and gardens; private
art collection.
☎ 0255 820492

PIERS AND PROMENADES

Clacton Pier
Large pleasure pier with rides,
amusements and fishing.
☎ 0255 421115

Water Sports

SWIMMING

Clacton Leisure Centre
☎ 0255 429647

WINDSURFING

Nucleus Sailboard and Leisure
204 Frinton Road, Horland-on-Sea
☎ 0255 812146

Point Clear Windsurfing
La Pointe, Clear Bay, St Osyth
RYA recognised.
☎ 0255 820651

Sailboard School
Gunfleet Beach
☎ 0255 812146 daytime only

YACHTING

Clacton Sailing Club
RYA affiliated.
☎ 0255 813027 Sundays only
☎ 0255 813463 for the Commodore

THEATRES

Princes Theatre
Station Road
☎ 0255 422998

West Cliff Theatre
Tower Road
☎ 0255 421479

Clare

Clare is an attractive woollen town with several 15th century houses including the Priory, named after the family of the Earl of Clare, the Church of St Peter and St Paul with its 13th century tower and 14th century interior and the 15th century priest's house – all good reasons to stroll around the village before going on to explore the country park and the neighbouring village of Stoke-by-Clare.

Market day Monday
Early closing Wednesday
Population 2060

Outdoor Leisure

HORSE RIDING

The Stoke-by-Clare Equitation Centre
On the A1092 at Stoke-by-Clare
General instruction.
☎ 0787 277266/278089

WALKING AND RAMBLING

St Peter's Way
45-mile walk from Chipping Ongar to the ancient chapel of St Peter's on the Wall at Bradwell.
☎ 0223 317404

Special Interests

COUNTRY PARKS

Clare Country Park
25 acres of land reclaimed from railway built through Clare Castle in 1850s; riverside walks, castle mound and keep, disused railway track walk, information centre in old station, butterfly garden and wildlife sanctuary in old moat.
☎ 0787 277491

FOOD AND DRINK

Boyton Vineyard
Hill Farm, Boyton End, Stoke-by-Clare
Vineyard tours, wine tasting lodge.
☎ 0440 61893

Cavendish Manor Vineyard
Cavendish
☎ 0787 280221

HERITAGE

Clare Castle
Ruins of motte and bailey castle and earthworks; surrounded by a country park.

MUSEUMS

Ancient House Museum
Local bygones in a 15th century priest's house.
☎ 0787 277865

Clare Priory
Priory founded in 1248, remains of the once extensive church, cloisters and foundations of the old chapter house. Gardens.

Sue Ryder Foundation Museum
Off the A1092 at Cavendish
Displays depicting Lady Ryder's life and the story of the foundation.
☎ 0787 280252

ESSEX / Coggeshall ESSEX

Coggeshall is a small mediaeval wool and lace-making centre with many lovely listed buildings. A very rewarding town to wander around before exploring the ancient woodlands in the surrounding countryside.

i **Braintree District Council**
☎ 0376 43140/552525

Market day Thursday
Early closing Wednesday
Population 3509

HERITAGE

Coggeshall Abbey
Founded in 1140 for Savignac Order.

Coggeshall Grange Barn
Oldest surviving timber-framed barn in Europe dates from the 12th century.
☎ 0376 562226

Outdoor Leisure

FISHING

Coarse Fishing
Fishing on the River Stour at Bures.
For information and permits contact the National Rivers Authority
☎ 0733 371811
   0473 727712

P Emson Tackle Shop
Earls Colne
☎ 0787 22341

HISTORIC BUILDINGS

St Peter ad Vincula
Church Green
Parish church containing brasses of the Paycocke family.

White Hart Hotel
The Old Wool Hall now forms part of this hotel.
☎ 0376 561654

Special Interests

ARTS AND CRAFTS

Colne Valley Arts
73 High Street, Earls Colne
☎ 0787 223044

COUNTRY PARKS

Chalkney Woods
4 miles from Coggeshall on the A1024 at Earls Colne
63 acres of ancient woodland.
☎ 0206 383868

HISTORIC HOUSES

Paycocke's
West Street
House of the wealthy textile family, built about 1500; half-timbered house with richly carved interior. Restored and presented to National Trust in 1924.
☎ 0376 561305

The Fleece
West Street
Adjoins Paycocke's, once belonged to wealthy textile merchants. Now a public house.
☎ 0376 561412

Colchester, established since 1000 BC, is Britain's oldest recorded town. It stands on a hill in rolling countryside. It's long history encompasses it being the capital city of the ancient British chieftan Cunobelin, 'Old King Cole', a Roman city built on the same site in AD 49–50 was sacked by Queen Boudicca (Boadicea) in AD 60 and a great castle was built here by the Normans. The town became a borough by Royal Charter in 1189. A Parliamentary town in the Civil War, the nursery rhyme *Humpty Dumpty* originated from a battle fought here with the Royalists. Huguenot weavers fleeing from persecution settled here leading to the growth of a Dutch Quarter in the town.

Modern Colchester is flourishing, it has a repertory company, two museums, art galleries and 180 acres of parks and gardens including the attractive Castle Park. There is a new sports centre and two major shopping complexes. There are seaside resorts with watersports facilities nearby as well as facilities to play golf, go birdwatching or spend a day at the zoo.

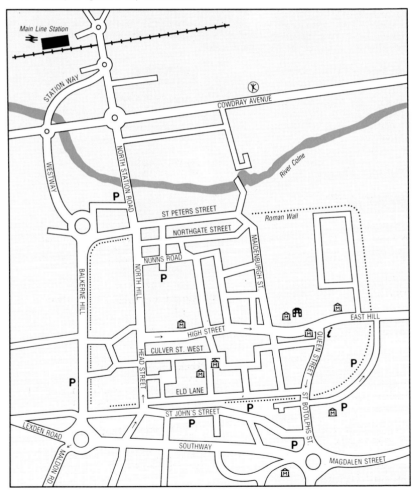

i ₁1 Queen Street
☎ 0206 712920

Market day Saturday
Early closing Thursday
Population 90,000

Adventure Sports

CLIMBING

University of Essex Sports Centre
Wivenhoe Park
☎ 0206 873250

Aerial Sports

GLIDING

Essex & Suffolk Gliding Club
Wormingford Airfield, Fairfields Farm
☎ 0473 822533
☎ 0245 467547

Indoor Sports

LEISURE CENTRES

Colchester Sports Centre
Cowdray Avenue
☎ 0206 766500

Monkwick Sports Hall
☎ 0206 564389

University of Essex Sports Centre
☎ 0206 873250

SQUASH

Colchester Sports Centre
☎ 0206 766500

Unversity of Essex Sports Centre
☎ 0206 766500

TENPIN BOWLING

Colchester Sports Centre
0206 766500

Multi-Activity Holidays

SPECIAL INTEREST CENTRES

Dorian Tours
Dundas Place, Colchester Road,
Ardleigh
Cycling holidays with own or hire
bikes, including bed and breakfast.
☎ 0206 230625

Outdoor Leisure

BIRDWATCHING

Abberton Reservoir
South of Colchester on the A1026

Wildfowl in winter and migrating
waders in spring and autumn. Bird
hide, visitor centre opening in 1990.
Contact the Essex Birdwatching
Society.

Fingringhoewick Nature Reserve
5 miles south-east of Colchester
Wide variety of habitats, freshwater
lake with hides, saltmarsh and
mudflats; nightingales, water birds and
waders; interpretive centre.
Contact the Essex Naturalists' Trust.
☎ 0206 28678/26879

CAMPING AND CARAVANNING

Colchester Camping
Lexden
☎ 0206 45551

Colchester Camping Caravan Park
Cymbeline Way
185 caravan and tent pitches. Lounge,
TV, showers and toilets, shop, games
room.
☎ 0206 45551

King's Vineyard
Fossetts Lane
☎ 0206 240377

CYCLING

Dorian Tours
☎ 0206 230625

FISHING

Coarse Fishing
Fishing at Birch Hall Lake and Layer
Pits, for information and permits
contact the National Rivers Authority.
☎ 0733 371811
☎ 0473 727712

Ardleigh Reservoir Trout Fishery
☎ 0206 230642

GOLF

Birch Grove Golf Club ⛳
Layer Road
Parkland course, restrictions on visitors
at weekends and Bank Holidays.
☎ 0206 34276

Stoke by Nayland Golf Club ⛳ ⛳
Keepers Lane, Leavenheath
Undulating course.
☎ 0206 262836

HORSE RACING

Marks Tey Racecourse
5 miles south of Colchester on the A12
Point-to-point and steeplechasing.

HORSE RIDING

Colchester Riding School
Berechurch Park Stables, Berechurch
Park Road
☎ 0206 575707

Park Farm Riding and Livery Centre
West Bergholt
☎ 0206 27153

WALKING AND RAMBLING

Essex Area Hundred Mile Walk
9-day walk from Stansted to Colchester
in Spetember.
Contact the West Essex Ramblers
☎ 0378 813350

**Roman River Valley Conservation
Centre**
Walks in woodland and open
countryside.
☎ 0206 330208

Special Interests

ANTIQUES

Trinity Antiques Centre
7 Trinity Street
15th century building with a wide
variety of antiques.
☎ 0206 577775

ART GALLERIES

The Minories
74 High Street
Exhibitions of contemporary art.
☎ 0206 577067

Vineyard Gallery
Vineyard Street
☎ 0206 767706

FESTIVALS AND FAIRS

June
Colchester Summer Show
Castle Park
☎ 0206 712460

July
Enterprise Exhibition
Castle Park
☎ 0206 712460

August
Colchester Military Tattoo, the
country's largest military tattoo, held
biannually.
☎ 0206 46015

October
Colchester Oyster Feast
Ceremony for the start of the season,
held in the Moot Hall and opened by
the Mayor.
☎ 0206 712206

FOOD AND DRINK

Colchester Oyster Fisheries
Oysters are a local speciality.
☎ 0206 384141

GARDENS

By-Pass Nurseries
Marks Tey
Holds the annual Primrose Festival in
March.
☎ 0206 211814

GUIDED TOURS

Regular and group tours available,
contact the Tourist Information Centre
for details.
☎ 0206 712920

HERITAGE

Balkerne Gate
Balkerne Hill
Preserved Roman gateway to the town.

Colchester Castle
Castle Park
Norman Keep built on the remains of a
Roman temple.
☎ 0206 712481

Roman Walls
Various locations, including Mersea
Road, Priory Street and Vineyard Street
(where a Roman vineyard was located).

St John's Abbey Gateway
St John's Road, near the town centre

St John's Abbey Gateway

HISTORIC BUILDINGS

Bourne Mill
Bourne Road
16th century fishing lodge converted to
a working mill.
☎ 0206 572422

Dutch Quarter
Former Jewish Quarter, colonised in
the early 1600s by Huguenot weavers.

Marquis of Granby
North Hill
Built in 1521, now a public house.
Impressive fireplace in the back room.
☎ 0206 577630

Siege House
East Street
Scene of the Siege of Colchester in
1648, now a restaurant.

HISTORIC HOUSES

Layer Marney Tower
6 miles south-west of Colchester on
the B1022
England's highest Tudor gate tower;
Italianate decoration, garden.

MUSEUMS

Colchester and Essex Museum
Colchester Castle
Archaeological material; Saxon,
excellent Roman and Norman artefacts.
☎ 0206 712222/712491

Hollytrees
High Street
Costume and social history displays in
1718 house.
☎ 0206 712222/712491

Museum of Natural History
All Saints Church, High Street
A natural history of Essex.

Social History Museum
Holy Trinity Church, Trinity Street
Country life and craft displays and a
collection of old bicycles.
☎ 0206 712222/712491

Tymperleys Clock Museum
Tymperleys, Trinity Street
Selection of Colchester-made clocks,
exhibited in a 15th century house.
☎ 0206 712222/712491

NATURAL HISTORY

Abberton Reservoir
South of Colchester on the B1026
Waterfowl.

Fingringhoewick Nature Reserve
5 miles south-east of Colchester, on the
Colne estuary

Wide variety of bird life, nature trails.
Contact the Essex Naturalists' Trust.
☎ 0206 28678/28679

Roman River Valley Reserve
3 miles south of Colchester
Meadows, marsh and woodland.
☎ 0206 28678/28679

RAILWAYS

East Anglian Railway Museum
6 miles west of Colchester on the A604
at Chappel Station
Steam railway, museum and shop.
Restoration work.
☎ 0206 242524

THEATRES

Arts Centre
☎ 0206 577301

Mercury Theatre
Balkerne Gate
☎ 0206 573948

University Theatre
University of Essex
☎ 0206 873333

ZOOS

Colchester Zoo
Maldon Road, Stanway
Animals and birds from around the
world. Daily events and displays.
☎ 0206 330253

Colchester Zoo

95

Water Sports

SWIMMING

Colchester Sports Centre
☎ 0206 766500

YACHTING

Ardleigh Sailing Club
Ardleigh Reservoir
RYA affiliated.
☎ 0206 581710/577846

University of Essex Sailing Association
Wivenhoe Park
RYA affiliated.

Wivenhoe Sailing Club
4 Quay Street, Wivenhoe

Colchester High Street

Cromer stands on a cliff with wide sandy beaches running down to the sea where fishing boats still work off the beach and sell fresh crabs from the boats. Narrow streets in the old town twist around the parish church of St Peter and Paul which dominates the town with its 60-foot tower, the tallest in Norfolk.

    Cromer became a seaside resort in the Victorian era with the arrival of the railway and it remains a popular family resort. Its pier is one of the few still existing in Norfolk and an 'End of Pier' show is staged in the summer at the Pier Theatre.

i Old Town Hall
Prince of Wales Road
☎ 0263 512497
Market day Friday
Early Closing Wednesday
Population 7385

Aerial Sports

FLYING

Norfolk & Norwich Aero Club
Northrepps Airfield
☎ 036283 274/581

Outdoor Leisure

FISHING

Coarse Fishing
For information and permits contact the National Rivers Authority
☎ 0733 371811
☎ 0473 727712

Felbrigg Hall Lake
½ mile south-west of Felbrigg Hall
5 acres with tench and rudd. Day and season tickets; book in advance from the Administrator, Felbrigg Hall
☎ 0263 75444

Gunton Lake
Gunton Park
16 acres with most coarse fish. Day tickets available from the bailiff on the bank.

Sea Fishing
Contact the Tourist Information Centre
☎ 0263 512497

GOLF

Links Country Park Golf Club ⛳₉
Downland, gorse-clad seaside course.
☎ 0263 75691

Royal Cromer Golf Club ⛳₁₈
145 Overstrand Road
Undulating seaside course alongside cliff edge.
☎ 0263 512497

HORSE RIDING

West Runton Riding Stables
2 miles from Cromer off the A149
BHS approved.
☎ 0263 75339

96

Special Interests

ARTS AND CRAFTS

Alby Crafts
5 miles south of Cromer on the A140
Restored farm buildings, furniture, lace
museum, bottle museum, honey.
☎ 0263 761590/768002

Old Forge Craft Gallery
3 miles south of Cromer on the B1436
☎ 0263 761403

FARM PARKS

The Norfolk Shire Horse Centre
2 miles from Cromer off the A149
Demonstrations and displays.
☎ 0263 75339

FOOD AND DRINK

Crabs
Sold direct from boats on the beach.

GARDENS

Alby Gardens
On the A140
4 acres of garden and wild areas,
interesting shrubs and plants, bee
garden and observation hide.

The Pleasaunce
Overstrand
Lutyens' house set in Gertrude Jekyll
gardens in need of restoration.
☎ 0603 78212

Wolterton Hall Gardens
Off the A140 at Erpingham
Georgian house set in parkland.
☎ 0603 31133

HERITAGE

Baconsthorpe Castle
6 miles south-west of Cromer
Semi-fortified moated house.
☎ 0263 77279

HISTORIC HOUSES

Felbrigg Hall
3 miles south-west of Cromer
Notable 17th century house with
original 18th century interior.
☎ 0263 77444

MUSEUMS

Alby Lace Museum and Study Centre
On the A140
Daily demonstrations; shop.
☎ 0263 768002

Cromer Museum
East Cottages, Tucker Street
Victorian fishermen's homes, local
history, geology and natural history.
☎ 0263 513543

Lifeboat Museum
Lifeboat House, The Pier
Modern lifeboat, models, pictures; talks
and films by appointment.
☎ 0263 512503

PIERS AND PROMENADES

Cromer Pier

THEATRES

The Pier Pavilion
Summer theatre.
☎ 0263 512281

Cromer beach and pier

Attractive old village on the Essex/Suffolk border, in the centre of Constable country.

Early Closing Wednesday
Population 1905

Adventure Sports

SHOOTING

Kings Arms Clay Club Suffolk Ground
Highfield, Lower Raydon
☎ 0473 310011

Outdoor Leisure

FISHING

Coarse Fishing
Fishing on the River Stour at Dedham, Flatford Mill and Nayland. For information and permits contact the National Rivers Authority.
☎ 0733 371811

WALKING AND RAMBLING

Constable Trail
9-mile walk through the landscape and villages associated with the artist's life.
☎ 0787 227823

Painters Way
24-mile walk along the River Stour between Sudbury and Maningtree through countryside associated with Gainsborough and Constable.
☎ 0787 227823

Special Interests

ARTS AND CRAFTS

Dedham Art and Craft Centre
High Street
Former Congregational church.
Working pottery, artists and craftsmen.
☎ 0206 322666

GARDENS

East Bergholt Lodge
Off the A12 at East Bergholt
Woodland garden with over 40 rose varieties and over 350 tree and shrub varieties.
☎ 0206 298278

Dedham village

HISTORIC BUILDINGS

Bridge Cottage
Flatford, East Bergholt
16th Century cottage beside the mill; teas and shop. National Trust.

Flatford Mill
Flatford, East Bergholt
Painted by John Constable, now a field study and arts and crafts centre.
☎ 0206 298283

Willie Lott's Cottage
Flatford, East Bergholt
Also featured by Constable. Private House.

MUSEUMS

Granary Bygones
Flatford, East Bergholt
Display of prints of John Constable's work. Collection of vintage bicycles.
☎ 0206 298111

Sir Alfred Munnings Art Museum
Castle House
Works by the late Sir Alfred Munnings, President of the Royal Academy 1944–49.
☎ 0206 322127

Toy Museum
Art and Craft Centre, High Street
Teddies, dolls, toys and games. Play corner and pictures, shop.
☎ 0206 322666

Water Sports

BOAT HIRE

D E Smeeth
The Boatyard, Mill Lane
Rowing boats, canoes, parties catered for.
☎ 0206 861748

Diss is a picturesque old market town with Tudor, Georgian and Victorian houses set around a beautiful six-acre mere. The 13th century church overlooks the sloping market place which holds a lively market on Fridays. Mere Street leads off from the market to Mere Mouth, an open area where ducks and other wildfowl gather.

Diss and its surroundings offer a diverse selection of attractions including a steam museum, a zoo and monkey sanctuary, a working towermill, and opportunities for ballooning, fishing, walking or even a vineyard visit where the visitor can taste some award-winning vintages.

i Meresmouth
Mere Street
☎ 0379 650523
Market day Friday
Early closing Tuesday

Aerial Sports

BALLOONING

Thomas Holt Wilson
The Cottage, The Green, Redgrave
Instruction in all aspects of ballooning.
Commercial flights.
☎ 0379 898079

Outdoor Leisure

FISHING

Diss Mere
5 acres in the centre of Diss with carp, roach and tench. Season tickets available.
☎ 0379 651222/75341

Zoe's Tackle Shop
Victoria Road
Information and tickets available.
☎ 0379 651222

GOLF

Diss Golf Club 🏌
Stuston Road
☎ 0379 642847
☎ 0379 644399 for the professional

HORSE RIDING

Reeves Hall
10 miles from Diss off the A143 at Hepworth
Residential instructional holidays. BHS approved.
☎ 0379 50217

Rosebrook Farm Equestrian Centre
6 miles from Diss off the A143 at South Lopham
Residential instructional holidays. BHS approved.
☎ 0379 88278

WALKING AND RAMBLING

Circular Walk
Free leaflets from South Norfolk District Council.
☎ 0508 31122

Special Interests

AQUARIUMS

Waveney Fish Farm
Park Road
Tropical and cold water aquarium.
Water gardens, ornamental fish.
☎ 0379 642697

ARTS AND CRAFTS

The Particular Pottery
North-west of Diss on the B1113 at Kenninghall
Pottery in a former Baptist Chapel.
Orders taken for dinner services.
☎ 0953 878476

FOOD AND DRINK

Pulham Vineyards
Pulham Market, near Diss
A vineyard since Roman times; has produced award-winning vintages.
☎ 0379 76672

GARDENS

Bressingham Gardens
2 miles west of Diss on the A1066
6 acres of informal and internationally famous gardens.
☎ 037 988 382/386

99

HISTORIC BUILDINGS

Thelnetham Windmill
Mill Road, Thelnetham, near Diss
Early 19th century towermill with four
floors and four sails, recently restored
and working. Flours for sale.
☎ 0473 726996

MUSEUMS

Bressingham Steam Museum
2 miles west of Diss on the A1066
5-mile narrow gauge railway, footplate
rides, exhibition and steam days.
☎ 037 988 382/386

Diss Museum
Market Place
Exhibits of old photographs of local
interest.

Strike School
3 miles north-west of Diss at Burston
Scene of the longest strike in British
history – 25 years. Keyholders' name in
porch if locked.

RAILWAYS

Bressingham Narrow Gauge Railway
Bressingham Steam Museum
☎ 037 988 382/386

ZOOS

Banham Zoo and Monkey Sanctuary
6 miles north-west of Diss on
the B1113
Extensive collection of wildlife and rare
primates in 20 acres of parkland.
Refreshments, farm shop, childrens
play area and woodland walk.
☎ 095 387 476

Water Sports

SWIMMING

Diss Swimming Pool
Victoria Road
25-metre pool, learner pool; weight
training and fitness room.
☎ 0379 652754

Downham Market is a small market town set on a hill on the edge of the Fens. A decorative clock tower stands in the town centre. Nearby Denver Mill is a landmark in the surrounding flat Fenland landscape and Denver Sluice marks the tidal limit on the Great Ouse River, it helps control the Fenland waterways. The masts of yachts and dinghies glide by above the banks of the sluices. The Ouse Washes lie to the south of the town, an expanse of land drained 200 years ago and now a rich habitat for many species of water bird.

Market day Friday
Early closing Wednesday
Population 5090

Adventure Sports

SHOOTING

Greenend Holiday and SG Ground
Off the A1101
☎ 03548 335

Outdoor Leisure

GOLF

Ryston Park Golf Club
Ely Road, Denver
Flat parkland course with lake.
Restrictions on visitors at weekends
and Bank Holidays.
☎ 0366 382133

Special Interests

FOOD AND DRINK

Norfolk Punch
Welle Manor Hall, Upwell
Herbal health drink made from an
ancient recipe.
☎ 0945 773333

HISTORIC BUILDINGS

Denver Windmill
South of town at Denver
A six-storey mill built in 1835 with a
former steam mill, granary, engine
shed, original machinery and a display
of old milling equipment. Tours by
appointment.
☎ 0366 383374

HISTORIC HOUSES

Welle Manor Hall
On the A1101 at Upwell
Mediaeval fortified manor house and
church, dating from 1202. Curio
museum in coachhouse includes
Lafayette Collection of Victorian
photographs. Guided tours by
appointment.
☎ 0945 773333

Water Sports

SWIMMING

Downham Market Swimming Pool
War Memorial Playing Fields
☎ 0366 383822

Duxford is a small village to the west of Cambridgeshire with some attractive
buildings and a notable chapel. It is famous as the home of the Imperial War Museum
and for its annual show. Wandlebury Camp, an Iron Age fort, is not far away and there
are several fascinating villages nearby.

Early closing Wednesday
Population 1718

Outdoor Leisure

BIRDWATCHING

Fowlmere
Access near Fowlmere village off the
A10 by Shepreth
Wildlife oasis of reedbeds and pools,
hides on stilts give panoramic views;
water rails and kingfishers.
☎ 0767 80551

Special Interests

FESTIVALS AND FAIRS

September
Air show at Duxford Airfield.
☎ 0223 833963

HERITAGE

Duxford Chapel
Located between Duxford and
Whittlesford

The chapel was founded soon after
1200 as a hospital, it became a 'free
chapel' in the 14th century until
dissolved by Edward VI. It was a
tollhouse for the nearby bridge before
being converted into a barn. It is open
all year and the key is available from
keyholders listed on the door.

MUSEUMS

Imperial War Museum
Off the M11 at Duxford
Former Battle of Britain fighter station.
Preserved military and civil aircraft and
a wide range of military vehicles,
special exhibits, ride simulator and
adventure playground.
☎ 0223 835075/833963

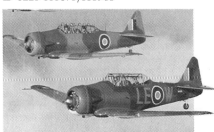

East Dereham, a lively market town, lies at the centre of Norfolk. Its church stands on the site of the nunnery founded in the 7th century by St Wighburga, daughter of King Anna of East Anglia. A well in the churchyard that bears her name was once a place of pilgrimage and a legend associated with her is depicted in the village sign. The local museum is housed in Bishop Bonner's Cottage noted for its decorative plasterwork known as pargetting.

Market days Tuesday, Friday
Early closing Wednesday
Population 13,444

Adventure Sports

SHOOTING

Wayland GC Ground
Mount Pleasant Farm, Carbroooke Lane, Shipham
☎ 0362 820943

Aerial Sports

MICROLIGHT FLYING

David Clarke Microlight Aircraft
Unit 1, The Black Hangar, Worthing
Trial flights, tuition and aircraft sales.
☎ 0362 83405

Outdoor Leisure

FISHING

Game Fishing
Bintree Mill Trout Fishery and Roosting Hills Trout Fishery, near Dereham are open to members of the Salmon and Trout Association only.

Tannery House Fishery
Tannery House, Worthing
3/4 acre lake with brown and rainbow trout. Tickets and information from Mr Eve.
☎ 0362 81202

GOLF

Dereham Golf Club ⓑ
Quebec Road
☎ 0362 5900

Special Interests

HERITAGE

North Elmham Saxon Cathedral and Bishop's Castle
Saxon cathedral, later a hunting lodge.

HISTORIC BUILDINGS

Dereham Windmill
Cherry Lane, Norwich Road
Brick tower mill built in 1836, restored 1984–87. Original machinery. Exhibition.

St Nicholas's Church
Partly Norman church on the site of 7th century St Withburga's nunnery. William Cowper, the poet, is buried here.

MUSEUMS

Bishop Bonner's Cottage
16th century cottage with local history, domestic and agricultural exhibits.
☎ 0362 693107

Norfolk Rural Life Museum
2 miles north-west of East Dereham
Last two centuries of Norfolk village life and agriculture depicted and housed in a former workhouse. Special events.
☎ 0362 860563

WILDLIFE PARKS

Badley Moor Fish, Bird and Butterfly Centre
Badley Moor
Water gardens, stream with fish, gardens with aviaries, 7000 sq.ft. covered area with British and tropical butterflies.

Water Sports

SWIMMING

East Dereham Swimming Pool
Quebec Road
☎ 0362 693419

Ely was once an island held by Hereward the Wake against the Normans, the island disappeared in the 17th and 18th centuries when the Fens were drained. It is a charming market town with ancient narrow streets, timbered houses, mediaeval gateways and a magnificent cathedral whose famous lantern tower can be seen for miles in any direction. The cathedral was begun in 1083 on the site of a 7th century Benedictine Abbey and the octagonal lantern tower was added in the 14th century after the collapse of the central tower. Oliver Cromwell caused the cathedral to close in 1644, it remained closed for 17 years.

A rich historical centre there are museums; including the new Oliver Cromwell's House opened in November 1990, windmills and fine opportunities for walking, birdwatching, fishing and, for the more adventurous, microlight flying.

i Oliver Cromwell's House
29 St Mary's Street
☎ 0353 662062

Market day Thursday
Early closing Tuesday
Population 9122

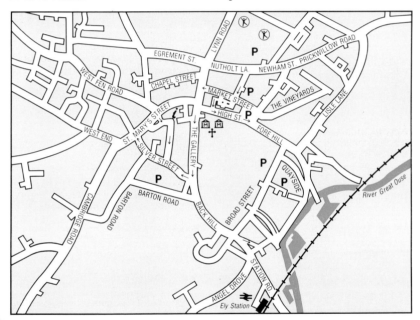

Oliver Cromwell's House

Detail of interior exhibit

103

Ely Cathedral

Adventure Sports

SHOOTING

Isleham GC Ground
Fen Bank, Waterside, Isleham
☎ 0638 750494

The Mepal Clay Target Centre Ground
Mepal Airfield
☎ 0354 53290

Aerial Sports

MICROLIGHT FLYING

Pegasus Flight Training
Sutton Meadows Airfield, The Gault, Sutton
☎ 0487 842360

Indoor Sports

LEISURE CENTRES

Paradise Centre
Newnham Street
☎ 0353 667580

Soham and District Sports Hall
Sand Street, Soham
☎ 0353 722662

SQUASH

Paradise Centre
☎ 0353 667580

Soham and District Sports Hall
☎ 0353 722662

Outdoor Leisure

BIRDWATCHING

Wicken Fen Wetland Reserve
Access via the William Thorpe Building, Lode Lane, Wicken
Waterfowl in winter, breeding marsh birds in summer seen in undrained fen.
☎ 0353 720274

FISHING

Coarse Fishing
For information and permits for fishing on the River Ouse contact the National Rivers Authority
☎ 0733 371811
☎ 0473 727712

GOLF

Ely City Golf Course
Cambridge Road
Well wooded parkland course. Green fee players and societies welcome.
☎ 0353 662751/663317

WALKING AND RAMBLING

Bishops Way
7–9 miles circular route on ancient tracks. Contact the Cambridgeshire County Council
☎ 0223 317404

Ely–Little Thetford–Ely
8½ or 6-mile walk starting from Barton Square, Ely, follows the River Ouse.
☎ 0353 666441

Ely–Witchford
6½-mile trail along old drover's road, tracks and fields.

Roswell Pits
Access from Springhead Lane off the B1382
Nature trail around flooded claypits close to the city.
☎ 0223 880788

Special Interests

ARTS AND CRAFTS

Steeplegate
Craft shop.
☎ 0353 664731

GARDENS

Herb Garden
5 miles south-west of Ely at Nigel House, Wilburton
Collection of culinary, aromatic, medicinal and Shakespearian herbs. Telephone to confirm garden is open.
☎ 0353 740824

GUIDED TOURS

Regular and special tours for the city and cathedral. Contact the Tourist Information Centre.
☎ 0353 662062

For the cathedral only, contact cathedral direct.
☎ 0353 667735

HERITAGE

Ely Cathedral
Mediaeval architecture, carpentry and stained glass. Brass-rubbing centre.
☎ 0353 667735

HISTORIC BUILDINGS

Downfield Windmill
5 miles south-east of Ely on the A142 at Soham
Brick tower mill dating from 1726 in full working order. Flours for sale.
☎ 0353 720333
☎ 0533 707625

MUSEUMS

Ely Museum
High Street
Local history, military collections,

recently re-furbished, new audio-visual displays.
☎ 0353 663488

Haddenham Farmland Museum
7 miles south-west of Ely at Haddenham
Collection of local bygones and agricultural tools. Special events and demonstrations.
☎ 0353 740381

Oliver Cromwell's House
29 St Mary's Street
Heritage centre furnished in Cromwellian period style; video display; opened November 1990.
☎ 0353 662062

Prickwillow Engine Museum
4 miles east of Ely at Prickwillow
☎ 0353 88230

Stained Glass Museum
Ely Cathedral
Stained glass windows from 14th century to the present day in lighted displays. History of the craft and style.
☎ 0353 663488

Stretham Beam Engine
Stretham, near Ely
1831 Watts parallel beam engine with 37-inch diameter scoopwheel.
☎ 0223 277346

NATURAL HISTORY

Roswell Pits
Off the B1382
Nature trail round flooded claypits. Rich vegetation and bird life. Contact the Cambridgeshire Wildlife Trust.
☎ 0223 880788

Wicken Fen
Off the A1123 at Wicken
One of the last undrained fens with general access. Varied plant, animal and bird life.
☎ 0353 720274

Water Sports

SWIMMING

Paradise Pool
Newnham Street
☎ 0353 665481

YACHTING

Ely Sailing Club
Prickwillow Road, 1 mile from the city on the B1382
RYA affiliated.
☎ 0353 663083/667717

Epping, a market town dating from the 13th century, was once an important coaching centre. It stands on the edge of Epping Forest, a 6,000-acre remnant of the 60,000-acre hunting ground of successive monarchs through Saxon, Norman and Tudor times. Great hornbeam trees, heaths and open glades characterize the forest which is ideal walking, rambling and riding country.

i 323 High Street
☎ 0378 560000

Market day Monday
Early closing Wednesday
Population 10,500

Adventure Sports

SHOOTING

Epping Sports Centre
25 Hemnall Street
☎ 0378 74895

Aerial Sports

GLIDING

Essex Gliding Club
North Weald Airfield, Bassett
☎ 0378 822222

PARAGLIDING

The Brigade Paragliding Club
North Weald
☎ 081 508 1991

North Weald Paragliding Club
Near Epping
Weekends and public holidays only, for prior bookings:
☎ 0702 540901

Indoor Sports

SQUASH

Epping Sports Centre
☎ 0378 784895

Loughton Hall
Rectory Lane, Loughton
☎ 081 508 4662 daytime
☎ 081 508 7772 evenings

Outdoor Leisure

CAMPING AND CARAVANNING

Debden House Camp Site
2½ miles from jctn 26 of the M25
75 caravan pitches and 150 tent
pitches. Showers, shop.
☎ 081 508 9435

FISHING

Coarse Fishing
For information about fishing in Epping
Forest contact the Superintendent, The
Warren, Loughton.

For information and permits contact
the National Rivers Authority
☎ 0733 371811
☎ 0473 727712

GOLF

Chigwell Golf Club 🏌18
High Road, Chigwell
☎ 081 500 2059

High Beech Golf Club 🏌9
Wellington Hill, High Beech, Loughton
☎ 081 508 7323

Theydon Bois Golf Club 🏌18
Theydon Road
Parkland and forest course, restrictions
on visitors at weekends and Bank
Holidays.
☎ 0992 813054

HORSE RIDING

Epping Forest
6000 acres of open heath with
bridleways.

Woodredon Riding School
Off the A121, ½ mile from the M25
jctn 26 at Upshire
Children's non-residential instruction.
Forest hacking.
☎ 0992 714312/711144

WALKING AND RAMBLING

Epping Forest Centenary Walk
15 miles from Manor Park to Epping
Contact the West Essex Ramblers
Association.
☎ 0378 813350

Essex Way
81-mile walk to Harwich
☎ 0378 813350

Hatfield Forest Nature Trail
Contact the Head Warden.
☎ 0279 870678

Three Forests Way
60-mile circular way linking Epping,
Hatfield and Hainault Forests.
☎ 0378 813350

Special Interests

COUNTRY PARKS

Epping Forest
5928 acres. Conservation centre at
High Beech, ancient earthworks.
☎ 081 508 7714

FARM PARKS

Hobbs Cross Farm Dairy
Theydon Garnon
Working farm with 400 cows, pigs,
hens and chicks. Adventure
playground, straw jump, farm trail and
shop.
☎ 0992 814862

MUSEUMS

Queen Elizabeth's Hunting Lodge
Rangers Road, Chingford, Epping Forest
Timber-framed lodge built for Henry
VIII; houses displays of local history
and wildlife.

Water Sports

SWIMMING

Loughton Pool
Traps Hill, Loughton
33-metre pool, learner pool, diving pit,
solarium.
☎ 081 508 1477

Eye is a sleepy Suffolk market town. The local squires refused to allow the railway to pass through their land in the mid-nineteenth century so the Stowmarket to Norwich line ran through Diss instead. Eye would no doubt have developed differently had the railway followed the route originally planned. Its impressive church has a 100-foot tower and a fine rood screen and the White Lion was once a centre for military, political and farming festivities.

i Wilkes Way Stowmarket
☎ 0449 676880
Market day Sunday
Early closing Wednesday
Population 1870

Outdoor Leisure

FISHING

Coarse Fishing
For information and permits for fishing on the River Waveney, contact the National Rivers Authority
☎ 0733 371811
☎ 0473 727712

Special Interests

HISTORIC BUILDINGS

Church of St Peter and St Paul
12th century church with notable tower and rood screen.

THEATRES

Somershey Theatre
☎ 0379 870519

Framlingham Castle, Suffolk

Fakenham

Fakenham, a busy market town, bustles with activity on Thursdays when both the open air market and the auctions are held, a good day to pick up a bargain! A visit to a unique collection showing the history of the gas industry, a working smithy, perhaps a day out in the world of steam engines accompanied by the nostalgic sound of the fairground organs, a visit to a waterfowl park or a day at the races

i Red Lion House
Market Place
☎ 0328 51981

Market day Thursday
Early closing Wednesday
Population 5555

Outdoor Leisure

FISHING

Coarse Fishing
For information and permits for fishing on the River Yare contact the National Rivers Authority
☎ 0733 371811
☎ 0473 727712

Davies Tackle Shop
Norwich Street
☎ 0328 2543

Game Fishing
Trout fishing in the River Wensum at the Fakenham Angling Club Fishery. For details contact Mr G Parsons
☎ 0328 4637

Willsmore Lake
Off Hayes Lane
1¼ acres with most coarse species. Tickets available from Mr G Parsons
☎ 0328 4637

GOLF

Fakenham and District Golf Club ⓗ
Gallows Sports Centre
☎ 0328 2867

Fakenham Golf Club
Hempton Road
Parkland course with water hazards, restrictions at weekends and Bank Holidays.
☎ 0328 3534

HORSE RACING

The Racecourse
☎ 0328 862388

HORSE RIDING

North Norfolk Riding Centre
Old Wells Road, Little Walsingham
Residential riding holidays and horse driving. BHS approved.
☎ 0328 820796

Special Interests

ANTIQUES

Fakenham Flea Market and Auctions
High Beck Auctions on Thursday mornings.
☎ 0328 51557

MUSEUMS

The Forge Museum
North Creake, near Fakenham
Blacksmiths at work, also bygones of village life.

Museum of Gas and Local History
Complete old town gas works with working gas engine; model of North Sea gas rig.
☎ 0328 51696

The Thursford Collection
Off the A148 at Thursford
World's largest collection of steam locomotives, showman's traction, fairground organs, ploughing and traction engines. Live concerts at the Wurlitzer.

NATURAL HISTORY

Pensthorpe Waterfowl Park
South-east off the A1067 Norwich road
200 acres of lakes, woodland and meadows with collection of rare and exotic birds. Visitors centre, conservation centre, wildlife exhibitions and adventure playground.
☎ 0328 851465

Water Sports

BOAT TRIPS

William Scoles
The Old Rectory, Great Snoring
Trips to Scolt Head Bird Sanctuary and Overy Beach.
☎ 0328 820597

109

Felixstowe is best known today as an international port, it is one of the largest 'roll-on, roll-off' cargo and container ports in Britain and a busy ferry port to the continent. Beautiful floral gardens and lawns separate the two-mile sea-front road round the bay from the promenade and the beach which is safe for swimming and windsurfing. Felixstowe has a large leisure centre and swimming pool, a golf course and a selection of seaside amusements.

i Felixstowe Leisure Centre
Sea Front
☎ 0394 276770

Market days Thursday, Sunday
Early closing Wednesday
Population 24,461

GOLF

Felixstowe Ferry Golf Club ⛳
Seaside links; self catering flats available including green fees. Visitors after 10.30am.
☎ 0394 286834

Indoor Sports

LEISURE CENTRES

Felixstowe Leisure Centre
Undercliffe Road West
☎ 0394 282126

Outdoor Leisure

FISHING

Sea Fishing
Contact the Tourist Information Centre for details.
☎ 0394 276770

Special Interests

FESTIVALS AND FAIRS

May
Folk Festival

June
Deben Week Regatta

August
Felixstowe Carnival

FUN PARKS

Charles Manning's Amusement Park
Many rides and attractions for children of all ages, arcade, bingo, food.
☎ 0394 282370

Felixstowe ferry

GARDENS

Cliff Gardens
Attractive floral displays along the
seafront.

MUSEUMS

Landguard Fort and Museum
View Point Road
18th century fort. Nautical, RAF and
local history displays, maps and
documents.
☎ 0394 286403

THEATRES

Spa Pavilion Theatre
☎ 0394 282126

Water Sports

SWIMMING

Felixstowe Leisure Centre
Swimming and free-form leisure pools.
☎ 0394 282126

WINDSURFING

Felixstowe Beach
In front of Cavendish Hotel
Car park, club, changing facilities,
toilets, rescue.
☎ 0394 644521 evenings

Windsurfing Seasports
The Beach, Sea Road
RYA recognised.
☎ 0394 248504

ESSEX — Finchingfield — ESSEX

Finchingfield is very picturesque with a church on a hill, a stream with a duckpond
and a green surrounded by houses of differing shapes, sizes and ages, elements that
combine to produce an enchanting and much photographed village scene.

i Braintree District Council
☎ 0376 552525

Population 1756

Outdoor Leisure

HORSE RIDING

Moor End Stables
3 miles from Finchingfield off the
B1053 at Great Sampford
Hunter hire and liveries, instruction in
riding and jumping.
☎ 079 986 338/282

Special Interests

GARDENS

Spains Hall
Manor House ground featuring Cedar of
Lebanon planted in 1670, flower and
kitchen gardens. Elizabethan house
open by appointment only.
☎ 0371 810266

MUSEUMS

Guildhall and Museum
Museum of local antiques, summer art
exhibitions.

Framlingham is a small market town dominated by the castle built by the Bigod family. The castle which has been partly restored houses a museum and also has a walk that links nine of the towers to other parts of the castle walls.

Population 2640

Adventure Sports

SHOOTING

Kettleburgh College CPSC
Kettleburgh Lodge Shooting School
☎ 0728 723783

Outdoor Leisure

ORIENTEERING

Suffolk Orienteering Club
Contact Stella Sills, 75a Fore Street
☎ 0278 723209

Special Interests

FOOD AND DRINK

Shawsgate Vineyard
Badingham Road
☎ 0728 724060

HERITAGE

Framlingham Castle
Impressive 12th century curtain walls, thirteen towers and Tudor brick chimneys. 17th century almshouses. Built by the Bigod family, Earls of Norfolk. Home of Mary Tudor in 1553. Wall walk.

HISTORIC BUILDINGS

Saxtead Green Windmill
18th century mill with original equipment.

MUSEUMS

390th Bomb Group Memorial Air Museum
Parham
Second World War East Anglian aviation history on former USAF base. RAF, USAF and Luftwaffe exhibits.

Lanman Museum
Framlingham Castle
Pictures and bygones concerning everyday life of Framlingham.
☎ 0278 723054

Laxfield and District Museum
6 miles north of Framlingham
Guildhall with archaeological, agricultural and natural history exhibits.
☎ 698683 218

Framlingham Castle

Godmanchester, an important Roman settlement, is sited on the crossroads of Ermine Street which ran from London to York and the Via Devana which ran from Colchester to Chester. It became one of the earliest boroughs receiving its charter in 1213. There are many fine period houses and a very attractive duck pond, one outlet of which is crossed by a distinctive Chinese-style bridge.

Outdoor Leisure

CAMPING AND CARAVANNING

Park Lane (Touring)
Park Lane
50 tent and 50 caravan pitches with
extensive facilities.
☎ 0480 453470

FISHING

Coarse Fishing
For information and permits for fishing
on the River Ouse contact the National
Rivers Authority
☎ 0480 414581

Stanjays Tackle Shop
7 Old Court Road
☎ 0480 453303

WALKING AND RAMBLING

Port Holme Meadow
300-acre meadow along the River Ouse,
pleasant walks along the footpaths.

Special Interests

HISTORIC HOUSES

Buckden Palace
Buckden
Restored parts of the ancient 12th
century palace of the Bishops of
Lincoln.
☎ 0480 810344

Island Hall
Entrance on Post Street
An elegant house built in the 1740s.
Wartime and historical interest.
☎ 0480 459670

NATURAL HISTORY

Wood Green Animal Centre
Follow brown tourist signs
50-acre shelter with over 1000
domestic animals. Restaurant, lake and
picnic area, gift shop.
☎ 0480 830014

Water Sports

WATER-SKIING

Buckden Marina and Leisure Club
Mill Road, Buckden
☎ 0480 810355

Grays

ESSEX ESSEX

Grays lies on the north bank of the River Thames between Tilbury and the M25. It is
in the middle of undergoing a massive rebirth as developers discover its potential.
The recently opened Thurrock Lakeside is the largest single shopping mall in the
country and one of the largest in Europe. It also boasts the largest private housing
development in the country and is the northern end of the new East London Thames
crossing – this bridge will become the last link in the M25 and should be open by the
end of 1991.

Market days Thursday, Friday, Saturday
Population 3858

Aerial Sports

MICROLIGHT FLYING

Essex Airsports
10 Dukes Avenue
☎ 0375 371172

Indoor Sports

LEISURE CENTRES

Grays Park Leisure Centre
Bridge Road
☎ 0375 382386

SQUASH

Grays Park Leisure Centre
☎ 0375 382386

Outdoor Leisure

GOLF

Belhus Park Golf Club ⌐18
Aveley
☎ 04025 854260

MUSEUMS

Thurrock Local History Museum
Thameside Complex
☎ 0375 390000

THEATRES

Thameside Theatre
Orsett Road
☎ 0375 838961

Water Sports

SWIMMING

Blackshots Swim and Leisure Complex
Blackshots Lane
33.3-metre pool, learner and splash
Three pools, sauna, weight lifting.
☎ 0375 375533

Great Dunmow is an attractive and ancient town sited at a junction of Roman roads. It has several interesting buildings including a timbered guildhall, an old inn and a village pond where the first lifeboat experiments were carried out in the 18th century.

To the south of the town are the Rodings, a group of eight villages along the River Roding. The countryside around the villages is picturesque with high hedges, water meadows and scattered woods.

i Council Offices
High Street
☎ 0371 874533

Market day Tuesday
Early closing Wednesday
Population 4048

Indoor Sports

SQUASH

Helena Romanes School
Parsonage Downs
☎ 0371 3782

Outdoor Leisure

FISHING

Coarse Fishing
For information and permits for fishing at Roding contact the National Rivers Authority
☎ 0733 371811
☎ 0473 727712

Special Interests

FESTIVALS AND FAIRS

Dunmow Flitch
A side of bacon is awarded annually to the 'happiest married couple' in Dunmow.

HISTORIC BUILDINGS

Aythorpe Roding Post Mill
Restored 18th century post mill
☎ 0245 352232

Little Easton Church
Norman chapel, brasses, wall paintings, many special memorials.

NATURAL HISTORY

Garnetts Wood
62 acres of ancient woodland.
☎ 0277 216297

Water Sports

SWIMMING

Helena Romanes School
☎ 0371 3782

114

Great Yarmouth is both a busy summer resort and an historic port. The seafront provides traditional seaside attractions, theatres, two piers, a funfair and the indoor facilities offered by the Marina Centre. The port around the River Quay has been home to the herring and merchant fleet for centuries, more recently it operates supply services to the North Sea gas and oil rigs. There is little of the old town remaining, one or two of the older buildings now house museums and a few sections of the mediaeval town wall are visible behind the Market Gates Shopping Centre. There is plenty to do to entertain and interest the visitor by day and by night in this colourful resort.

i Marine Parade
☎ 0493 84219

Market days Wednesday, Friday
Early closing Thursday
Population 62,429

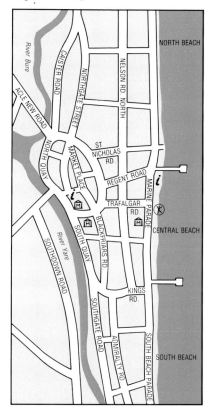

Aerial Sports

PARAGLIDING

Apollo Tavern Paragliding Club
Marine Parade
Club operates over water. Social facilities.
☎ 0493 856052

Indoor Sports

LEISURE CENTRES

Great Yarmouth Marina Leisure Centre
Marine Parade
Pool with tropical beach, sports hall, table tennis, snooker, pool, squash, sauna and solarium, restaurants, bars, gym, indoor bowls and children's play area.
☎ 0493 851521

SQUASH

Great Yarmouth Marina Leisure Centre
☎ 0493 851521

TENPIN BOWLING

Regent Bowl
Regent Road
☎ 0493 856830

Outdoor Leisure

BIRDWATCHING

Breydon Water
Footpaths from Great Yarmouth
Tidal waters and mud flats. Nature reserve.

FISHING

Coarse Fishing
Fishing on the River Yare and at Ormesby
For information and permits contact the National Rivers Authority
☎ 0733 371811
☎ 0473 727712

Sea Fishing
Contact the Tourist Information Centre.

GOLF

Gorleston Golf Club ⛳
Warren Road, Gorleston
Cliffside course.
☎ 0493 661911

Great Yarmouth and Caister Golf Club ⛳
¹/₂ mile north of Great Yarmouth on the A149
Natural links course by dunes and beach.
☎ 0493 728699

HORSE RACING

Great Yarmouth Racecourse
North Denes
1 mile 5 furlong course.
☎ 0493 842527

HORSE RIDING

Belton Riding Centre
Station Road, Belton
Instruction in riding and jumping.
☎ 0493 781164/780247

Hillcrest Riding School Ltd
Hillcrest Farm, Yarmouth Road, Filby Heath
Instruction in riding and jumping.
☎ 0493 730394

Willow Farm Riding School
Ormesby St Margaret
Instruction in riding and jumping.
☎ 0493 730297

WALKING AND RAMBLING

Around Norfolk Walk
220-mile walk taking in most of Norfolk's scenery. Send stamped addressed envelope to Norfolk County Council, Martineau Lane, Norwich. Lane, Norwich.

Peddars Way
Peddars Way Association, 150 Armes Street, Norwich
97-mile footpath through woodland and along the coast. Official guide can be purchased from HMSO, or the East Anglia Tourist Board.
☎ 0473 822922

Special Interests

ART GALLERIES

Great Yarmouth Museums Exhibition Galleries
Centre Library
Paintings, arts and crafts, displays from local collections.
☎ 0493 858900

FUN PARKS

Great Yarmouth Pleasure Beach
70 rides, sideshows and attractions, bar, food, exhibitions.
☎ 0493 844585

House of Wax
18 Regent Street
Exhibition, torture chambers, chamber of horrors, hall of mirrors.
☎ 0493 844851

World of Wax
Regent Road
Open all year round, weekends and holidays only during winter months.
☎ 0493 842203

GARDENS

Fritton Lake
6 miles south-west of Great Yarmouth on the A143
232 acres of woodlands and picnic area, wildfowl reserve, launch trips, fishing, assault course.
☎ 0493 488208

HERITAGE

Burgh Castle
Remains of Roman fort overlooking the River Waveney.

Nelson's Monument
Erected 1819, 144 feet high, 217 steps.

St Olave's Priory
St Olave's Bridge, near Great Yarmouth
Early 14th century undercroft with brick-vaulted ceiling.

HISTORIC BUILDINGS

St Olave's Windpump
St Olave's Bridge, near Great Yarmouth
Tiny timber windpump in working order. Apply at Bridge Stores for the key.

MUSEUMS

Broadland Tractor Museum
Ormesby St Michael
7 miles north of Great Yarmouth on the A149
Collection of tractors and unusual agricultural machinery.

Elizabethan House Museum
South Quay
Built in 1596. Panelled rooms, Victorian toys, porcelain, displays.
☎ 0493 855746

Maritime Museum for East Anglia
Shipbuilding, fishing, lifesaving and inland waterways.
☎ 0493 842267

Old Merchant's House
Row 111, South Quay
17th and 19th century domestic ironwork in partly restored house.
☎ 0493 857900

Tolhouse Museum
Tolhouse Street
Mediaeval courthouse and jail. Local history and brass-rubbing.
☎ 0493 858900

THEATRES

Britannia Theatre
☎ 0493 842209

Hippodrome
☎ 0493 844172

Royalty Theatre
☎ 0493 842043

St Georges Theatre
☎ 0493 858387

Wally Windmill's Playhouse
☎ 0493 843504

Wellington Pier Theatre
☎ 0493 843635/042244

Winter Garden Theatre
☎ 0493 844945

THEME PARKS

Merrivale Model
Marine Parade
200 models in landscaped gardens.
☎ 0493 842097

The Venetian Waterways
North Drive
Trips in launch through gardens, illuminated at night.
☎ 0493 853886

Great Yarmouth illuminations

ZOOS

Great Yarmouth Butterflies and Tropical Gardens
Tropical world under glass, exotic plants, birds and butterflies. Shop.
☎ 0493 842202

Water Sports

BOAT HIRE

Johnson's Yacht Station
St Olave's Bridge
Motor launches and cruisers.
☎ 049 379218

BOAT TRIPS

Norfolk Yacht Tours
Riverside, Martham
Accompanied sailing trips through nature reserves for parties up to four per yacht. Optional sailing tuition.
☎ 0493 653597

SWIMMING

Great Yarmouth Marina Leisure Centre
25-metre pool with tropical beach, waves and aqua slide. Wavemaking machine.
☎ 0493 851521

Phoenix Pool
Mallard Way, Bradwell
25-metre pool.
☎ 0493 64575

WINDSURFING

Fritton Lake
Windsurfing school
☎ 0493 488208

YACHT CHARTER

Norfolk Yacht Tours
☎ 0493 653597

YACHTING

Blakeney Sailing Club
Gorleston-on-Sea
RYA affiliated.

Great Yarmouth and Gorleston Sailing Club
Pier Plain, Harbour entrance, Gorleston
RYA affiliated.
☎ 0603 612035/629992

Rollesby Broad Sailing Club
Great Yarmouth
☎ 0603 610217

Hadleigh

Hadleigh is a thriving market town set in fine countryside. It has a wealth of timber-framed buildings built during the 14th to 16th centuries when the town was an important wool trading centre. The spire of the parish church dominates the town and opposite it is a complex of fine mediaeval buildings that incorporate the Guildhall and the Town Hall, both Grade I listed buildings. The River Brett is spanned by the 500-year-old red brick Toppesfield Bridge, one of the oldest bridges still in use and nearby Toppesfield Hall has been beautifully restored, it is now the headquarters of the English Tourist Board. Hadleigh has good shopping facilities and an interesting selection of restaurants.

i Toppesfield Hall
☎ 0374 822922

Market days Friday, Saturday
Early closing Wednesday
Population 8500

Adventure Sports

SHOOTING

East Anglia Shooting
Toppesfield Hall
Books parties and individuals for pheasant and partridge shooting at a wide variety of estates. Operates in co-operation with the East Anglia Tourist Board. Contact Jackey Mayes.
☎ 0473 822922

Outdoor Leisure

BIRDWATCHING

Wolves Wood
2 miles east of Hadleigh access from the A1071
Mixed woodland with signposted paths. Woodland birds. RSPB.
☎ 0255 886043

WALKING AND RAMBLING

Railway Walk
A peaceful walk along the disused railway line from Hadleigh to Rayden.

Special Interests

ARTS AND CRAFTS

Playthings of the Past
102a High Street
Collectors' toys, teddies and dolls, railways, jigsaw puzzles.
☎ 0473 82443

FESTIVALS AND FAIRS

May
Hadleigh Show
Millfield Fete

August
Deanery Fete

HISTORIC BUILDINGS

The Deanery Tower
1495 Tudor gatehouse in the churchyard, designed to be the entrance of a new rectory for Archdeacon Pykenham, he died and the old rectory remained until 1831.

The Guildhall
A Grade I listed building; the centre of the town's commercial and social life for many centuries. The central portion was the original market hall donated by William de Clopton in 1438.
☎ 0473 823576

St Mary's Church
Tower built in 1250 to replace Saxon one, fine organ and unfinished vaulted ceiling.

Topplesfield Hall
Once the home of William de Clopton, now restored and the headquarters of the English Tourist Board
☎ 0374 822922

Water Sports

SWIMMING

Hadleigh Swimming Pool
Stonehouse Road
25-metre pool, sauna and sunbed.
☎ 0473 823470

Halesworth

Halesworth is a small, quiet market town situated close to the River Blyth and the Suffolk coast. It has an art gallery and local museum that will give the visitor a fascinating insight into the history of the town and the surrounding Suffolk farmland.

Market day Wednesday
Early closing Thursday
Population 4798

Special Interests

ART GALLERIES

Halesworth Gallery
The Almshouses, Steeple End

Elizabethan house built from parts of 15th century almshouses. Exhibitions of paintings and sculptures.
☎ 0986 873064

MUSEUMS

Halesworth and District Museum
The Almshouses, Steeple End
Local history and archaeological exhibits in old almshouses.

Halstead

Halstead, a small former spinning and weaving town, is sited in the Colne Valley where heaths, woodland and rich farming country combine in a largely unspoilt landscape. The town has some interesting buildings and the nearby Tudor Gosfield Hall is open to visitors. Walking, fishing, an unusual museum and a theatre offer a range of entertainment by day and by night.

Market day Friday

Indoor Sports

LEISURE CENTRES

Halstead Sports Centre
Colne Road
☎ 0787 472480

SQUASH

Halstead Sports Centre
☎ 0787 472480

Outdoor Leisure

CAMPING AND CARAVANNING

Gosfield Lake Caravan Park
2¹/₂ miles south-west of Halstead off the A131 at Gosfield
25 touring caravan pitches; speedboat rides and pitch 'n' putt.
☎ 0787 475043

FISHING

Coarse Fishing
For information and permits contact the National Rivers Authority
☎ 0733 371811
☎ 0473 727712

Gosfield Lake
☎ 0787 475043

Special Interests

COUNTRY PARKS

Gosfield Lake and Pleasure Park
Lake and parkland with sports facilities
and camping.
☎ 0787 475043

HISTORIC HOUSES

Gosfield Hall
Gosfield
Tudor house with later alterations.
Courtyard, well and pump house.
☎ 0787 472914

MUSEUMS

Brewery Chapel Museum
Adams Court
Unique consecrated chapel within a
brewery. Items of local interest.

THEATRES

Empire Theatre
Berridge Road
Primarily a cinema, but with live theatre
and musical performances.
☎ 0787 477001

Water Sports

WATER SKIING

Halstead Water Ski Club
Gosfield Lake
☎ 0787 475043

Harlow is a large, newly-developed town with a strong commercial bias. The town's
history can be explored at the study and visitor's centre where the archives are kept.
Harlow has a fully equipped multi-purpose sports centre with extensive outdoor
facilities. Opportunities exist to try out a range of watersports and there are several
parks and a conservation area to explore before tackling the Harcamlow Way! The
town provides lots of entertainments and has a popular shopping centre.

Market days Tuesday, Friday, Saturday
Early closing Wednesday
Population 79,521

Adventure Sports

CLIMBING

Harlow Outdoor Pursuits Centre
Climbing courses, 21 foot wall; caving,
mountaineering, camping and canoeing
trips and courses arranged.
☎ 0279 432031

LEISURE CENTRES

Harlow Sportcentre
Hammarskjold Road
25 indoor sports catered for in the Sports
Hall; indoor tennis, table tennis; outdoor
facilities include international standard
running track, all-weather training area,
ski-run and tennis courts. Sauna,
solarium, café and bars.
☎ 0279 635100

SQUASH

Harlow Sportcentre
☎ 0279 635100

Outdoor Leisure

CAMPING AND CARAVANNING

Roydon Mill Caravan Park
Next to Roydon Station on the B181
60 caravan pitches, 50 tent pitches,
electric hook-ups. Club, adventure
playground, restaurant and many other
facilities. No dogs allowed.
☎ 0279 792777

CYCLING

Harlow Cycling Club
Recreational riding, touring road and
track racing.
☎ 0279 412416

Harlow Velodrome
Cycle racing track, stadium and clubhouse.
☎ 0279 415967

FISHING

Coarse Fishing
For information and permits for fishing on the River Stort contact the National Rivers Authority
☎ 0733 371811

Roydon
☎ 0279 792777

Ryemeads
Contact the Chertsey Angling Club.
☎ 0932 564872

Sea Fishing
Deep sea angling trips are arranged by a local club, Titelines.
☎ 0932 414081

GOLF

Canons Brook Golf Club ⁂
☎ 0279 421482

Four Provinces Driving Range
Floodlit range and golf shop.
☎ 0279 417271

HORSE RIDING

Churchgate Farm
Churchgate Street, Old Harlow
Holiday instruction. BHS approved.
☎ 0279 35195

WALKING AND RAMBLING

Harcamlow Way
140-mile route in a figure of eight from Harlow to Cambridge and back.
☎ 0378 813350

Special Interests

ART GALLERIES

The Playhouse
Art gallery and theatre; restaurant and bars.
☎ 0279 31945

GARDENS

Mark Hall Gardens
Muskham Road
Three walled gardens, each of differing character. Part of the cycle museum.
☎ 0279 4396801

HERITAGE

Harlow Study and Visitors' Centre
Netteswellbury Farm
13th century church and mediaeval tithe barn containing town's archives. Walled garden and churchyard, displays and lecture theatres.
☎ 0279 446744

MUSEUMS

Harlow Museum
Passmores House, Third Avenue
Georgian manor house, park, butterfly garden, local exhibits.
☎ 0279 446422

Mark Hall Cycle Museum
Muskham Road
Over 60 exhibits dating from 1818 housed in a 19th century stable building.

Mark Hall Cycle Museum

NATURAL HISTORY

Maymeads Marsh Conservation Area
Harlow Town Park
☎ 0279 446402

Parndon Wood Nature Reserve
Study centre, nature trails with observation hides.
☎ 0279 30005

ORNAMENTAL PARKS

Harlow Town Park
Contains Pets Corner, conservation area, pitch 'n' putt, adventure playground, paddling pool, road safety training ground and café.
☎ 0279 446402

Latton Bush Park and Woods
Southern Way
☎ 0279 446402

121

Mulberry Green Nursery
Gilden Way
☎ 0279 422638

Peldon Road Park
Peldon Road
☎ 0279 446402

The Moorhen
Burnt Mill Lane
Alongside Stort Navigation; woods,
meadows, walks and water sports.
☎ 0279 410181

THEATRES

The Playhouse
Main house and studio theatres;
restaurant, bars, art gallery.
☎ 0279 31945

Water Sports

DINGHY SAILING

The Moorhen
☎ 0279 410181

CANOEING

Harlow Outdoor Pursuits Centre
Canoeing courses held at weekends.
☎ 0279 432031

SWIMMING

Harlow Pool
First Avenue (Mandela Avenue)
Main pool, paddling and learner pools,
aquatubes, gym, steam room, dance
studio, weight training, sunbeds,
refreshments.
☎ 0279 446420

Stewards School Pool
Pincey Brook Road, Staple Tye
18-metre pool.
☎ 0279 444503

WINDSURFING

The Moorhen
Contact Mark Groves to book. Hire
charge includes wet suit.
☎ 0279 413500
☎ 0277 354 886

YACHTING

Harlow (Blackwater) Sailing Club
☎ 0279 730682 evenings

Winter Sports

SKIING

Harlow Sportcentre
☎ 0279 635100

Harwich, a seafaring town since mediaeval times, was where Charles II embarked for
the first pleasure cruise during the time that Samuel Pepys was MP for the town.
Harwich was the headquarters of the King's navy. A busy port for cargo and
passengers to and from the Hook of Holland or Denmark, the nine-sided High
Lighthouse is the first landmark seen by the ferry passengers as they arrive. A little to
the south along the coast is Dovercourt, the residential and holiday suburb of
Harwich.

i Parkeston Quay
☎ 0255 506139

Early closing Wednesday
Population 17,329

Indoor Sports

LEISURE CENTRES

Harwich Sports Hall
Hall Lane, Dovercourt
☎ 0255 504380

SQUASH

Harwich Sports Hall
☎ 0255 504380

Outdoor Leisure

BIRDWATCHING

Stour Wood and Copperas Bay
1 mile east of Wrabness on the B1352
☎ 0255 886043

122

CAMPING AND CARAVANNING

Greenacres Caravan Park
Low Road, Dovercourt
For tent and caravan overnight stops;
facilities available.
☎ 0255 502657

FISHING

Sea Fishing
Fishing at Harwich and Dovercourt.
Contact the Tourist Information Centre
for details.
☎ 0255 506139

GOLF

Harwich and Dovercourt Golf Club ⚑
Parkeston Road, Dovercourt
☎ 0255 503616

Special Interests

HISTORIC BUILDINGS

Electric Palace Cinema
Kings Quay Street
Purpose built in 1911.
☎ 0255 553333/553404

Harwich Redoubt
Main Road
Circular fort built 1808; cannon, cells,
moat, museum.
☎ 0255 508920

MUSEUMS

Maritime Museum
Low Lighthouse, Harwich Green
Royal Navy, lifeboat and commercial
shipping displays.
☎ 0255 508920

The High Lighthouse, Harwich

Water Sports

BOAT TRIPS

Orwell and Harwich Navigation Ltd
The Quay
Morning and afternoon cruises on *MS
Brightlingsea* with commentary on
Rivers Stour and Orwell and Harwich
Harbour. Discos, folk nights. Twelve-
seater launch for hire. Ferry service runs
to Felixstowe and Shotley.
☎ 0255 502004

SWIMMING

Dovercourt Swimming Pool
Wick Lane, Dovercourt
25-metre pool.
☎ 0255 508266

YACHTING

Harwich and Dovercourt Sailing Club
RYA affiliated. Contact the secretary,
John Kemp, for details.
☎ 0255 508205

Harwich Town Sailing Club
Angel Gate
☎ 0255 503200

SUFFOLK   **Haverhill**   SUFFOLK

Haverhill lies on the Suffolk – Essex border in the south-western corner of Suffolk. It
is surrounded by some lovely countryside and boasts a well equipped leisure centre
and good shopping.

Market days Friday, Saturday
Early closing Wednesday
Population 19,790

Adventure Sports

CLIMBING

Haverhill Sports Centre
Ehringshausen Way
☎ 0440 702548

SHOOTING

Haverhill Sports Centre
☎ 0440 702548

Indoor Sports

LEISURE CENTRES

Haverhill Sports Centre
Golf net, cricket nets, sauna and
solarium suite, fitness room, indoor
tennis, badminton, weight training, bar
and café as well as swimming pools and
squash courts.
☎ 0440 702548

SQUASH

Haverhill Sports Centre
☎ 0440 702548

Outdoor Leisure

GOLF

Haverhill Golf Club Ltd ⚐
Coupals Road
Parkland course with river.
☎ 0440 61951

Special Interests

MUSEUMS

**Haverhill and District Local History
Centre**
Town Hall, High Street
Local artefacts, documents and
photographs. For details about the centre
contact the Haverhill History Group.
☎ 0440 62594

Water Sports

SWIMMING

Haverhill Sports Centre
☎ 0440 702548

NORFOLK / **Holt** / NORFOLK

Holt, an attractive market town, has a main street lined with Georgian buildings. The
town is well known for Gresham's, a school founded in 1555 by the founder of the
Royal Exchange in London. Holt has a regular craft market and many picture galleries
and bookshops. The North Norfolk Steam Railway runs between Holt and the sea at
Sheringham providing a delightful means of enjoying the surrounding countryside.

Market day Friday
Early closing Thursday
Population 2510

Outdoor Leisure

BIRDWATCHING

Cley Marshes
Freshwater and salt marshes with rare
migrant birds. Access by permits only –
available at the Visitor Centre.
☎ 0263 740380

ORIENTEERING

Holt Country Park
Maps from the Ranger at the park.
Enquiries to the Forestry Officer at
North Norfolk District Council.
☎ 0263 513811

Special Interests

ARTS AND CRAFTS

The Handworkers' Market
18 Chapel Yard
Embroidery and needlecraft specialists.
Materials and books for sale.
☎ 0263 711251

Wansbeck Dolls Houses
2 Chapel Yard
Craftsman-made houses, interiors and
dolls to 1:12 scale.
☎ 0263 713933

COUNTRY PARKS

Holt Country Park
Coniferous woodland and heathland, waymarked walks, nature trail, fishing, adventure playground, Ranger Service. Information from the North Norfolk District Council.
☎ 0263 513811

FACTORY VISITS

Langham Glass
Langham
Traditional glassmaking in historic barn.
☎ 0328 75511

GARDENS

Glavenside Gardens
1 mile west of Holt on the A148 at Letheringsett
4 acres of gardens around working watermill; 1903 hydraulic ram raises water for kitchen garden. Picnic areas, water and rock gardens, streams, boating and fishing in the River Glaven.

HISTORIC BUILDINGS

Letheringsett Watermill
1 mile west of Holt on the A148
Restored working watermill. Demonstrations, flours for sale.
☎ 0263 713153

NATURAL HISTORY

Holt Lowes
1 mile south of Holt on the B1149
98 acres of conifer wood and 113 acres of heathland with walks and a nature trail.

RAILWAYS

North Norfolk Railway
Steam railway runs from Sheringham to Holt.
☎ 0263 822045

North Norfolk Railway

WILDLIFE PARKS

Kelly's Birds and Aviaries
Weybourne Road
Collection of wildfowl and exotic birds in 6 acres of grounds.
☎ 0263 711185

Hunstanton

Hunstanton is the largest of West Norfolk's coastal resorts and the only East Anglian coastal town facing west. Developed by a local landowner during the latter part of the last century it retains its Victorian atmosphere. The town has extensive sandy beaches, distinctively striped cliffs, attractive esplanade gardens and attractions such as the Sea Life Centre, heated pools, extensive sports facilities and the Princess Theatre, all of which make Hunstanton a very popular local resort.

i The Green
☎ 04853 2610

Market day Wednesday
Early closing Thursday
Population 4069

Adventure Sports

SHOOTING

Heacham and North West Norfolk Wildfowlers Association
Heacham Chalk Pit
☎ 0553 674837

Indoor Sports

LEISURE CENTRES

Oasis Leisure Centre
Seagate
Heated leisure pools, whirlpool spa, sun lounge, rollerskating, multi-activities hall, cafeteria, bar and squash courts.
☎ 04853 34227

SQUASH

Oasis Leisure Centre
☎ 04853 32447

125

Outdoor Leisure

CYCLING

A E Wallis
High Street, Heacham
Cycle hire for all ages.
☎ 0485 713683

FISHING

Sea Fishing
Fishing trips arranged by Searles Hire
Boats.
☎ 0485 532342

GOLF

Hunstanton Golf Club ⚐₁₈
1¹/₂ miles north off the A129
Championship links course with fast
greens.
☎ 0485 532811

HORSE RIDING

Home Farm Riding Stables
Holme-next-the-Sea
Instructions in riding and jumping.
☎ 048 525 233

WALKING AND RAMBLING

Peddars Way
97-mile walk between Holme and
Knettishall Heath. Guide from the East
Anglia Tourist Board
☎ 0473 822922

Special Interests

AQUARIUMS

Sea Life Centre
South Beach Road
Variety of marine life on display, walk
underwater in the Ocean Tunnel to see
sealife in over twenty natural settings.
New seal pool opened in 1990.
☎ 0485 533576

ARTS AND CRAFTS

Norfolk Lavender Ltd
4 miles south of Hunstanton on the
A149 at Heacham
England's only lavender farm, show-
gardens including the National
Collection of Lavenders, and herb
garden. Shop and tea room.
☎ 0485 570384

FARM PARKS

Park Farm
4 miles south of Hunstanton off the
A149 at Snettisham
Working farm; crops, livestock, red deer,
safari rides, walks, adventure
playground. Guided tours.
☎ 0485 542425

HISTORIC BUILDINGS

Great Bircham Windmill
8 miles south-east of Hunstanton on the
B1153
Preserved corn mill in working order.
Group tours by arrangement. Cycles for
hire.
☎ 048 523 393

Snettisham Watermill
4 miles south of Hunstanton off the
A149 at Snettisham
18th century machinery restored to
working order. Flour for sale. 'Lego' mill
museum. Demonstrations.
☎ 0485 542180

THEATRES

The Princess Theatre
☎ 0485 532252

Water Sports

BOAT TRIPS

Searle's Hire Boats
Trips to Seal Island to view seals of the
Wash, coastal and fishing trips.
Speedboat rides.
☎ 04853 2342

SWIMMING

Oasis Leisure Centre
Swimming pool with flume and toddler
pool in a tropical environment. Café.
☎ 0485 34227

WATER-SKIING

Heacham Boat Owners Association
Heacham North Beach
Contact the secretary, Rod Winter, for
details.
☎ 0523 890818

Hunstanton and District Water Ski Club
South Beach Road
Contact the secretary, Mandy Abberley,
for details.
☎ 0638 77320

Huntingdon

Huntingdon, formerly a county town, is situated on the northern bank of the Great Ouse separated from Godmanchester by a beautiful 13th century bridge. There are several fine Georgian buildings to be seen in Huntingdon. Its associations with Oliver Cromwell are well documented, he was born there in 1599 and educated in the old grammar school, the school also attended by Samuel Pepys for a year, now the Cromwell Museum. Hinchingbrooke House, an Elizabethan mansion, was built by Cromwell's great-grandfather around the remains of a nunnery, it is now a school and its grounds a country park. More recently Huntingdon has been in the political headlines for being the constituency and home of the newly elected Prime Minister, John Major.

i The Library
Princes Street
☎ 0480 425831

Market days Wednesday, Saturday
Early closing Wednesday
Population 14,500

Multi-Activity Holidays

MULTI-ACTIVITY CENTRES

Grafham Water Centre
Perry
Residential centre for 54 students, courses related to water sports and environmental studies in the summer, creative arts and languages in the winter.
☎ 0480 810521

Outdoor Leisure

BIRDWATCHING

Grafham Water
5 miles south-west of Huntingdon on the B661
Nature reserve at western end of reservoir has hides; wintering ducks – mallards, tufted duck, wigeon and coot flocks of over 1000 birds. For information contact the Beds and Hunts Wildlife Trust
☎ 0234 64213

FISHING

Coarse Fishing
There is good coarse fishing on the Rivers Great Ouse and Nene, at reclaimed gravel pits, at Grafham Water and Hinchingbrooke Country Park. For information and permits contact the National Rivers Authority
☎ 0733 371811
☎ 0473 727712

Tim's Tackle
18 High Street
☎ 0480 450039

Game Fishing
Boat and fly fishing for trout at Grafham Water. Fishing lodge and tackle shop on site. Competition venue.
☎ 0480 810531

HORSE RACING

Huntingdon Racecourse
Brampton Road
A right-handed, 1½ mile, oval track founded in 1886. It hosts 15 national hunt race days each year.
☎ 0480 453373

HORSE RIDING

Great Gransden
☎ 07677 366

Mill Cottage Riding and Livery Stables
Gidding Road, Sawtry
Basic instruction in riding and jumping. BHS approved.
☎ 0487 831497

Warboys
Wislow Fen
☎ 0487 822076

ORIENTEERING

West Anglian Orienteering Club
Contact Mary Palmer, 10 Hall Close, Hartford
☎ 0480 458628

WALKING AND RAMBLING

The Huntingdon Amble/Town Trails
Details from the Tourist Information Centre

Ouse Valley Long Distance Footpath
Details from the Huntingdon District Council
☎ 0480 561561

Special Interests

COUNTRY PARKS

Grafham Water
Man-made reservoir with a nature reserve, nature trails, bird hides, fishing and sailing.

Hinchingbrooke Country Park
156 acres of meadows, lakes, woods and ponds open to the public for walking, riding, fishing and picnics. Watersports, visitors' centre.
☎ 0480 51568

FESTIVALS AND FAIRS

June
Carnival week

Shakespeare at the George
Performances held in the galleried courtyard of the George Hotel. Contact the Tourist Information Centre
☎ 0480 425831

GARDENS

Abbots Ripton Hall
North of Huntingdon at Abbots Ripton Garden of the de Ramsey family, it retains a drive of impressive elms.

HISTORIC BUILDINGS

Houghton Mill
3 miles south-east at Houghton Massive timbered mid-17th century mill, original machinery, used until 1930, owned by the National Trust.
☎ 0480 301494

HISTORIC HOUSES

Hinchingbrooke House
13th century Benedictine nunnery with later conversions and additions. Ancestral home of the Cromwells and the Earls of Sandwich, now a school. Guided tours on summer Sundays.
☎ 0480 51121

MUSEUMS

Cromwell Museum
Grammar School Walk
Once part of St John's Hospital, founded in 1160, later a grammar school where both Oliver Cromwell and Samuel Pepys were educated. The museum relates specifically to Oliver Cromwell.
☎ 0480 425830

NATURAL HISTORY

Aversley Wood
Off the A1 at Sawtry

Holme Fen
Off the A1 to Peterborough
Nature reserve lowest point of dry land in the British Isles, 10 ft below sea level.

Monks Wood and Woodwalton Fen
Off the A1 at Woodwalton
Nature reserve and environmental research centre.

WILDLIFE PARKS

Hamerton Wildlife Centre
North-west at Hamerton
Unique bird collection with rare species of mammals from around the world, wallabies, lemurs and meerkats set in 15 acres with children's farm.
☎ 08323 362

Water Sports

BOAT HIRE

Huntingdon Marine and Leisure Ltd
Small powered day boats with tapes available in French or German giving history of the area.
☎ 0480 413517

Purvis Marine Boatyard
Canoes, motor launches and day boats.
☎ 0480 53628

CANOEING

Purvis Marine Boatyard
☎ 0480 53628

DINGHY SAILING

Grafham Water Sailing Club
Clubhouse, Grafham Water
1600 acres of water, day membership, championship course, beginners.
☎ 0480 810478

SWIMMING

Huntingdon Recreation Centre
St Peters Road
☎ 0480 454130

WINDSURFING

Grafham Water Residential Centre
☎ 0480 810478/810521

Jonti Sailboards
Grafham Water Sailing Club, Perry Instruction, video tuition, board hire.
☎ 0480 811242

Ipswich is the county town of Suffolk, England's oldest heritage town, and a major commercial and shopping centre. The town is a thriving port on the River Orwell and can boast twelve mediaeval churches, a Tudor mansion, an excellent art gallery and museum. Ipswich was the birthplace of Cardinal Wolsey and a resting place for Dickens during his days as a reporter.

Sports and leisure facilities in the town are excellent with the award-winning Crown pools and most indoor and outdoor sports being catered for. The Wolsey Theatre and the Corn Exchange provide first-rate live entertainment.

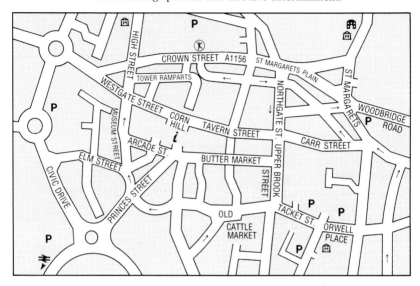

i Town Hall
Princes Street
☎ 0473 258070
Market days Tuesday, Friday, Saturday
Early Closing Wednesday
Population 131,137

Aerial Sports

PARACHUTING

Ipswich Parachute Centre
Ipswich Airport, Nacton Road
All facilities including food and accommodation.
☎ 0473 710044

Indoor Sports

LEISURE CENTRES

Gainsborough Sports and Community Centre
Braziers Wood Road
☎ 0473 716900

Maidenhall Sports Centre
Maidenhall Approach
☎ 0473 680644

Northgate Sports Centre
Sidegate Lane West
☎ 0473 717402

Whitton Sports and Community Centre
Whitton Church Lane
☎ 0473 462711

SQUASH

There are squash courts at the leisure centres listed above. Please phone to confirm and make your bookings.

TENPIN BOWLING

Kingpin Bowling Centre
Gloster Road, Martlesham Heath
☎ 0473 61111

Solar Bowl
Sproughton Road
☎ 0473 47525

129

Outdoor Leisure

FISHING

Coarse Fishing
For information and permits contact
the National Rivers Authority
☎ 0733 371811
☎ 0473 727712

Alton Water and River Stour
For additional information contact the
Chertsey Angling Club
☎ 0932 564872

GOLF

Ipswich Golf Club ⛳ ⛳
Purdis Heath, Bucklesham Road
Heathland course.
☎ 0473 728941

Rushmere Golf Club ⛳
2 miles east of Ipswich on the A12 at
Rushmere Heath
Natural flat heathland course.
☎ 0473 795648

HORSE RIDING

Newton Hall Equitation Centre
1 mile off the B1078 at Swilland
Residential instructional holidays. BHS
approved.
☎ 047 385 616

WALKING AND RAMBLING

Gipping Valley River Path
17-mile long former tow path between
Ipswich and Stowmarket by the River
Gipping. Leaflets from the Suffolk
County Council.

Shotley Peninsula
Signposted walks through the area.
☎ 0473 822801

Special Interests

ART GALLERIES

John Russell Gallery
Orwell Place
☎ 0473 212051

Wolsey Art Gallery
Christchurch Mansion
Famous collection of Constables,
Gainsboroughs and other treasures.
☎ 0473 253246

FESTIVALS AND FAIRS

May
East Coast Boat Show at Bourne Park

Suffolk Show at Suffolk Showground

GARDENS

Helmingham Hall
On the B1077 Debenham road
Elizabethan moated gardens with
highland cattle and safari rides.
☎ 0473 890363

Thompson and Morgan Seed Trials
Poplar Lane, London Road
Flowers, vegetables and house plants.
☎ 0473 690743

GUIDED TOURS

Regular and group tours available.
Contact the Tourist Information Centre.
☎ 0473 258070

Central Ipswich

HISTORIC BUILDINGS

Ancient House Bookshop
Excellent example of pargetting on the outside walls.

HISTORIC HOUSES

Christchurch Mansion
Town centre
Tudor mansion in its own park. Art collection, china, glass, attached art gallery.
☎ 0473 253246

Otley Hall
8 miles north-east of Ipswich on the B1079 at Otley
Grade I listed 15th century moated hall with interesting architecture and gardens.
☎ 047339 264

MUSEUMS

Ipswich Musuem
High Street
Archaeology, geology, natural sciences and ethnography.
☎ 0473 213761

PARKS

Suffolk Water Park
Bramford
☎ 0473 830191

THEATRES

Wolsey Theatre
Civic Drive
☎ 0473 253725

Water Sports

BOAT HIRE

Suffolk Water Park
☎ 0473 830191

CANOEING

Suffolk Water Park
☎ 0473 830191

SWIMMING

Crown Pools
Crown Street
Leisure pool, wave machine, fountain, waterfall. Award winning pools.
☎ 0473 219231

Fore Street Baths
Fore Street
25-yard pool.
☎ 0473 253089

WINDSURFING

Oysterworld Sailboard School
Based in the heart of the fashionable Ipswich docklands. Instruction and residential tuition, club and restaurant. 27 acres of safe water.
☎ 0473 230109

Surf-Ace
Suffolk Water Park, Bramford
Windsurfing, tuition, sales, changing. RYA recognised.
☎ 0473 830191

YACHTING

East Anglian School of Sailing
Studio 1 Fox's Marina
Weekend and 5-day courses.
☎ 0473 684884

Orwell Yacht Club
Washbrook
☎ 0473 602288

Oysterworld Nautical Training Centre
1 Wherry Lane, Wherry Quay
RYA powerboat and sailing courses.
☎ 0473 230109

P & Q Sailing Centre
Deer Park Lodge, Mannings Lane, Woolverstone
Two cruising yachts for parties of up to five people. Tuition available. RYA courses.
☎ 0473 84293

Pin Mill Sailing Club
River Orwell
RYA affiliated.
☎ 0473 84731/728685

Shotley Sailing Club
Shotley Promenade, Queen Victoria Drive, Shotley Gate
RYA affiliated.
☎ 0473 34434

Winter Sports

SKIING

Suffolk Ski Centre
Bourne Terrace, Whearstead Road
☎ 0473 602347

Suffolk Ski Club
Belstead House
☎ 0473 686321

Kessingland is part of the Suffolk coastline that has been invaded from the sea at various times by Romans, Angles and Danes. Its church tower has been a navigational marker for seafarers for centuries and now it is very much a coastal resort well known for its Wildlife Park. This dry sunny coast can be explored by taking a walk along the Suffolk Coast Path.

Market day Tuesday
Population 4070

Outdoor Leisure

FISHING

Coarse Fishing
For information and permits for fishing on the River Waveney contact the National Rivers Authority
☎ 0733 371811
☎ 0473 727712

WALKING AND RAMBLING

Suffolk Coast Path
45-mile path along the coast from Bawdsey to Kessingland. Details from the Suffolk County Council.

Special Interests

RAILWAYS

Suffolk Wildlife and Rare Breeds Park
East Anglia's longest miniature railway ride.
☎ 0502 740291

WILDLIFE PARKS

Suffolk Wildlife and Rare Breeds Park
Exotic birds with beavers, otters, monkeys and deer housed in 70 acres. The rare breeds include cattle, sheep, pigs, poultry, miniature horses and shire horses. Large children's play area and educational facilities.
☎ 0502 740291

Kimbolton is a very attractive red-roofed village situated on the western boundary of Cambridgeshire. It has many fine buildings but the 13th century church with its fine spire and the mediaeval castle where Catherine of Aragon spent her last years dominate, the castle is now a school. The town has an inviting atmosphere and several interesting shops.

Special Interests

FESTIVALS AND FAIRS

November
Firework Display
Elaborate display of exceptional fireworks made in Kimbolton by the Reverend Lancaster.

HISTORIC BUILDINGS

St Andrew's Church
13th century church with a 16th century screen partially decorated with paintings of Kings and angels. Impressive monuments to the Manchester family – Henry Montagu became the first Earl of Manchester.

HERITAGE

Kimbolton Castle
Mediaeval castle where Catherine of Aragon spent her last four years; extended by Henry Montagu; renovated by Vanbrugh in the 17th century; Robert Adams added the outer gatehouse and north gateway. It is now a school open to the public on Bank Holidays and Sunday afternoons in summer.

Water Sports

DINGHY SAILING

Kimbolton School Sailing Club
Kimbolton School, Kimbolton
RYA affiliated.

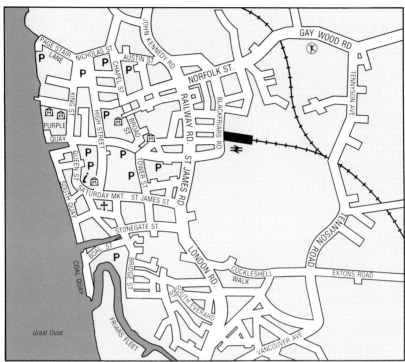

King's Lynn, an ancient market town, has been an important port since the 11th century. It has a wealth of historic buildings reflecting its colourful maritime past. It is unusual in having two market places and two mediaeval guildhalls, one of which has become the Town Hall – it has a dazzling chequered flintwork front. Amongst the town's array of graceful buildings is the Georgian Customs House built by Henry Bell when mayor of 'Lynn' as the locals refer to the town. The wealth generated by the shipping trade is evident in the mediaeval merchants' houses that back onto the river. Now a thriving commercial and shopping centre the town has extensive sports and leisure facilities and a Centre for the Arts that hosts an international festival annually.

i The Old Gaol House
Saturday Market Place
☎ 0553 763044
Market days Tuesday, Friday, Saturday
Early closing Wednesday
Population 37,966

Adventure Sports

SHOOTING

Pentney Abbey SC Ground
Off the A47 at Pentney Abbey
☎ 0760 337300

Sandringham SS Ground
5 miles from King's Lynn on the A149
at Wolferton
☎ 0485 40255

Aerial Sports

HANG GLIDING

Flexiwing Training
'Shetland', Chapel Lane, Beeston
Towing School.
☎ 0328 701602

Indoor Sports

LEISURE CENTRES

King's Lynn Sports Centre
Gaywood Road
☎ 0553 760923

SQUASH

King's Lynn Sports Centre
☎ 0553 762923

TENPIN BOWLING

King's Lynn Bowl
1–5 Lynn Road, Gaywood
☎ 0553 760333

Outdoor Leisure

CYCLING

Norfolk Cycling Holidays
Sandy Way, Ingoldisthorpe
Cycling holidays around the broads,
brecklands and fens.
☎ 0485 560642

FISHING

Coarse Fishing
For information and permits for fishing
on the River Ouse contact the National
Rivers Authority
☎ 0733 371811
☎ 0473 727712

GOLF

Granary Golf Club ♙
Little Dunham
☎ 0328 701310

King's Lynn Golf Club ♙
4 miles north-east of King's Lynn off
the A148 at Castle Rising
Woodland course.
☎ 0553 631654

Middleton Hall ♙
Middleton
☎ 0553 841513

HORSE RIDING

Runcton Hall Stud
Church Farm, North Runcton
Instruction in riding and jumping.
☎ 0553 840676

ORIENTEERING

Wash Orienteers
Contact Jeremy Widdowson, 31 Corbyn
Shaw Road, Churchill Park
☎ 0553 760294

WALKING AND RAMBLING

Wash Coast Path
10-mile path between Sutton Bridge
Lighthouse and West Lynn.

Special Interests

COUNTRY PARKS

Sandringham
600 acres of wood and heathland on the
Royal estate. Nature trails, information
room, Ranger service, picnic area,
scenic drive.

FACTORY VISITS

Caithness Crystal
Oldmedow Road, Hardwick Industrial
Estate
Conducted tours to see glassmaking,
cutting by hand and polishing.
☎ 0553 765111

FESTIVALS AND FAIRS

Easter
Craft and Art Fair at the King's Lynn
Centre for the Arts

Castle Rising

July
Festival of Music and the Arts at the King's Lynn Centre for the Arts

Norwich Union Carriage Driving Trials at Sandringham House, Sandringham

Sandringham Flower Show at Sandringham House, Sandringham

FOOD AND DRINK

Grimston
Specialist herbs and vegetables, guided tours including lunch.
☎ 0485 600250

GARDENS

Cougham Hall Herb Garden
7 miles east of King's Lynn
Formal gardens, 200 varieties of herbs, wild flowers and herb shop.
☎ 0485 600250

Gooderstone Water Gardens
11 miles south-east of King's Lynn on the A47
Lake, pools, bridges, landscaped garden, walks, shrubs, flowers.
☎ 0366 21645

Wellbank's Orchid World
West of King's Lynn on the A17 at Terrington St Clement
20,000 orchid plants under glass.
☎ 0553 671925

GUIDED TOURS

Regular and group tours available.
Contact Town Guides
☎ 0553 671925

HERITAGE

Castle Rising
5 miles north-east of King's Lynn
Fine mid-12th century keep with notable history set in the centre of massive earthworks. Remains include gatehouse and bridge; English Heritage.
☎ 0553 631330

HISTORIC BUILDINGS

St Margaret's Church
Saturday Market Place
Part of a Benedictine priory with an unusual tide clock.

HISTORIC HOUSES

Houghton Hall
14 miles east on the A148
Built for Prime Minister Sir Robert Walpole. 20,000 model soldiers.
☎ 0485 22569

Sandringham House
Royal residence, car and doll museums, gardens, woods, heath, trail. Not open when Royal Family is in residence.
☎ 0553 772675

Trinity Hospital
5 miles north-east at Castle Rising
17th century almshouses, chapel, dining hall and treasury.
☎ 0558 7241

MUSEUMS

Guildhall of St George
15th century, largest surviving mediaeval Guildhall, now part of King's Lynn Arts Centre. National Trust.
0553 774725

Lynn Museum
Natural and social history, exhibitions.
☎ 0553 775001

Musuem of Social History
27 King Street
18th century house and brass rubbing centre.
☎ 0553 775004

Regalia Rooms and Heritage Centre
Trinity Guildhall, Undercroft
Town treasures, King John Cup, Royal Charters and exhibitions.
☎ 0553 763044

Wolferton Station Museum
6 miles north-east on the A149
Edwardian Royal Travel.
☎ 0485 40674

THEATRES

Fermoy Centre
☎ 0553 773578

Water Sports

SWIMMING

St James Swimming Pool
Blackfriars Street
25-metre pool, learner pool.
☎ 0553 764888

WATER-SKIING

Pentney Water Sports Club
Pentney Pits
Contact the Secretary, Lyn York, for details.
☎ 0223 290391

Lavenham, with its fine mediaeval timber-framed houses leaning over narrow streets, is the most splendid of the Suffolk wool towns. It derived its wealth for over 500 years from the manufacture of cloth and the preparation of wool and yarn and was ranked as the fourteenth richest town in England in the reign of Henry VIII. The market place is a triangular space atop a hill dominated by a 16th century cross and the Guildhall which has been a prison, a workhouse and almshouse and is now a National Trust property.

i The Guildhall
Market Place
☎ 0787 248207 summer only
Early closing Wednesday
Population 1800

Outdoor Leisure

WALKING AND RAMBLING

Railway Walks
Short walks along dismantled railway lines through beautiful countryside. Leaflet from the Suffolk County Council.

Special Interests

GARDENS

The Priory
Water Street
Over one hundred varieties of herbs in herb garden of unique design.
☎ 0787 247417

HISTORIC BUILDINGS

Church of St Peter and St Paul
A mediaeval church with a tower, 141 feet high.

Lavenham Guildhall
Display of local history and industry including unique exhibition of mediaeval woollen cloth trade. National Trust.
☎ 0787 247646

Little Hall
Market Place
15th century house. Gayer Anderson collection. Headquarters of the Suffok Preservation Society.
☎ 0787 247179

The Priory
Benedictine priory. Grade I listed timber-framed building under restoration. Collections of paintings, drawings and stained glass. Tours.
☎ 0787 247417

Leiston is situated a few miles inland from the Suffolk coastline on one of the attractive link-roads that joins the seaside towns. The continual erosion of the shoreline makes the building of a through road along the coastline impracticable. The landscape is clothed in broom and heather and well populated by wildfowl making this a very rewarding region for birdwatchers.

Market day Friday
Early closing Wednesday
Population 5370

Indoor Sports

LEISURE CENTRES

Leiston Sports Centre
Redhouse Lane
☎ 0728 830364

136

SQUASH

Leiston Sports Centre
☎ 0728 830364

Outdoor Leisure

BIRDWATCHING

Minsmere (RSPB)
East of Yoxford on the A12 near Westleton
The RSPB's most celebrated reserve. Woodland and heathland leading to the shingle beach. Nature trails and hides where you can see marsh harriers or kingfishers. Information centre and shop.
☎ 072 873 281

Special Interests

ARTS AND CRAFTS

Aldringham Craft Market
Near Leiston
British crafts, frequent exhibitions. Evening visits by arrangement.
☎ 0728 830397

FACTORY VISITS

Sizewell Power Station
Group tours of nuclear power station by appointment only.
☎ 0728 642139

HERITAGE

Leiston Abbey
14th century abbey remains including transepts of church and a range of cloisters.

MUSEUMS

The Long Shop
Main Street
Built in 1853 as a prototype production line manufacture and assembly of steam engines. Steam machinery display.
☎ 07218 832189

Linton is situated ten miles south-east of Cambridge. The village has some very attractive timbered houses and a zoo, well known for its wildlife breeding centre.

Population 4020

Outdoor Leisure

WALKING AND RAMBLING

Roman Walk
6½-mile walk along a Roman trackway.
☎ 0223 317404

Special Interests

ART GALLERIES

Chilford Hundred Vineyard
Balsham Road
Art gallery with prints and sculpture in historic buildings with ornamental stonework.
☎ 0223 892641

FOOD AND DRINK

Chilford Hundred Vineyard
Cambridgeshire's largest vineyard. Wine tasting and tours. Farm and industrial artefacts, children's play area.
☎ 0223 892641

Culpepers Ltd
Hadstock Road
Warehouse and mail order department for the famous herbalists.
☎ 0223 891196

ZOOS

Linton Zoo
Hadstock Road
Zoo and wildlife breeding centre in 10 acres of gardens. Children's play area and picnic site.
☎ 0223 891308

137

Long Melford is set along an impressive, broad, tree-lined thoroughfare, over a mile in length. Most of the 18th and 19th century shops and houses are timber-framed interspersed with original Tudor buildings. It has grown into a centre for the local antiques trade and there are several shops to browse. The triangular green at the west end of the main street is dominated by the church and hospital almshouses. Parkland and great manors abound, they include the Tudor red-bricked Melford Hall and the moated Kentwell Hall which is approached by a delightful avenue of limes.

Early Closing Thursday
Population 3370

Outdoor Leisure

WALKING AND RAMBLING

Railway Walk
Short walks along dismantled railway lines. Leaflet from the Suffolk County Council.

Special Interests

FESTIVALS AND FAIRS

June–July
Kentwell Hall Tudor Event. 200 participants live, dress, behave and talk as in the Tudor period.

GARDENS

Kentwell Hall
17th century walled gardens, moats; fruit trees, spring bulbs; rare breed domestic farm animals.
☎ 0787 310207

HISTORIC BUILDINGS

Holy Trinity Church
The Green
Magnificent 15th century church with ornately carved stonework and nearly one hundred windows. Flanked by the Holy Trinity Hospital Almshouse.

HISTORIC HOUSES

Kentwell Hall
Moated Tudor manor with Victorian detail, maze, costume display, special events.
☎ 0787 310207

Melford Hall
Turreted brick Tudor mansion little changed since 1578; original panelled banqueting hall, 18th century and Regency interiors, fine furniture and Chinese porcelain collection. Beatrix Potter display and garden with an octagonal summer house and imposing gatehouse. National Trust.
☎ 0787 880286

Long Melford

Lowestoft is both a leading holiday resort and a commercial port and modern fishing centre. Fresh fish are landed daily and can be selected at the fish market, herrings are a local speciality. Behind the inner harbour and Lake Lothing is Oulton Broad, one of the finest stretches of inland water in England, and the scene of yacht, dinghy and motor-boat racing, it has extensive moorings, boat-yards and hire facilities. The wide range of family entertainments that includes both old favourites like Punch and Judy, seaside amusement, seafront cafes, the shows and events at the Edwardian Marina Theatre as well as an American Theme Park make Lowestoft a very popular resort.

i The Esplanade
☎ 0502 514274/565989

Market days Friday, Saturday, Sunday
Early closing Thursday
Population 59,875

Indoor Sports

LEISURE CENTRES

Waveney Sports and Leisure Centre
Water Lane
Sauna, solarium, roller skating, sports hall, bar, fitness centre, gym, pool and squash courts.
☎ 0502 569116

SQUASH

Waveney Sports and Leisure Centre
☎ 0502 569116

Outdoor Leisure

CAMPING AND CARAVANNING

Beach Farm Caravan Park
Arbor Lane, Pakefield
60 pitches for tourers or tents in 6-acre site, extensive facilities.
☎ 0502 572794

Touring Caravan Park
White House Farm, Gisleham
Country site by sea, all facilities,
Caravan Club approved, fishing.
☎ 0502 740218

FISHING

Coarse Fishing
Fishing on the River Waveney. For information and permits contact the National Rivers Authority
☎ 0733 371811
☎ 0473 727712

Sea Fishing
Contact the Tourist Information Centre
☎ 0502 514274/565989

GOLF

Rookney Park Golf Club
3½ miles south-west of Lowestoft on the A146 at Carlton Colville
Flat, parkland course.
☎ 0502 560380

HORSE RIDING

Pakefield Riding Centre
Carlton Road
Instruction in riding and jumping.
☎ 0502 572257/562410

139

WALKING AND RAMBLING

Angles Way
70-mile walk along the Waveney and Little Ouse Valleys. Details are available from Norfolk County Council.

Waveney District Walks
Five walks of varying distances around the villages. Contact the Tourist Information Centre for details.

Special Interests

FACTORY VISITS

Lowestoft Fishing Industry and Harbour Tour
Visit the working harbour and fishing industry with a chance to board a trawler. By appointment only.
☎ 0502 514274

Oulton Road Brewery
20 Harbour Road, Oulton Broad
Tours by appointment.
☎ 0502 587905

Raglan Smokehouse
Raglan Street
Kippers a speciality. Herrings cured by real oak smoke.
☎ 0502 581929

FESTIVALS AND FAIRS

July
Lowestoft Regatta

August
Lowestoft Carnival
Oulton Broad Regatta

October–November
Sea-angling Festival

FOOD AND DRINK

Herrings
A local speciality caught and landed at Lowestoft. Tours available.
☎ 0502 573318

GARDENS

Somerleyton Hall Maze
5 miles north-west on the B1074
Garden trail, maze and miniature railway through part of the 12 acres of gardens. Azaleas and rhododendrons.
☎ 0502 730308

HISTORIC BUILDINGS

Herringfleet Marsh Mill
Herringfleet
Last full-size surviving working mill of its type in the country with four common sails and a tailpole.
☎ 0473 230000

HISTORIC HOUSES

Somerleyton Hall
5 miles north-west on the B1074
Rebuilt in Anglo-Italian style in 1846. Home of the Lord and Lady Somerleyton the Hall is open to the public during most afternoons in the summer; magnificent furniture and art.
☎ 0502 730308

MUSEUMS

East Anglia Transport Museum
3 miles south-west of Lowestoft on the B1384 at Carlton Colville
Working trams, trolleybuses, commercial vehicles and narrow gauge railway.
☎ 0502 518459

Lowestoft and East Suffolk Maritime Museum
Whapload Road
Models of boats, paintings, tools and fishing gear.
☎ 0502 561963

Lowestoft Museum
Broad House, Nicholas Everitt Park, Oulton Broad
Local history and archaeology. Lowestoft china.
☎ 0502 565371

Royal Naval Patrol Service Museum
Sparrows Nest
Naval documents, photographs, uniforms, certificates, models, memorial.
☎ 0502 586250

NATURAL HISTORY

Carlton Marshes
Marsh and fen with wetland birds. Access by public footpath. Guided tours by arrangement.
☎ 0502 564250

RAILWAYS

Narrow gauge and miniature railways. Rides can be enjoyed at the East Anglia Transport Museum and Somerleyton Hall.

THEATRES

Marina Theatre
☎ 0502 573318

THEME PARK

Pleasurewood Hills
Corton Road
American Theme Park, rides and shows.
☎ 0502 513626/513627

Water Sports

BOAT HIRE

Waveney River Tours Ltd
Mutford Lock, Bridge Road, Oulton Broad
Inboard motor launches from Easter to September inclusive.
☎ 0502 574903

BOAT TRIPS

Hoseasons Holidays Ltd
Sunway House
Hire of cruisers and houseboats.
☎ 0502 501010

Waveney River Tours Ltd
Mutford Lock, Bridge Road, Oulton Broad
Broads trips on *Enchantress* and *Waveney Princess* at Easter and during the summer season. Light refreshments and bar.
☎ 0502 574903

SWIMMING

Waveney Sports and Leisure Centre
25-metre heated indoor pool.
☎ 0502 569116

YACHTING

Excelsior
The historic Lowestoft sailing trawler *Excelsior* sails to Europe during the summer season taking individuals or groups of over 16 people. Voyages from 2 days to 2 weeks.
☎ 0502 585302

Waveney and Oulton Broad Yacht Club
Oulton Broad
☎ 0502 574100/565888

Lowestoft Harbour

Ludham is a village in the Norfolk Broads and, not surprisingly, there are many venues nearby where it is possible to take to the water and appreciate the real character of the Broads. An ideal location for birdwatchers, this area is noted for its varied birdlife.

Outdoor Leisure

BIRDWATCHING

Hickling Broad
Reed, sedge and oak woodland, passage waders in spring and autumn. Heron and bearded tit in summer. Water trail – 2 hour trip in boat.
☎ 069261 276

Horsey Mere
Winter wildfowl with occasional swans, extensive reedbeds, restricted access by boat.

How Hill Nature Reserve
Walks to hides; marshes and fens; guide will describe area on water trail by electric launch. Contact the Broads Authority.
☎ 0603 610734

141

Special Interests

GARDENS

How Hill Trust Garden
Off the A1062 at How Hill
Nature trail, cottage museum, azaleas a
speciality. Open three times a year.
☎ 0692 6255

HERITAGE

St Benet's Abbey
Access by farm track from minor road
signposted Hall Common
Ruins of monastery founded in 1020AD
by King Canute.

HISTORIC BUILDINGS

Boardman's Mill
How Hill
Interesting open-framed timber trestle
windpump with working turbine, open
daily.

Thurne Dyke Windpump
West of Thurne on the A149
Fully restored windpump. Exhibition of
Broadland windpumps.

MUSEUMS

Toad Hall Cottage
Work and domestic life of a marshman
and his family from the last century.

NATURAL HISTORY

Broadland Conservation Centre
Ranworth
Conservation in the Norfolk Broads;
wildlife and birdwatching gallery.
☎ 0605 49479

Hickling Broad
Reed, sedge and woodland.
Birdwatching, boat trips.
☎ 0692 61276

How Hill Nature Reserve
Rivers, dykes, marshes and fens. Water
trail by small electric launch.
Contact the Broads Authority
☎ 0603 610734

Water Sports

BOAT HIRE

Horning Pleasurecraft Ltd
Ferry View Estate, Horning
Self-drive holiday cruisers.
☎ 0692 630366

Maycraft Ltd
River Bank, Potter Heigham
Motor launches, dinghies, sailing boats
and cruisers.
☎ 0692 670241

Pennant Holidays
Potter Heigham
Hire cruisers, day trips.
☎ 0692 670711

Stalham Yacht Services Ltd
The Staithe, Stalham
Motor launches, house boats, canoes,
motor cruises.
☎ 069 280 288

BOAT TRIPS

Mississippi River Boats
The Little House, Irstead
Broadland trips on 100-seater double-
decked Mississippi paddle boat.
☎ 0692 630262

Pennant Cruises
Broads Haven, Potter Heigham
☎ 0692 670711

Stalham Water Tours
28 St Nicholas Way, Potter Heigham
Broads cruises on luxury boat.
☎ 0692 670530

Sailing on the Broads

Maldon, an important yachting centre and home to the Thames sailing barges, stands on a hill by the Rivers Chelmer and Blackwater. It was here, in 991, that the Vikings defeated the English at the Battle of Maldon. The town, granted its charter in 1171, retains both atmosphere and many of its older buildings such as the 15th century Moot Hall and the 17th century Plume library amongst its attractive lively lanes and 'chases'. Fishing boats and the sailing barges can be seen moored at the picturesque and colourful Hythe quay, at the east end of the town.

i The Maritime Centre, The Hythe
☎ 0621 856503

Market days Thursday, Friday, Saturday
Early closing Wednesday
Population 11,564

Indoor Sports

LEISURE CENTRES

Tiptree Sports Centre
Thurstable School, Maypole Road, Tiptree
☎ 0621 817499

SQUASH

Tiptree Sports Centre
☎ 0621 817449

Outdoor Leisure

BIRDWATCHING

Northey Island
Access by a causeway at low tide
The island surface is treacherous, contact the warden before you visit. Details from the Essex Naturalists' Trust.
☎ 020628 678/679

CAMPING AND CARAVANNING

Barrow Marsh Camping Site
Millbeach, Heybridge
Close to the Blackwater estuary.
5–6 tent pitches, facilities.
☎ 0621 852859

Beacon Hill Leisure Park
St Lawrence Bay
20 caravan and tent pitches; all facilities.
☎ 0621 187248

St Lawrence Caravans
St Lawrence Bay
10 caravan pitches on friendly site, boat launching facilities, sailing club, inn, restaurant, children's room.

FISHING

Coarse Fishing
Fishing sites include the River Blackwater, Beeleigh Lock, Railway Pond, Totham Pit and Totham Reservoir. For information and permits contact the National Rivers Authority
☎ 0733 371811
☎ 0473 727712

GAME FISHING

Chigborough Fisheries
Trout fishery
☎ 0621 57368

Chigborough Gravel Pits
Contact the Chertsey Angling Club
☎ 0932 564872

GOLF

Bunsay Downs ⛳
Little Baddow Pond, Woodham Walter
Indoor golf range.
☎ 024541 2648

Maldon Golf Club ⛳
Beeleigh, Langford
Flat, parkland course.
☎ 0621 853212

Quietwaters Golf Club ⛳ ⛳
North-east of Tolleshunt d'Arcy on the B1026
Coastal courses with many bunkers and water hazards.
☎ 0621 860410

Three Rivers Country Club ⛳ ⛳
Cold Norton
☎ 0621 828631

The Warren Golf Club ⛳
Woodham Walter
☎ 024541 3258

WALKING AND RAMBLING

Dengie Coastal Walks
☎ 0621 854477

143

Special Interests

ARTS AND CRAFTS

The Friary Arts Centre
Fambridge Road
☎ 0621 853331

FACTORY VISITS

Bradwell Power Station
By appointment only.
☎ 0621 76331

Maldon Crystal Salt Co
The Downs
The last remaining producers of sea salt
in Britain.
☎ 0621 853315

FESTIVALS AND FAIRS

June
Barge Match – sailing barges.
☎ 0621 855058

July
Heybridge Basin Regatta

December
Christmas Victorian Evenings.
Shopkeepers and townspeople revive
Victorian dress, customs and
entertainment for the Christmas
shopping evenings. Contact the
Chamber of Trade.
☎ 0621 853711

FOOD AND DRINK

New Hall Vineyards
Purleigh, near Maldon
Tours by appointment.
☎ 0621 828343

HERITAGE

St Peter's on the Wall
Ancient chapel founded by St. Cedd
during the Roman occupation; it was
later used as a barn, then reconsecrated.

HISTORIC BUILDINGS

All Saints Church
13th century church with a unique
triangular tower.

Moot Hall
High Street
Built by the d'Arcy family in 15th
century. Now headquarters of the
Town Council. Tours by arrangement.
☎ 0621 857373

St Giles Leper Hospital
Spital Road
12th century hospital built by order of
Henry II for local lepers.
☎ 0621 854477

MUSEUMS

Agricultural Museum
Goldhanger
4 miles north-east of Maldon on the
B1026
Items of agricultural interest.

Jaguar Motor Museum
3 Mill Lane
History of Jaguar cars up to the present.
Many cars and photographs.
☎ 0621 853311

Maldon Museum
High Street
Local history and a programme of
exhibitions.
☎ 0621 852493

Hythe quay, Maldon

Maritime Centre
The Hythe
Artefacts, models, plans, photographs of local maritime interest.

Plume Library
St Peter's Church
Collection of 16th and 17th century books left by Sir Thomas Plume.
☎ 0621 853556

NATURAL HISTORY

Northey Island
Bird and wildlife sanctuary.
☎ 0621 853142

ORNAMENTAL PARKS

Maldon Promenade
100 acres of formal and informal parkland adjoining River Blackwater.

RAILWAYS

Promenade Park Railway
Miniature railway.

Water Sports

WATER-SKIING

Stone Watersports Club Ltd
Stone, St Lawrence Bay
☎ 0621 87332

YACHT CHARTER

Ostrea Rose
Day trips and cruises and gaff rig tutorial.
☎ 0245 261362

YACHTING

Anglian Yacht Services
The Hythe
Thames sailing barge *Reminder* for individuals or groups up to twelve.
☎ 0621 852290

Essex Sailing School
35 Bramley Way, Mayland
RYA courses and sailing on traditional craft. Weekend sailing and cruises to Holland.
☎ 0621 741818

Lawling Sailing Association
Maylandsea
RYA affiliated.
☎ 0279 70295

Maldon Little Ship Club
Hythe Quay
☎ 0621 58859

Maldon Yacht Club
The Promenade Extension
☎ 0621 659658

Stone Sailing Club
Tinnocks Lane, Stone
RYA affiliated.
☎ 0245 76942

Manningtree is an attractive, small, Essex port. There are many Victorian, Georgian and older houses in the town and at nearby Mistley the church boasts two towers designed by Robert Adam. The town is known for its sailing barges, the maltings for fermenting barley and for its swans.

Market days Saturday, Wednesday
Early closing Wednesday
Population 764

Outdoor Leisure

CAMPING AND CARAVANNING

Strangers Home Inn
The Street, Bradfield
25 caravan pitches and 40 tent sites near River Stour; all facilities.
☎ 0255 870304

FISHING

Coarse Fishing
Fishing on the River Stour.
For information and permits contact the National Rivers Authority
☎ 0733 371811
☎ 0473 727712

Special Interests

COUNTRY PARKS

Mistley Environmental Centre
New Road, Mistley
20 acres of woodland by River Stour.
Horses, goats, hens and geese. Lakeside and woodland walks.
☎ 0206 396483

GARDENS

East Bergholt Lodge
East Bergholt
Over 350 different trees and shrubs and over 140 varieties of rose. Plants for sale.
☎ 0206 298278

The Fens
Old Mill Road, Langham, near Manningtree
2 acres of traditional cottage garden.
Plants for sale.
☎ 0206 262259

HERITAGE

Mistley Towers
4 miles east of Manningtree on the B1070
Two towers designed by Robert Adam in 1776. Keyholder's name is displayed.

HISTORIC BUILDINGS

The Wooden Fender
Ardleigh
Once the haunt of the Witchfinder General, Matthew Hopkins, now a public house.

Water Sports

YACHTING

Stour Sailing Club
10 Quay Street
☎ 0206 393924

March, like many other Fenland towns and villages was once an island surrounded by marshes. As the land was drained the town grew and prospered, initially as a trading and religious centre and a minor port and more recently as a market town and railway centre. The town offers a good range of shopping facilities and its new marina gives easy access to the pleasures of boating on the region's waterways.

Market days Wednesday, Saturday
Early closing Tuesday

Adventure Sports

SHOOTING

Greenend Shooting Ground
Off the A1101 jctn 1098
☎ 03548 335

Outdoor Leisure

BIRDWATCHING

Welney Wildfowl Refuge
800 acres of the Ouse washes with
thousands of wild birds. Observatory
and hides, information rooms and shop.
☎ 0353 860711

FISHING

Coarse Fishing
Fishing on the River Nene. For
information and permits contact the
National Rivers Authority
☎ 0733 371811
☎ 0473 727712

GOLF

March Golf Club ▶
Frogs Abbey, Grange Road, Knightsend
☎ 0354 52364

HORSE RIDING

Knightsend Farm
Knightsend Road
Lessons, livery, schooling, riding for the
disabled.
☎ 0354 57444

WALKING AND RAMBLING

The Hereward Way
110-mile long distance path between
Oakham and Thetford passes through
March. Leaflet from the Ely Tourist
Information Centre.

Woodman's Way
6½ mile circular walk around March
and Wimblington. Contact
Cambridgeshire County Council for
details.
☎ 0223 317404

Special Interests

FARM PARKS

Stags Holt Farm Park
Fridaybridge
Suffolk Punch horses and farming
bygones in Victorian buildings set in 20
acres of ancient parkland.
☎ 0354 52406

HISTORIC BUILDINGS

St Wendreda's Church
16th century carved double-hammer
roof decorated with 120 carved angels
open in flight.

MUSEUMS

March and District Museum
High Street
Agricultural and domestic exhibits,
photographs and local records in
restored blacksmith's forge. Guided
tours by arrangement.
☎ 0354 55300

Water Sports

BOAT HIRE

Fox's Boats
10 Marina Drive
5 narrowboats for off-peak weekend
hire and weekly hire during the
summer.

Boating at March

SWIMMING

George Campbell Pool
City Road
☎ 0345 53511

Mildenhall can be found ten miles north-east of Newmarket beside the River Lark. The town centres around its market place and church, an area of the town that has retained its historic character in several fine timber-framed buildings and a row of attractive 18th century almshouses. The town has a long history and several interesting antiquities have been found here including the famous Mildenhall Treasure, over 30 pieces of 4th century Roman silverware that were ploughed up in the 1940s. The parish of Mildenhall is one of the largest in the country and it is well served with sports and leisure facilities. The Mildenhall air field is one of the largest strategic NATO air bases in Europe and is home to a unit of the United States Air Force who have named the passenger and freight terminal there the 'Gateway to England'.

Market day Friday
Early closing Thursday

Adventure Sports

SHOOTING

Hereward CS Ground
Lakenheath Road, Lakenheath
☎ 0353 721432

Lakenheath Rod and GC Ground
Off the A1065 between Barton Hill roundabout and Brandon
☎ 0892 835770

Mildenhall town centre

Indoor Sports

LEISURE CENTRES

Dome Sports Centre
Bury Road
☎ 0638 717737

SQUASH

Dome Sports Centre
☎ 0638 717737

Outdoor Leisure

FISHING

Coarse Fishing
Fishing on the River Lark and in the local dykes. For information and permits contact the National Rivers Authority
☎ 0733 371811
☎ 0480 414581

Special Interests

FESTIVALS AND FAIRS

May
Mildenhall Air Fete
June
Forest Heath Arts Festival

HISTORIC BUILDINGS

St Mary's Church
Attractive tower and Lady Chapel rebuilt in the 15th century with many 12th and 13th century features. Carved hammer beam ceiling.

MUSEUMS

Mildenhall and District Museum
King Street
Local history including the Mildenhall Treasure, a hoard of 4th century Roman silver tableware.

Water Sports

SWIMMING

Mildenhall and District Swimming Pool
Recreation Way
☎ 0638 712515

Mundesley is a quiet holiday village, its sandy beaches and shallow water providing safe bathing. Nearby Paston was once home to the influential Paston family whose papers have given historians a vivid insight into the reigns of several monarchs. Today this is a very popular resort area for families.

i 2a Station Road
☎ 0263 721070 summer only

Outdoor Leisure

GOLF

Mundesley Golf Club 🏌
Links Road
Parkland course, part flat, part hilly.
☎ 0263 720095

HORSE RIDING

Rose-Acre Riding Stables
Back Mundesley Road, Gimingham
Instruction in riding and jumping.
☎ 0262 720671

Special Interests

HISTORIC BUILDINGS

Stow Mill
1 mile south of Mundesley at Paston
1827 tower mill with working fantail and sails. Restoration in progress.
☎ 0263 720298

Nearby Cromer

Needham Market is a small attractive town sited in the pleasant countryside of the Gipping Valley with several riverside walks. It is close to Needham Lake, popular for its excellent fishing and picnic facilities. Many interesting buildings can be found in the town and the interior roof of the church with its fine hammerbeam roof is of particular interest. There are also several craft and antique shops to encapsulate quality in both the past and the present.

Early closing Tuesday
Population 4370

Outdoor Leisure

FISHING

Coarse Fishing
Fishing on Needham Lake. For information and permits contact the National Rivers Authority
☎ 0733 371811
☎ 0473 727712

WALKING AND RAMBLING

Gipping Valley Walks
Waymarked circular walks linked to the River Gipping path. Walkcards available from the Suffolk County Council.

Special Interests

GARDENS

Blakenham Woodland Garden
4 miles south-east of Needham Market at Little Blakenham
5-acre woodland garden with many rare trees and shrubs.

Newmarket

Newmarket has been the home of horse racing since 1605 when James I and his Scottish nobles discovered the springy turf of the heath, ideal for horse racing. Charles II was a great racing enthusiast and the Rowley Mile Racecourse was named after his horse, Old Rowley. The turrets and cupolas of studs and stables can be seen all around the heath where strings of horses exercising is an everyday scene. The Jockey Club, the controlling body of racing, can be found in the High Street, it was founded in 1772 and has grown considerably over the years. Newmarket is also home to the National Horseracing Museum and the National Stud which is situated southwest of the town next to the racecourse.

i Public Library
Rookery Precinct
☎ 0638 661216

Market days Tuesday, Saturday
Early closing Wednesday
Population 16,000

Adventure Sports

SHOOTING

Newmarket Gun Club
Rectory Pitts, Kennett
☎ 0487 830454

Indoor Sports

LEISURE CENTRES

Newmarket Sports Centre
Exning Road
☎ 0638 662726

151

Newmarket Sports Centre
☎ 0638 662726

Outdoor Leisure

Newmarket Golf Course ⓘ
1 mile south-west of Newmarket on
the A1034
Flat parkland course.
☎ 0638 663000

The National Stud
Conducted tours to see top racehorses,
mares and foals. By appointment only.
☎ 0368 663464

Newmarket Racecourses
Rowley Mile
There are two racecourses, the Rowley
Mile Course used for spring and autumn
meetings and the July course for
meetings between June and August. The
two courses host 37 flat race days each
year. Newmarket is very much the home
of racing.
☎ 0638 662762

Special Interests

Newmarket Equine Tours
The National Horseracing Museum,
99 High Street
Tours of the famous studs around
Newmarket. Book in advance.
☎ 0638 667333

Stevens Mill
4 miles north-west of Newmarket at
Burwell
Three-stone clunch tower mill
undergoing extensive restoration.
☎ 0223 811233

Horse training on the heath

At the races

National Horse Racing Museum
99 High Street
Complete history of horseracing in five
galleries of exhibits and art.
☎ 0638 667333

Water Sports

SWIMMING

Newmarket Swimming Pool
High Street
22-metre pool.
☎ 0638 661736

North Walsham

North Walsham became a centre for the wool trade and a focus for the local farming community in the 14th century. The revenue from this trade financed the large church close to the Market Cross in the town centre and the Paston School built during the same era educated Horatio Nelson before he embarked on his famous naval career. It remains an attractive market town and popular shopping centre.

Market day Thursday
Early closing Wednesday
Population 7941

Indoor Sports

LEISURE CENTRES

North Walsham Sports Hall
Spencer Avenue
☎ 0692 402293

Multi-Activity Holidays

MULTI-ACTIVITY CENTRES

Broadland Outdoor Adventure
Sailing, windsurfing, canoeing, orienteering, fishing based on board a 60-year old cruiser.
☎ 069260 527

Outdoor Leisure

FISHING

Coarse Fishing
Contact the National Rivers Authority for information and permits for fishing on the Norfolk Broads.
☎ 0733 371811

WALKING AND RAMBLING

Bacton Wood Forest Walks
Forest walks through gentle hilly woodland east of the town.

Special Interests

ARTS AND CRAFTS

Cat Pottery
1 Grammar School Road
Pottery cats and dogs made in traditional workshops. Collection of railway and other curiosities.
☎ 0692 402692

GARDENS

Rose World
Landscaped gardens. 5 acres of roses (over 400 varieties), garden centre and shop.
☎ 0693 402591

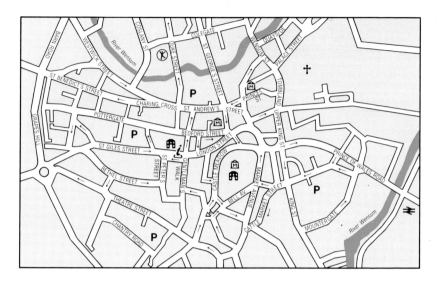

Norwich, a fortified city on the River Wensum, has been the See of East Anglian bishops for almost 900 years. It is a cathedral city, the county town of Norfolk, a port and an industrial centre. It thrived initially as a weaving centre for worsted cloth, named after the village of Worsted, that lies to the north of the city, and later prospered through the manufacture of shoes, mustard and chocolate. The Cathedral of the Holy Trinity dominates the city, its 315-foot spire overshadowing the towers of the other thirty-three mediaeval churches within the city walls. The most substantial of the city's hills is crowned by the Norman keep of Norwich Castle, it is surrounded by attractive moated gardens and steep walks. The open market place is overlooked by the old Guildhall and narrow flint-cobbled streets lead off it past elegant town houses and many intriguing specialist shops. In addition to the many museums, entertainment is provided for all tastes by the theatres and art galleries. For an elevated view of the city a journey to Mousehold Heath, a tract of furze and heather north of the city, is well worth the effort.

i The Guildhall
Gaol Hill
☎ 0603 666071

Market days Monday, Wednesday, Saturday
Population 173,286

Michael C Litton
International Sporting Agent
☎ 0603 880043

Adventure Sports

CLIMBING

University of East Anglia Sports Centre
University Plain
☎ 0603 56161

SHOOTING

Deighton Hills Gun Club
Mid Norfolk Shooting Ground,
Taverham
☎ 0603 860436

Aerial Sports

BALLOONING

Anglia Balloons
Peacock Lodge, Marlingfield
Ballooning holidays.
☎ 0603 880819/871636

FLYING

Norwich School of Flying
Norwich Airport
☎ 0603 403107

154

PARAGLIDING

Pegasus Scouts P C
20 miles west of Norwich at Watton Airfield
Open at weekends during the season.
☎ 0603 37147

Indoor Sports

SPORTS AND LEISURE CENTRES

Crome Recreation Centre
Telegraph Lane East, Thorpe Hamlet
☎ 0603 36697

Duke Street Centre
Duke Street
☎ 0603 623469

Long Stratton Leisure Centre
Swan Lane, Long Stratton
☎ 0508 31444

The Norman Centre
Bignold Road
☎ 0603 408140

Norwich Sports Village
Drayton High Road, Hellesdon
☎ 0603 788898

University of East Anglia Sports Centre
☎ 0603 56161

Wensum Lodge Sports Block
King Street
☎ 0603 624326

SQUASH

There are squash courts at all the sports and leisure centres listed above.

TENPIN BOWLING

Crome Bowl
Telegraph Lane East
☎ 0603 700203

Norwich Club Bowl
193c Plumstead Road
☎ 0603 37609

Multi-Activity Holidays

SPECIAL INTEREST CENTRES

Wensum Lodge
King Street
Resident and non-resident arts and crafts weekend courses and summer schools in former Victorian brewery.
☎ 0603 666021

Outdoor Leisure

BIRD WATCHING

Strumpshaw Fen
Access off the A47
Wide range of habitats; marsh harriers, the rare Cetti's warbler and many other birds.
☎ 0603 715191

Surlingham and Rockland Marshes
Access from Surlingham Church car park off the A146
2-mile circular route with hides and screens; reed warblers and other wild fowl. Wellingtons essential. RSPB.
☎ 0603 615920

FISHING

Coarse Fishing
For information and permits contact the National Rivers Authority
☎ 0733 371811
☎ 0473 727712

Norfolk Broads and River Yare
Contact the Tourist Information Centre.
☎ 0603 666071

FOOTBALL

Norwich City Football Club
Carrow Road
☎ 0603 612131

GOLF

Costessey Park Golf Course ⚑18
Old Costessey
☎ 0603 746333

Eaton Golf Club ⚑18
2¹/₂ miles south-west of Norwich on the A11
Undulating, old established course.
☎ 0603 51686

Norwich Golf Course ⚑9
Long Lane, Banburgh
☎ 0603 746390

Royal Norwich Golf Club ⚑18
2¹/₂ miles north-west of Norwich on the A1067 at Hellesdon
Undulating parkland course.
☎ 0603 429928

HORSE RIDING

Newin Equestrian Centre
Woodrow Lane, Great Moulton
Instruction in riding, jumping and show jumping.
☎ 0263 720671

Salhouse Equestrian Centre
Vicarage Farm, Salhouse
Equestrian holiday courses. BHS
approved.
☎ 0603 782749/720921

Strumpshaw Riding
Buckenham Road, Strumpshaw Centre
Instruction in riding and jumping.
Young children welcomed.
☎ 0603 712815

ORIENTEERING

Mousehold Heath
Map packs from Norfolk City Tourist
office. Contact Norwich Orienteering
Club for details.

Norwich Orienteering Club
Contact Peter Softley, 34 Lowther Road
☎ 0603 52859

TENNIS

Norwich Sports Village
☎ 0603 788898

WALKING AND RAMBLING

Marriott's Way
7-mile footpath and bridleway between
Norwich and Attlebridge along former
railway line. Leaflet from Norfolk
County Council.

Norfolk's Changing Heritage
2-3 mile walks around Norfolk guided by
local experts. Details from the
Department of Planning and Property,
Norfolk County Council.

Special Interests

ART GALLERIES

Norwich Gallery
Norfolk Institute of Art and Design,
St George Street
Exhibitions of contemporary art.
☎ 0603 610561

Sainsbury Centre for Visual Arts
University of East Anglia
Art, sculpture and antiquities from
around the world. Collection includes
works by Henry Moore and Francis
Bacon.
☎ 0603 56060

ARTS AND CRAFTS

The Dolls' House
7 Bagleys Court, Pottergate
Handmade dolls' houses, kits and all
accessories.
☎ 0603 610807

Towerham Craft Centre
Fir Covert Road, Taverham
Purpose-built centre for many local
crafts; manufacture and sales.
☎ 0603 860522

Wensum Lodge
King Street
Resident and non-resident arts and crafts
weekend courses and summer schools in
former Victorian brewery.
☎ 0603 666021

FACTORY TOURS

Lotus Cars
Off the A11 at Hethel
Guided tours and demonstrations of
sports car production. By appointment
only.
☎ 0953 608000

FOOD AND DRINK

Colmans Mustard
3 Bridewell Alley
Mustard manufacturers for over 160
years. Shop-cum-museum of mustard
making.
☎ 0603 627889

Pickering and Son
30 The Street, Costessy
Forty kinds of home-made sausage with
no artificial additives.
☎ 0603 742002

Samphire
A marsh plant of the Norfolk coast
known as 'poor man's asparagus'.
Harvested in July and August and
available at Norwich market.

Woodfords Norfolk Plus
Broadland Brewery, Woodbastwick
Local ales.
☎ 0603 720353

GARDENS

Rainthorpe Hall Gardens
8 miles south of Norwich on the A140 at
Tasburgh
Large gardens with specialist trees
including bamboo.
☎ 0508 470618

GUIDED TOURS

Regular and group tours. Contact the
Tourist Information Centre.
☎ 0603 666071

Dragon Hall Tours
☎ 0603 663922

HERITAGE

Norwich Castle
12th century Norman keep, now
headquarters of Norfolk Museums
Service.
☎ 0603 621154

Norwich Cathedral
Anglican cathedral founded in 1096.
Norman style architecture with 15th
century carvings. Edith Cavell buried
here.

St John's Cathedral
Roman Catholic cathedral with 19th
century Gothic style buildings. Tours of
tower available.

St Peter Mancroft Church
Market Place
15th century parish church on Norman
foundations with Flemish tapestry and
other treasures.

HISTORIC BUILDINGS

Dragon Hall
King Street
Mediaeval timber-framed merchants
hall originally built as a cloth
showroom, with an intricately carved
and painted dragon. Guided tours.
☎ 0603 663922

The Guildhall
Market Place
Mediaeval Guildhall dating from the
time of the cloth trade.

HISTORIC HOUSES

Rainthorpe Hall
8 miles south of Norwich on the A140 at
Tasburgh
Elizabethan manor house, open by
appointment only.
☎ 0508 470618

MUSEUMS

Bridewell Museum
Bridewell Alley
History of trades and industries in
Norwich since the 17th century.
☎ 0603 222222 extn 71224

City of Norwich Aviation Museum
Old Norwich Road, Horsham St Faith
Aeronautical history, aero engines,
Vulcan bomber and other aircraft.
☎ 0603 625309

Forncett Industrial Steam Museum
10 mile south-west of Norwich on the
A140
Collection of large industrial stationary
steam engines.
☎ 050841 8277

John Jarrold Printing Museum
Whitefriars
Working museum of printing and
binding housed in a 12th century crypt.
☎ 0603 660211

Norwich Castle Museum
Very wide range of exhibits covering
archaeology, geology, natural and social
history. Also the largest specialist
collection of British teapots in the world.
Exhibition programme.
☎ 0603 621154

Royal Norfolk Regiment Museum
1 mile north-east of the city centre off
the B1140
Regimental history since 1685.

St Peter Hungate Church Museum
Princes Street
Mediaeval church displaying church art
and furnishings. Brass rubbing.
☎ 0603 222222 extn 71224

**Station 146 Seeting Airfield Control
Tower**
Brooke, Norwich
Original wartime control tower with
exhibits and pictures from Second World
War, including 448th Bomb Group
collection.
☎ 0508 50787

Strangers Hall Museum of Domestic Life
Mediaeval town house, rooms furnished
in 16th to 19th century styles.
☎ 0603 222222 extn 71224

NATURAL HISTORY

Redwings Horse Sanctuary
6 miles north of Norwich
Rescued horses, ponies and donkeys.

Stumpshaw Fen
Off the A47 Norwich to Great Yarmouth
road
Small broad, reedbeds and woodland
with wildfowl. Hides available.
☎ 0603 715191

Surlingham and Rockland Marshes
Access from Surlingham Church car
park off the A146 Norwich to Lowestoft
road
Wildfowl can be seen on 2-mile circular
route with hides and screens.
Wellingtons essential. RSPB.
☎ 0603 615920
☎ 050 88 661

THEATRES

Arts Centre
☎ 0603 660352

Maddermarket Theatres
☎ 0603 620917

Puppet Theatre
☎ 0603 629961

Theatre Royal
☎ 0603 628205

WILDLIFE PARKS

Norfolk Wildlife Park
12 miles north-west of Norwich on the
A1067 at Great Witchingham
Largest collection of British and
European wildlife in 40 acres of
parkland. Flowering shrubs and unusual
trees. Woodland steam railway. Unique
team of trained reindeer.
☎ 0603 872274

Water Sports

BOAT HIRE

Harbour Cruisers
Riverside, Brundall
Motor cruisers.
☎ 0603 712146

Highcraft
Griffin Lane, Thorpe St Andrew
Motor cabin cruisers.
☎ 0603 701701

BOAT TRIPS

Southern River Steamers
Elm Hill
Broadland river and city cruises.
Available for private hire.
☎ 0603 501220

SWIMMING

Norwich City Baths
St Augustine's Gate
33-metre pool, squash courts, sauna,
solarium, gym.
☎ 0603 620164

WATER-SKIING

Bluebird Deaf Water Ski Club
Costessey Pits, Costessey
Contact the secretary, Paul Dennis, for
details.
☎ 0263 761727

Buckenham Ferry Water Ski Club
Buckenham
Contact the secretary, Graham Orpet at
2 Snowhill, Chedgrave, near Codden, for
details.

Norwich and District Water Ski Club
Taverham Lakes, Taverham
☎ 0603 967373

YACHTING

Brundall Motor Yacht Club
Bells Marine, Riverside, Brundall
☎ 0603 630345/667196

Buckenham Sailing Club
Buckenham Ferry, Claxton
☎ 0603 53317/660011 extn 303

Coldham Hall Sailing Club
Coldham Hall Tavern, Surlingham
☎ 0603 715781

Norfolk Broads Yacht Club
Wroxham Road
☎ 0603 58255

Tama Sailing
55 Eastern Road, Thorpe St Andrew
Weekend or longer cruising courses
around the east coast and further afield.
☎ 0603 35431

Yare Sailing Club
River Yare
☎ 0508 8542
☎ 0603 619261

YACHT CHARTER

Norfolk Wherry Albion
63 Whitehall Road
Charter of *Albion* for parites of up to
twelve people.
☎ 0603 624642

Wherry Yacht Charter
Barton House, Hartwell Road, The
Avenue
Broadland cruising for groups up to
twelve people on the historic wherry
yachts *Olive* and *Norada* or the pleasure
wherry *Hathor*.
☎ 0603 782470

Winter Sports

SKIING

Norwich Ski Club
Whitlingham Lane, Trowse
☎ 0692 662781

Dry slope skiing at Norwich

Orford is a coastal town on the restless Suffolk coast. The fate of Dunwich, a former East Anglian capital, can be seen in an exhibition here – coastal erosion has left most of it underwater! Orford is approached by passing through the gnarled and ancient Staverton Forest and crossing the River Bute in which there are oyster beds. Salmon, eel and trout are all smoked locally. Orford provides good sailing and a boat trip from the quay to Havergate Island might be rewarded with a glimpse of the avocets that nest there.

Outdoor Leisure

BIRDWATCHING

Havergate Island (RSPB)
Access by boat from Orford Quay
Low embanked island in the River Ore.
Britain's largest nesting colony of
avocets. Write to book: J Partridge, 30
Mundays Lane, Orford, Woodbridge
enclosing SAE.

WALKING AND RAMBLING

Orford Walks
4 walks in and around Orford including
one suitable for wheelchairs. Leaflets
available from Suffolk County Council.

Orford Castle

Special Interests

HERITAGE

Butley Priory
Off the B1084 Woodbridge to Orford road
Huge 14th century gatehouse remains
with heraldic carvings; set in Staverton
Forest, an ancient woodland.

Orford Castle
90-foot high, 18-sided keep with views
across the River Alde to Orford Ness.
Built by Henry II for coastal defence in
the 12th century.

MUSEUMS

**Dunwich Underwater Exploration
Exhibition**
The Craft Shop, Front Street
Underwater exploration of Dunwich,
once the capital of East Anglia. Coastal
erosion has reduced it to a tiny village
with most of the former town
underwater.
☎ 0394 450678

Water Sports

BOAT TRIPS

Lady Florence
Cruising the Rivers Alde and Ore.
Maximum twelve passengers, food and
bar.
☎ 0394 450210

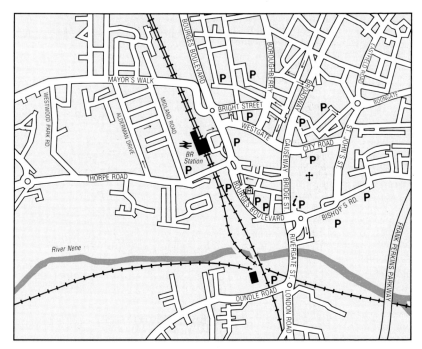

The Soke of Peterborough has moved from the jurisdiction of Northamptonshire to that of Huntingdonshire and now Cambridgeshire. The city has a long history, the Bronze Age 'Lake Village' excavations at Flag Fen date back to 1000 B.C. The Romans had a main fortress and a pottery here and the cathedral, built over 750 years ago, was built on the site of an earlier church that was sacked by Hereward the Wake in his efforts to defeat William the Conqueror. Largely rebuilt by the Normans it has a magnificent triple-arched west front. Catherine of Aragon was entombed here as was Mary Queen of Scots until her son James, moved her body to Westminster Abbey.

The city offers sports and leisure facilities that are hard for any town to beat. Ferry Meadows Country Park has lakes for fishing and watersports, there are golf courses, an excellent ice rink and a purpose-built rowing and canoeing centre, a roller skating centre and the riverside Key Theatre. Steam trains ply the Nene Valley and Britain's second biggest agricultural show, the East of England Show is staged at the permanent showground here which also hosts a variety of other national shows.

i Town Hall
Bridge Street
☎ 0733 317336

Market days Tuesday, Wednesday, Friday, Saturday
Early closing Monday, Thursday
Population 114,733

Adventure Sports

SHOOTING

Manor Leisure Centre
Station Road, Whittlesey
☎ 0733 202298

Aerial Sports

GLIDING

Peterborough and Spalding Gliding Club
Crowland Airfield, near Peterborough
☎ 0733 210463/235964

PARACHUTING

Action Enterprise Ltd
Sibson Airfield, Wansford
Rapid progression courses.
☎ 0832 280677

Peterborough Cathedral

Peterborough Parachute Centre
Sibson Airfield, Wansford
Full-time centre, accommodation, food,
tandem available.
☎ 0832 280490

Indoor Sports

ICE SKATING

Peterborough Ice Rink
Bretton Way
☎ 0733 260222

LEISURE CENTRES

Bushfield Sports Centre
Bushfield
☎ 0733 234018

The Cressett
Bretton Centre
☎ 0733 265705

Manor Leisure Centre
Station Road, Whittlesey
☎ 0733 202298

Werrington Sports Centre
Staniland Way, Werrington

SQUASH

Bushfield Sports Centre
☎ 0733 234018

The Cressett
☎ 0733 265705

Werrington Sports Centre
☎ 0733 76606

TENPIN BOWLING

Peterborough Bowl
Sturrock Way, Bretton
☎ 0733 264182

Outdoor Leisure

BIRD WATCHING

Nene Washes (RSPB)
Near Peterborough
Grass washlands of River Nene with
breeding and wintering waders and
wildfowl. Visits by appointment only.
☎ 0603 615920

CYCLING

Surface Watersports
Ham Lane, Orton Waterville
Cycle hire.
☎ 0733 234418

FISHING

Coarse Fishing
For information and permits contact the
National Rivers Authority
☎ 0733 371811

161

GOLF

Burghley Park Golf Club 🏌
St Martins Without, Stamford
☎ 0780 53789

Milton Golf Club 🏌
3 miles west of Peterborough on the A47
at Milton Ferry
Parkland course.
☎ 0733 380489

Orton Meadows Golf Course 🏌
Ham Lane
☎ 0733 237478

Thorpe Wood Golf Course 🏌
Thorpe Wood, Nene Parkway
☎ 0733 267701

HORSE RIDING

Lynch Farm Equitation Centre
Wistow Way, Orton Wistow
Instruction in riding and jumping.
☎ 0733 234445

TENNIS

Court Tennis Centre
6 Mallard Road, Bretton
Indoor tennis.
☎ 0733 269747

WALKING AND RAMBLING

Circular Walks
13 walks in rural Peterborough between
4–7 miles through farmland, ancient
woodland and riverside scenery. Leaflet
guides from the Town Hall.
☎ 0733 63141

Nene Way
Ferry Meadows Country Park, Ham Lane
9-mile walk along the Nene Valley from
Peterborough to Wansford.
☎ 0733 234443

Torpel Way
11¹/₂-mile walk to Stamford through
open countryside. Leaflets from the
Town Hall.
☎ 0733 63141

Special Interests

ART GALLERIES

Peterborough Arts Centre
Orton Gallery
Three galleries, studios, workshops and
performance areas. Programme of
events.
☎ 0733 27075

COUNTRY PARKS

Ferry Meadows Country park
2 miles west of city centre on the A605
Nature reserve, miniature railway,
visitor centre, water sports and boat hire.
☎ 0733 234443

FARM PARKS

Sacrewell Farm and Country Centre
8 miles west on the A47 at Thornhaugh
530-acre farming centre with working
watermill, farm animals and a large
collection of agricultural, rural and
domestic bygones.
☎ 0780 782222/782277

FESTIVALS AND FAIRS

January
Straw Bear Festival at Whittlesey

March
Shire Horse Show at the East of England
Showground
☎ 0733 234451

May
Truckfest at the East of England
Showground

Stilton cheese rolling at Stilton.
July
East of England Show at the East of
England Showground
☎ 0733 234451

HERITAGE

Flag Fen
Off Fourth Drove, Fengate
Bronze Age excavation. Small-scale
reconstruction of Flag Fen as it was and
Bronze Age countryside with fields,
animals and buildings. Visitors centre
and play area.
☎ 0733 313414

Longthorpe Tower
Three storey tower of fortified 14th
century manor house with best
collection of biblical wall paintings in
Britain.
☎ 0733 268482

Peterborough Cathedral
Built of local Barnack limestone between
1118 and 1238. It has an exquisite West
front and a magnificent 13th century
hand-painted nave ceiling. Both
Catherine of Aragon and Mary Queen of
Scots were buried here. Also contains
the Hedda Stone, an early Saxon
sculpture.
☎ 0733 43342/62125

Thorney Abbey Church
7 miles north-east of Peterborough
Abbey church dates from 1100. Guided
tours by appointment.
☎ 0733 270388

HISTORIC BUILDINGS

Sacrewell Farm and Country Centre
Working watermill, farm gardens and
museum.
☎ 0780 782222/782277

HISTORIC HOUSES

Elton Hall
8 miles west on the A605 at Elton
15th century gatehouse, tower, chapel,
library, paintings, furniture.
☎ 08324 468/223

MUSEUMS

City Museum and Art Gallery
Priestgate
Local and natural history, industry, folk
life, militaria and costume displays.
☎ 0733 43329

NATURAL HISTORY

Nene Washes
☎ 0603 615920

RAILWAYS

Nene Valley Railway
Regular steam service with English and
Continental rolling stock, 15 miles of
line; special steam weekends including
Thomas the Tank Engine.
☎ 0780 782854

THEATRES

Cresset Theatre
☎ 0733 265705

Key Theatre
☎ 0733 52437

WILDLIFE PARKS

Peakirk Wildfowl Trust
7 miles north on the B1443 at Peakirk
Flamingoes, ducks, geese and swans in
17 acres of water gardens.
☎ 0733 252271

Water Sports

DIVING

Gildenburgh Water
Eastrea Road, Whittlesey
☎ 0733 202867

JET-SKIING

Tallington Lakes Leisure Park
Near Stamford
RYA recognised.
☎ 0778 347000

SWIMMING

Embankment Sports Complex
25-metre swimming pool and diving
pool.

Jack Hunt Swimming Pool
Bradwell Road
25-metre pool, gym.

Manor Leisure Centre
Station Road, Whittlesey
☎ 0733 202298

Orton Longueville Swimming Pool
Orton Longueville School, Oundle Road
25-metre pool.
☎ 0733 231313

Regional Swimming Pool
Lancashire Gate, Bishops Road
25-metre pool, learner pool, diving pit,
solarium.
☎ 0733 41474

WATER-SKIING

King's Water Ski Club
King's Dyke, Whittlesey
Contact the secretary, Yvonne
McCormack for details
☎ 053 652 3583

Tallington Lakes Leisure Park
☎ 0778 347000

WINDSURFING

Surface Watersports
Ferry Meadows, Orton Waterville
Windsurfing specialist courses.
☎ 0733 234418

Tallington Windsurfing Club
Tallington Lakes Leisure Park
RYA recognised.
☎ 0778 346342

YACHTING

Fenland Sailing Club
Whittlesey
☎ 0733 66888/26200 extn 2767

Winter Sports

SKIING

Tallington Lakes Leisure Park
☎ 0778 344990

Ramsey, an ancient market town, has developed a distinctive character born out of its location at the edge of Fenland and its relative remoteness from the rest of what were Huntingdonshire towns. The area around the remains of the mediaeval Ramsey Abbey, now a school, is extremely attractive and the Abbey Gatehouse can be visited as can the St Thomas A Becket Church which was originally used as a hospital for the Abbey.

Ramsey Abbey Gatehouse

Aerial Sports

GLIDING

Nene Valley Gliding Club
RAF Upwood
Contact Eric Yeardley, 22 Burns Way,
St Ives
☎ 0480 301316

Outdoor Leisure

FISHING

Coarse Fishing
Fishing on the River Nene. For information and permits contact the National Rivers Authority
☎ 0733 371811
☎ 0480 414581

GOLF

Ramsey Golf Club ⚑₁₈
4 Abbey Terrace
Flat parkland course.
☎ 0487 812600

HORSE RIDING

Ramsey St Marys
☎ 0731 29580

Special Interests

HISTORIC BUILDINGS

Ramsey Abbey
Abbey Green
17th century house, now a school, on the ruins of a Benedictine abbey founded in 969.
☎ 0487 813285

Ramsey Abbey Gatehouse
Ruins of the 15th century gatehouse, now owned by the National Trust.
☎ 0263 733471

MUSEUMS

Ramsey Rural Museum
The Woodyard
Crafts, trades and social history in what were the De Ramsey Estate workshops. Several agricultural buildings have been re-erected on the site. Reconstructions of a Fenland kitchen, washroom and a late Victorian schoolroom.
☎ 0487 813229

Water Sports

SWIMMING

Ailwyn School Pool
Hollow Lane
20-metre pool.
☎ 0487 812352

Saffron Walden remains a relatively unspoilt small town with a wealth of mediaeval houses and yet it is only 40 miles from London. Another of the region's wool towns it also derived its wealth from its saffron crop which was used as both a dye and a medicine. The mediaeval market rows are well preserved and mediaeval houses and cottages are scattered throughout the town, many decorated by pargetting. The High Street has several late Georgian houses and many interesting and unusual shops. The church, reputedly the largest in Essex, dominates the town and there are the remains of a Norman castle. On the common is a rare earth maze that attracts many archaeologists.

i 1 Market Palce
☎ 0799 24282

Market days Tuesday, Saturday
Early closing Thursday
Population 12,058

Indoor Sports

LEISURE CENTRES

Lord Butler Leisure Centre
Peasland Road
☎ 0799 26600

SQUASH

Lord Butler Leisure Centre
☎ 0799 26600

Outdoor Leisure

GOLF

Saffron Walden Golf Club ⛳
Windmill Hill
Parkland course, visitors need handicap certificate.
☎ 0799 22786

HORSE RIDING

Brook Farm Equestrian Centre
Radwinter
Instruction in riding and jumping.
☎ 079 987 262

Special Interests

GARDENS

Bridge End Gardens
Victorian garden and maze, Dutch garden, rose garden, pavilions.

GUIDED TOURS

Regular and group tours available.
Contact the Tourist Information Centre.
☎ 0799 24282

HERITAGE

Priors Hall Barn
4 miles south of Saffron Walden at Widdington
One of the finest surviving English mediaeval aisled barns in south-east England, typical of north-west Essex.
☎ 0799 41047

Saffron Walden Maze
The Common
Rare, ancient earth maze.

HISTORIC BUILDINGS

The Eight Bells
Tudor building, part of which used to be the old Wool Hall, now a public house.

The Sun Inn
Reputed to be Oliver Cromwell's headquarters, although this has never been proven, now a public house.

The Sun Inn

HISTORIC HOUSES

Audley End House
Jacobean house, remodelled in the 18th and 19th centuries, with decorated interiors and collections of pictures and furniture, magnificent Great Hall. Grounds were landscaped by Capability Brown.
☎ 0799 22342/22399

MUSEUMS

Audley End House
19th century vehicles and farm tools from Saffron Walden Museum displayed in stable block.
☎ 0799 22342

Saffron Walden Museum
Museum Street
Ethnography, archeology, local history and many other exhibits. Special exhibitions.
☎ 0799 22494

RAILWAYS

Audley End Miniature Railway
Three steam and two diesel engines run 1 mile through attractive woodland over the River Cam.
☎ 0799 22354

WILDLIFE PARKS

Mole Hall Wildlife Park
4 miles south of Saffron Walden at Widdington
Birds and animals, butterfly pavilion, gardens and picnic area.
☎ 0799 40400

Water Sports

SWIMMING

Lord Butler Leisure Centre
☎ 0799 26600

St Ives is a very attractive riverside market town formerly called Slepe. It changed its name after a priory dedicated to St Ivo was built in the town in 1050. A 15th century bridge spans the river, it has a chapel in its centre and is one of only four such mediaeval bridge chapels still surviving. A statue of Cromwell in the market square is a reminder of his connection with the area, he had a farm nearby. The town is very enjoyable to wander around, there are several specialist shops and many intriguing streets to explore as well as the ducks and swans on the river to feed while the launches and narrowboats glide by.

Market day Monday
Early closing Wednesday
Population 13,489

Bridge Chapel and quay

Adventure Sports

CLIMBING

St Ivo Recreation Centre
Westwood Road
☎ 0480 64601

SHOOTING

St Ivo Recreation Centre
☎ 0480 64601

Indoor Sports

LEISURE CENTRES

St Ivo Recreation Centre
Range of indoor and outdoor sports, weight training and Civic Hall for concerts and dances.

SQUASH

St Ivo Recreation Centre
☎ 0480 64601

Outdoor Leisure

FISHING

Coarse Fishing
The River Ouse and reclaimed gravel
pits in Ouse Valley provide good fishing.
For information and permits contact the
National Rivers Authority
☎ 0733 371811

Central Region
Bromholme Lane, Brampton,
Huntingdon
☎ 0480 414581

GOLF

St Ives Golf Club ⚑
Westwood Road
☎ 0480 68392

Special Interests

HISTORIC BUILDINGS

Bridge Chapel
15th century bridge over the River Ouse
with chapel built into it in midstream.
One of only four such buildings in
England. Information from the Norris
Museum. List of keyholders on door.

MUSEUMS

Norris Library and Museum
Local exhibits. Industries, agricultural
and domestic.

Water Sports

BOAT HIRE

List of hirers available from the Tourist
Information Centre.
☎ 0480 425831

Westover Boat Company Ltd
PO Box 43, Hemingford Grey
Week long barge cruises on River Ouse.
Full board and excursions.
☎ 0860 516343

DINGHY SAILING

Meadow Lane Pits
All facilities are available.

SWIMMING

St Ivo Recreation Centre
☎ 0480 64601

WINDSURFING

Meadow Lane Pits
All facilities are available.

St Neots

St Neots, a pleasant market town owing much to the Great North Road, is sited on
the Great Ouse and has historical links back to the 10th century. The market square
backs on to the river on one side and is flanked on another by the church with its
arresting 15th century perpendicular tower and elaborate interior roof carvings of
angels, birds and animals. The expansive riverside gardens provide a very popular and
attractive recreational area. The town also has a wide selection of sporting and leisure
facilities.

Market day Thursday

Adventure Sports

SHOOTING

Waresley and District GC Ground
St Neots Leisure Centre, Eynesbury
☎ 0480 586953

Indoor Sports

LEISURE CENTRES

St Neots Sports Centre
Barford Road, Eynesbury
☎ 0480 74748

SQUASH

Abbotsley Golf and Squash Club
Eynesbury, Hardwicke
☎ 0480 215153

MUSEUMS

Longsands Museum
Longsands Road
Local history, domestic bygones,
farming, trade, geology and archaeology.
☎ 0480 72740

Outdoor Leisure

FISHING

Coarse Fishing
Fishing at the gravel pits at Little Paxton
or in the River Ouse; for further details
and permits contact the National Rivers
Authority.
☎ 0733 371811

GOLF

Abbotsley Golf and Squash Club 🏌
Eynesbury Golf Club, Hardwicke
☎ 0480 215153

St Neots Golf Club 🏌
Crosshall Road
Undulating parkland course with lake
and water hazards.
☎ 0480 72363

WALKING AND RAMBLING

River Walk
Waymarked riverside walk along the
River Ouse from Little Paxton to Offord
Mill. Leaflet from Huntingdon District
Council.
☎ 0480 456161

Special Interests

FESTIVALS AND FAIRS

August
St Neots Carnvial

November
St Neots Arts Festival

Water Sports

SWIMMING

St Neots Sports Centre
Pool with aquaslides.
☎ 0480 74748

WATER-SKIING

Boughton Lodge Water Sports Club
Little Paxton
Contact the secretary, Clive Gillam, for
details.
☎ 0480 411704

Riverside Gardens

SUFFOLK — Saxmundham — SUFFOLK

Saxmundham lies on the main Ipswich to Lowestoft road a few miles inland from the
attractive Suffolk coast. It offers opportunities for walking and fishing, there is a
vineyard and herb garden to visit, a park with acres of woodland and two lakes to
explore and for those who enjoy hunting for antiques or bargains there is an auction
every other week.

Market day Wednesday
Early closing Thursday
Population 2410

Outdoor Leisure

CAMPING AND CARAVANNING

Lakeside Caravan Park
West of Saxmundham on the B1119
47 acres of woodland and grassland with
a 4-acre and 2-acre lake, trout and coarse
fishing. Caravan park and facilities.
☎ 0728 603344

CYCLING

Byways Bicycle Centre
☎ 0728 77764

FISHING

Coarse Fishing
Fishing on the River Blythe at Henham
Dairy Ponds; coarse and trout fishing on
the River Wang at Peasenhall and at
Lakeside Caravan Park. For information
and permits contact the National Rivers
Authority
☎ 0473 727712

River Alde
Contact the Saxmundham Angling
Centre.
☎ 0728 603443

Special Interests

ANTIQUES

Auctions every other Wednesday.
Contact Flick and Son for details.
☎ 0728 603232

FOOD AND DRINK

Bruisyard Vineyard
Church Road, Bruisyard
Open to the public. Wines, vines and
herbs for sale.
☎ 072875 281

GARDENS

Bruisyard Herb Gardens
Church Road, Bruisyard
Herb and water garden, shop selling
herbs.
☎ 072875 281

NATURAL HISTORY

Suffolk Wildlife Trust
Park Cottage
Information on wildlife throughout
Suffolk.
☎ 0728 603765

NORFOLK / **Saxthorpe** / NORFOLK

Saxthorpe is a Norfolk village on the Aylsham to Thursford road. It has an attractive
15th century moated manor house, the gardens of which have an outstanding rose
collection, a Saxon church and Victorian follies to see before trying one of the
waymarked walks.

Outdoor Leisure

WALKING AND RAMBLING

Mannington Walks
20 miles of waymarked walks and trails
through woodlands, meadows and
farmland. Information Centre at
Mannington Hall Gardens.

Special Interests

GARDENS

Mannington Hall Gardens
Exceptional rose collection, lake, moat
and woodland. Victorian follies and
Saxon church.
☎ 026 387 4175

HISTORIC HOUSES

Mannington Hall
15th century moated manor house.
Restricted entry by appointment only.
☎ 026 387 4175

Sheringham, on the North Norfolk coast, is a holiday resort that grew up around the old fishing village of Lower Sheringham at the end of the last century. There are attractive Victorian and Edwardian houses as well as distinctive houses faced with pebbles, used for building in Norfolk since Saxon times. There are extensive sandy beaches and a steam railway as well as a theatre and a splash pool to enjoy.

Upper Sheringham, on the hill, was once dependent on agriculture and is now a residential area where Sheringham Hall with its rhododendron gardens can be found.

i Station Approach
☎ 0263 824329

Market day Saturday
Early closing Wednesday
Population 7138

The Temple in Sheringham Park

Outdoor Leisure

FISHING

Sea Fishing
Fishing at Salthouse. Contact the Tourist Information Centre for details.
☎ 0263 824329

GOLF

Sheringham Golf Club ♿
Clifftop course, visitors must have handicaps.
☎ 0263 823488

WALKING AND RAMBLING

Kelling Heath Nature Trail
$2^1/2$ mile woodland trail with conservation lake, good views, historic sites. It runs adjacent to the North Norfolk Railway.

Pretty Corner Walks
Pretty Corner main car park
Walks around 250 acres of woodland.
Maps available at the site.

Special Interests

FARM PARKS

Norfolk Shire Horse Centre
2 miles east of Sheringham on the A149
Shire and Suffolk horses working and on display.
☎ 0263 75339

FOOD AND DRINK

Lobsters
Lobsters are the fishing speciality at Sheringham and can be purchased locally and along the Norfolk coast.

GARDENS

Sheringham Park
Woodlands and rhododendron gardens. Spectacular coastline views.
☎ 0263 733471

MUSEUMS

The Muckleborough Collection
Weybourne Military Camp
Britain's largest privately-owned collection of military vehicles. Second World War artefacts and memorabilia.
☎ 0263 70425

RAILWAYS

North Norfolk Railway
Sheringham Station
Full size steam railway. 5-mile run to Holt via Weybourne.
☎ 0263 822045

Water Sports

SWIMMING

The Splash
Weybourne Road
25-metre pool, wave machine, fountains, slides and landing pool, 50-metre flume.
☎ 0263 825675

Southend-on-Sea

Southend-on-Sea, now one of the biggest seaside resorts in Britain, was once a hamlet called the South End of Prittlewell. It had, by the 1930s incorporated Leigh-on-Sea, Westcliff, Thorpe Bay and Prittlewell. Once the favoured resort of a Prince Regent it has many elegant period streets including the Royal Terrace overlooking the sea. The town boasts the longest pleasure pier in the world, 1¹/₃ miles long, and its seven miles of seafront offer traditional seaside entertainment, fairs, a fantasy park, cliff gardens and seafood stalls. A new shopping development adjoining the seafront adds to the already extensive range of specialist shops and markets.

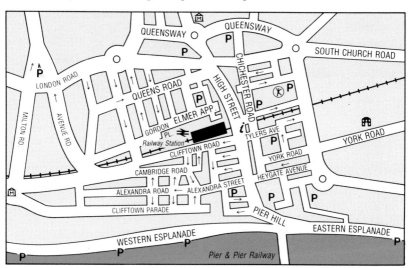

i Civic Centre
Victoria Avenue
☎ 0702 355122

Market days Tuesday, Thursday, Sunday
Early closing Wednesday
Population 156,969

Adventure Sports

CLIMBING

Clements Hall Leisure Centre
Clements Hall Way, Hawkwell
☎ 0702 207777

SHOOTING

Clements Hall Leisure Centre
☎ 0702 207777

Southend Flying Club
Southend Airport
☎ 0702 545198

Aerial Sports

FLYING

Park Sports Centre
Rawreth Lane, Rayleigh
☎ 0268 781233

Indoor Sports

LEISURE CENTRES

Clements Hall Leisure Centre
Clements Hall Way, Hawkwell
☎ 0702 207777

171

Park Sports Centre
Rawreth Lane, Rayleigh
☎ 0268 781233

Westcliff Leisure Centre
Westcliff-on-Sea Esplanade
☎ 0702 353822

ROLLER SKATING

Roller City
Aviation Way
Skating, hire, professional shop, bar and food.
☎ 0702 546344/541111

SQUASH

Clements Hall Leisure Centre
☎ 0702 207777

Park Sports Centre
☎ 0268 781233

TENPIN BOWLING

Pavilion Lanes
The Pier
Bowling, fast food, bar, amusements.
☎ 0702 463081

Outdoor Leisure

CAMPING AND CARAVANNING

Hayes Farm Caravan park
Hayes Chase, Burnham Road, Battlesbridge
75 caravan pitches, no tent pitches. Club with children's room, extensive facilities.
☎ 0245 320309

Lansdowne Country Club
Poynters Lane, Shoeburyness
Country club, bars, restaurant, 3 caravan pitches and 1 caravan for hire, facilities available. No dogs allowed.

Riverside Village Holiday Park
Creeksea Ferry, Wallasea Island
Adjacent to nature, reserve and Essex Yacht Marina. 60 caravan pitches, extensive facilities, restaurant, playspace. Access for launching and windsurfing.
☎ 0702 258297/258484/258441

FISHING

Coarse Fishing
Fishing is good at Eastwood Pit, Shoebury Park Lake and Essex Carp Fishery in Rayleigh. For information and permits contact the National Rivers Authority
☎ 0473 727712

Sea Fishing
Fishing from the pier and foreshore, for details of boat trips contact the Tourist Information Centre.

FOOTBALL

Southend United
Roots Hall Ground, Victoria Avenue
☎ 0702 340707

GOLF

Ballards Gore Golf Club ⛳18
Gore Road, Canewdon
☎ 0370 68917

Belfairs Golf Club ⛳18
Belfairs Park, Eastwood Road
☎ 0702 525345

Rochford Hundred Golf Club ⛳18
Hall Road, Rochford
☎ 0702 544302

Thorpe Hall Golf Club ⛳18
Thorpe Hall Avenue, Thorpe Bay
Flat parkland course.
☎ 0702 582205

ORIENTEERING

Havering and South Essex Orienteering Club
Contact John Flay, 31 Windsor Way, Rayleigh
☎ 0268 772151

Special Interests

ANTIQUES

Battlesbridge Antiques Centre
Off the A130 to Chelmsford.
Shops, antiques warehouse and motorcycle museum housed in 17th and 18th century buildings; warehouse and workshops; pubs, teas.

ART GALLERIES

Beecroft Art Gallery
Station Road, Westcliff-on-Sea
Permanent topographical collection, temporary exhibitions.
☎ 0702 347318

Delta Fine Arts Gallery
179 West Road, Westcliff-on-Sea
Original paintings of local scenes.
☎ 0702 333749

Leigh Heritage Centre
High Street, Old Leigh
Display illustrating local and natural history of Old Leigh. Exhibitions.
☎ 0702 470834

COUNTRY PARKS

Belfairs Park
Leigh-on-Sea
318 acres of woodland; golf course, horse trail, riding school, nature reserve.
☎ 0702 523817

Grove Woods
Eastwood
Forty acres of old orchards and smallholdings.
☎ 0702 546366

Hadleigh Castle Country Park
Hadleigh
450 acres of woodland, marshes and downland. Wildlife area and Ranger service.
☎ 081 973 3000

Hockley Woods
250 acres of coppice woodlands, walks and a horse trail.
☎ 0702 546366

FESTIVALS AND FAIRS

April - May
Festival of Flowers and Craft at Priory Park.

May
Southend Airshow, the biggest free airshow of its kind in Western Europe with displays along the seafront.

June - July
Southend-on-Sea Historic Transport Rally
Punch and Judy Weekend
Raft Race
Southend Festival, street theatre, music and dance.

August
Carnival, illuminations and fireworks, two processions.
Thames Barge Race

September
Whitebait Festival
☎ 0702 78380

Old Leigh Regatta
Two days of fun and water sports.

For more details of all the events contact the Tourist Information Centre.

FOOD AND DRINK

Seafood
Cockles and whelks, shellfish, on sale in Old Leigh.

Annual Whitebait Festival
Organised by the Chamber of Commerce.

FUN PARKS

Peter Pan's Playground
Western Esplanade, next to Pier
Fun rides, crooked house and free playground with swings. Children's parties arranged.
☎ 0702 468023

GARDENS

Churchill Gardens
Victoria Avenue
Pleasant tree-lined walk, stream, ponds, lawns.

Cliff Gardens
Sea front between Southend and Westcliff
Landscaped walks and flower beds, part of which is illuminated during the summer. Views over estuary.

Library Gardens
Leigh-on-Sea
Flowers and shrubs, scented herb garden with signs in braille.

Old World Garden
Priory Park
Ornamental sunken garden with goldfish pond, flowers, shrubs and climbing plants.

Warrior Square Garden
Behind the main shopping area
Lawns and flower beds.

HERITAGE

Hadleigh Castle
Hadleigh
50-foot high single bailey and 13th and 14th century remains.
☎ 081 973 3000

HISTORIC BUILDINGS

Rayleigh Windmill
6 miles north-west of Southend
Non-operating mill with local history museum.
☎ 0268 775867

HISTORIC HOUSES

The Old House
South Street, Rochford
Timber-framed hall house dating from 1270, refurbished in 1983.
☎ 0702 546366 extn 3602

MUSEUMS

Battlesbridge Motor Cycle Museum
☎ 0268 769392/734005

Central Museum
Victoria Avenue
Natural and social history of south-west Essex.
☎ 0702 330214

Leigh Heritage Centre
☎ 0702 470834

Priory Park

Prittlewell Priory Museum
Priory Park, Prittlewell
12th century Cluniac priory with radio and communications equipment, local and natural history and bees.

NATURAL HISTORY

Leigh Mudflats
NCC and Essex Naturalists Trust
Mudflats and salt marsh with nature trail.
☎ 0603 620558
☎ 0206 28678

ORNAMENTAL PARKS

Blenheim Park
Leigh-on-Sea
Children's play area, playing fields and gardens.

Chalkwell Park
London Road, Chalkwell
Park and playing fields, rose gardens, tennis courts, Essex County Cricket Ground, children's playground.
☎ 0702 76603

Priory Park
Victoria Avenue
Grounds of a 14th century priory. Gardens, duck and fish ponds. Playing fields, bowls, tennis.

PIERS AND PROMENADES

Southend Pier
World's longest pleasure pier. Electric trains, amusements and fishing. Visit the Lifeboat. Promenades with gardens.
☎ 0702 618747

THEATRES

Cliffs Pavilion
Theatre, bars and exhibition centre on the cliffs at Westcliff.
☎ 0702 351135

Palace Theatre
London Road, Westcliff-on-Sea
☎ 0702 342564

THEME PARKS

Never Never Land
Western Esplanade
Fantasy park for children, illuminated after dark. Open Easter to October.
☎ 0702 46018

Water Sports

SWIMMING

Belfairs Swimming Pool
Fairview Gardens, Leigh-on-Sea
25-metre pool and learner pool.
☎ 0702 712155

Clements Hall Leisure Centre
☎ 0702 207777

Shoeburyness Swimming Pool
Delaware Road, Shoeburyness
20-metre pool and learner pool.
☎ 0370 83558

Westcliff Leisure Centre
Westcliff-on-Sea Esplanade
Swimming pool and country club.
☎ 0702 353822

WATER-SKIING

Southend Water Sports Club
Shoebury Common, Thorpe Bay
☎ 0702 219351

WINDSURFING

Chalkwell Windsurfing Club
Chalkwell Beach
Tuition arranged.
☎ 0702 75788/0702 554864 (racing)

Channels SOS
☎ 0245 441000

Thorpe Bay
2 miles east of Southend-on-Sea car park
Tuition, board and suit hire.

YACHTING

Alexandra Yacht Club
Clifton Terrace
☎ 0702 66652/340363

Thorpe Bay Yacht Club
☎ 0702 587563

Up River Yacht Club
Pooles Lane, Hullbridge
☎ 0702 232129

Wakering Yacht Club
Millhead, Great Wakering
☎ 0702 217088

Southwold is an elegant small town set up on the cliffs of the Suffolk coast overlooking the sea. The town was devastated by fire in the 1600s and was rebuilt around wide greens. The town retains a distinctive charm, with its Victorian terraces looking down on Edwardian style beach huts, a reminder of the town's popularity as a Victorian bathing place. Services at St Edmund's Church begin only when 'Southwold Jack', a 15th century figure of a man-at-arms, strikes his bell. Southwold provides good sailing and is famous for its inland lighthouse. There are pleasant walks along the abandoned railway line, cliffs, shore and dyke to Walberswick and Dunwich, both ports to the south, and to Dunwich Common.

i Town Hall
☎ 0502 722366

Market days Monday, Thursday
Early closing Wednesday
Population 3877

Adventure Sports

SHOOTING

High Lodge SS Ground
Henham Park, Blytheburgh
☎ 0502 70709

Outdoor Leisure

FISHING

Sea Fishing
Contact the Tourist Information Centre.

GOLF

Southwold Golf Club
The Common
☎ 0502 723248

Special Interests

ARTS AND CRAFTS

The Parish Lantern
Walberswick Village Green
☎ 0502 724425

FOOD AND DRINK

Adnams and Co
East Green
Local brewery with range of real ales.
☎ 0502 722424

MUSEUMS

Dunwich Museum
4 miles south-west of Southwold
History of Dunwich and its
disappearance into the sea.

Southwold Lifeboat Museum
RNLI history with models, photographs and relics.
☎ 0502 722422

Southwold Museum
Local and natural history. Exhibits connected with Southwold Railway.

Southwold Sailors Reading Room
Maritime books.

NATURAL HISTORY

Dunwich Heath
214 acres of heathland, 1 mile of sandy beach. National Trust.
☎ 0203 733471

Minsmere (RSPB)
1500 acres of heath, woodlands, marsh and lagoon. Birdwatching facilities.
☎ 0603 615920

Water Sports

YACHTING

Southwold Sailing Club
Buss Creek, Bridge Road, Reydon

175

Stansted Mountfitchet

Stansted Mountfitchet lies close to Stansted Airport and has recently lost a long battle to prevent the third London Airport from being situated in a tract of countryside that has innumerable buildings of architectural interest apart from churches. The town has many old houses of charm including Stansted Hall, which stands in a great park with a lake, and a mediaeval church and historic windmill.

Special Interests

HERITAGE

Mountfitchet Castle
Reconstruction of a Norman castle and village; experience life as it was in 1066.
☎ 0279 813237

HISTORIC BUILDINGS

Stansted Mountfitchet Windmill
Built in 1787, the best-preserved red-brick tower mill in Essex; 65-feet high with original machinery. Restored in 1966.
☎ 0279 813160

MUSEUMS

Aklowa African Traditional Heritage Village
Takeley
Reconstructed African village with African activities. By appointment only.
☎ 0279 871062

NATURAL HISTORY

Hatfield Forest
Off the A120
1000 acres of woodland and pasture, nature reserve, nature trail. National Trust.

WILDLIFE PARK

Mole Hall Wildlife Park
4 miles north-east at Widdington

Stowmarket

Stowmarket was once the county town of Suffolk and an important centre for the wool industry; it is now a busy market town and agricultural centre. It offers a wide range of leisure activities both indoor at its leisure centre and outdoor playing golf or walking along the River Gipping.

i Wilkes Way
☎ 0449 676800
Market days Thursday, Saturday
Early closing Tuesday
Population 11,050

Adventure Sports

SHOOTING

ICI Gun Club
Off the A45 at Drinkstone near Woolpit
☎ 0449 612047

Indoor Sports

LEISURE CENTRES

Mid Suffolk Leisure Centre
Gainsborough Road
Extensive facilities include three pools, a bowls hall, fitness suite, solariums, bar, cafeteria and newly opened health suite.
☎ 0449 674980

Multi-Activity Holidays

MULTI-ACTIVITY CENTRES

'Kids Klub
Finborough Hall, Great Finborough
Professionally supervised activity
holidays for children aged 6–15.
☎ 0449 675907

Outdoor Leisure

GOLF

Stowmarket Golf Club ⚑₈
Lower Road, Onehouse
☎ 0449 3392

WALKING AND RAMBLING

Gipping Valley River Path
17-mile towpath along the Gipping
Valley.

Special Interests

ARTS AND CRAFTS

Ascot House Crafts
Earl Stanham
Pictures, pine furniture, pottery,
metalwork, jewellery and other crafts.

FOOD AND DRINK

Aspall Cider
Cider House, Aspall
Local cider. 1728 press room on view.
☎ 0728 860510

GARDENS

**Mickfield Fish and Water Garden
Centre**
Mickfield
Landscaped water gardens with fish and
aquatic plants.
☎ 0449 711336

HISTORIC HOUSES

Haughley Park
3 miles west of Stowmarket on the A45
Jacobean manor house with beautiful
gardens.
☎ 0359 40205

MUSEUMS

Cotton Mechanical Music Museum
5 miles north of Southwold
Organs, pianos, music boxes and other
musical devices. Concerts held.
☎ 0449 781354

Museum of East Anglian Life
Extensive working collection of
agricultural, domestic and craft exhibits
demonstrating East Anglia's heritage.
Special events.
☎ 0449 612229

Water Sports

SWIMMING

Mid Suffolk Leisure Centre
☎ 0449 674980

Sudbury, a thriving market town and rural centre, was a settlement in Saxon times. It has an attractive market place, 15th century church and several old and interesting buildings, many dating from the Georgian period when it was a prosperous wool trading centre. The town, a weaving centre since the 13th century, still weaves fine silk including that used recently in the Princess of Wales' wedding dress. Sudbury is also famous for being the birthplace of the painter Thomas Gainsborough, his father's Tudor house is now an exhibition gallery and museum.

i The Library
Market Place
☎ 0787 72092

Market days Thursday, Saturday
Early closing Wednesday
Population 17,911

Aerial Sports

PARAGLIDING

Suffolk Eagles PC
34 First Avenue
☎ 0787 77186

Indoor Sports

LEISURE CENTRES

Great Cornard Sports Centre
Head Lane, Great Cornard
☎ 0787 73132

Sudbury Sports Centre
Tudor Road
☎ 0787 73132

Outdoor Leisure

FISHING

Coarse Fishing
For information and permits for fishing
on the River Stour contact the National
Rivers Authority
☎ 0733 371811
☎ 0473 727712

GOLF

Newton Green Golf Club ⌘
Newton Green

WALKING AND RAMBLING

Constable Trail
9-mile walk through landscape
associated with the artist. Leaflet from
Peddar Publications.
☎ 0787 227823

River Stour at Sudbury

Painters Way
24-mile walk to Manningtree along the
River Stour, through the countryside
that inspired Gainsborough and
Constable. Leaflet from Peddar
Publications.
☎ 0787 227823

Sudbury Walk
Walk along dismantled railway line.
Leaflet from Suffolk County Council.

Special Interests

ART GALLERIES

Gainsborough's House
Georgian town house and gardens,
birthplace of Thomas Gainsborough.
Gainsborough's paintings and
contemporary furniture. Exhibition
programme.
☎ 0787 72958

Laurimore Gallery
The Mews, Boxford
☎ 0787 210138

FOOD AND DRINK

Mauldons Brewery
7 Addison Road
Local ales.
☎ 0787 311055

HISTORIC BUILDINGS

St Peter's Church
15th century church with painted
screen panels and the 'Sudbury Pall', an
exquisite piece of embroidery on velvet.

HISTORIC HOUSES

Gainsborough's House
☎ 0787 72958

MUSEUMS

Gainsborough's House
☎ 0787 72958

THEATRES

The Quay Theatre
☎ 0787 74745

Water Sports

SWIMMING

Kingfisher Leisure Pool
Station Road
25-metre pool, fitness area, sauna.
☎ 0787 75656

Swaffham has an impressive market place which comes alive on Saturdays with a busy open-air market and auction. The unusual 18th century 'market cross' was built, in fact, as a rotunda by Horace Walpole. There are several fine Georgian buildings around the marketplace and the 16th century church has a magnificent hammerbeam roof with carved angels, it is regarded as one of the finest mediaeval churches in the eastern counties. Swaffham is well situated as a touring centre for north-west Norfolk and has the fascinating village of Castle Acre with its famous priory nearby.

Market day Saturday
Early closing Thursday
Population 4798

Adventure Sports

SHOOTING

Beeston Gun Club
Watery Lane, Beestonett, near Litcham
☎ 0328 700462

Marham Guns Ground
Hoggs Drove, Marham
☎ 0760 337449

Indoor Sports

LEISURE CENTRES

Swaffham Leisure Centre
Brandon Road
☎ 0760 23974

SQUASH

Swaffham Leisure Centre
☎ 0760 23974

Outdoor Leisure

GOLF

Swaffham Golf Club ⓑ
Cley Road
☎ 0760 21611

Special Interests

FOOD AND DRINK

The Norfolk Pickling Centre
Hill Farm, Castle Acre Road, Great Dunham
Pickles, chutney, jam and other preserves.

HERITAGE

Castle Acre Priory
Cluniac priory founded by William de Warenne in 1090, remains clearly show the original dimensions, west front has a fine tier of Norman arcading, displays of mediaeval masonry can be seen in some of the rooms.

Castle Acre Village
North of Swaffham on the A1065
A village on the old Roman Peddars Way, it is enclosed by the earthworks of the castle of William the Conqueror's son-in-law, William de Warenne. Imposing 13th century bailey gate and fine priory.

Cockley Cley Iceni Village
3 miles south-west of Swaffham
Saxon church from circa 630; reconstruction of Iceni encampment.
☎ 0760 721339

HISTORIC HOUSES

Oxburgh Hall
7 miles south-west of Swaffham
15th century moated and fortified red-brick manor house. Magnificent 80-foot gatehouse. Pugin chapel and French parterre garden. Woodland walks.
☎ 036612 258

MUSEUMS

Cockley Cley
Folk and East Anglian Museum in Elizabethan cottage. Engine and carriage museums.
☎ 0760 721339

Dunham Museum
Working tools and machinery; dairy, leathersmith, shoemakers; stationary engines.
☎ 0760 23073

Swaffham Musuem
Off London Street
Local history exhibits.
☎ 0760 721230

179

Thaxted

Thaxted is a small town with a magnificent church of cathedral proportions, its 181-foot spire is a local landmark. A settlement has existed here since Saxon times. The town prospered during the 14th and 15th centuries when it had a thriving cutlery industry and it was during this period that the Guildhall and many of the half-timbered houses that characterise the streets leading to Cutlers Green were built.

Market day Friday
Early closing Wednesday
Population 2600

Special Interests

FESTIVALS AND FAIRS

Thaxted Church

June
Morris Weekend when two to three hundred Morris Men gather. The Morris Ring was formed in Thaxted.

HISTORIC BUILDINGS

John Webb's Windmill
Preserved tower mill built in 1804 by John Webb. Fine views from the top floor.

Thaxted Guildhall
Mediaeval timbered building. For details contact Mr Marc Arman.
☎ 0371 830366

MUSEUMS

John Webb's Windmill
Rural bygones and a restored 1835 fire engine. Open from May to September.

Thaxted Guildhall
Local history, exhibitions and demonstrations.
☎ 0371 830366

Thetford

Thetford, a busy market town since before the Norman Conquest, has many traces of its rich and fascinating past. It is one of the few places in Britain to have Saxon remains and there are Iron Age earthworks at Castle Hill overlooking the Icknield Way, the oldest trade route in England. The town was the See of East Anglian bishops until 1091 and is surrounded by the ruins and remains of religious foundations. The fine ancient buildings of the town centre are now a conservation area, interesting to explore before strolling down to the attractive riverside walks along the Rivers Thet and Ouse. Thetford is a good centre from which to explore the beautiful surrounding countryside including walks in the ancient Thetford Forest.

i Ancient House Museum
White Hart Street
☎ 0842 752599

Market day Tuesday, Saturday
Early closing Wednesday
Population 19,513

Adventure Sports

SHOOTING

Ashill Clay Pigeon Club
Cutbush Farm, Ashill
☎ 0760 721771

180

Aerial Sports

GLIDING

Norfolk Gliding Club
Tibenham Airfield, Long Stratton
☎ 037 977 207
☎ 0359 31548

Indoor Sports

LEISURE CENTRES

Breckland Sports Centre
Croxton Road
☎ 0842 753110

SQUASH

Breckland Sports Centre
☎ 0842 753110

Outdoor Leisure

FISHING

Coarse Fishing
Fishing on the River Ouse. For
information and permits contact the
National Rivers Authority
☎ 0733 371811
☎ 0473 727712

GOLF

Thetford Golf Club ⚐₁₈
Brandon Road
☎ 0842 752162

HORSE RIDING

Hockwold Lodge Riding School
Davey Lodge, Cowles Drove, Hockwold
Instruction in riding, jumping and side
saddle.
☎ 0842 828376

Stanbrook Riding Centre
Paddock Farm, Lower Road, Holme Hale
Instruction in riding and jumping. Small
groups welcome. Breaking and schooling
of ponies.
☎ 0760 22125

WALKING AND RAMBLING

King's Forest Trail
2¹/₂-mile waymarked walk through
Thetford Forest.

Santon Downham Forest Trail
2-mile circular walk starting from the
forest centre.

Special Interests

ARTS AND CRAFTS

The Art Gallery
The Guildhall
Exhibitions of local artists.
☎ 0842 766599

HERITAGE

Thetford Castle
Norman castle mound surrounded by
Iron Age ramparts.

Thetford Priory
Founded by Norman warrior Roger
Bigod. English Heritage.

Thetford Warren Lodge
Ruins of a 14th century two-storey
hunting lodge built for the Prior of
Thetford's gamekeeper.

MUSEUMS

Ancient House Museum
White Hart Street
15th century house with local and
natural history displays.
☎ 0842 752599

NATURAL HISTORY

Thetford Forest
Ancient forest with nature and bird
trails. Contact Santon Downham Forest
Office or the Forestry Commission.
☎ 0842 810271

WILDLIFE PARKS

Kilverston Wildlife Park
1 mile east of Thetford on the A11
The only Latin American wildlife park
in the world with exotic and endangered
wildlife from every habitat. 800 birds
and mammals in 50 acres of garden and
parkland including Falabella miniature
horses from Argentina.
☎ 0842 755369

Water Sports

SWIMMING

Breckland Sports Centre
Swimming and learner pools.
☎ 0842 753110

Tilbury

Tilbury, an old established town, is a major commercial port with a busy docks area. Tilbury Fort is a popular tourist attraction and there are excellent facilities for shopping, sports, leisure and entertainment.

Population 11,500

Indoor Sports

LEISURE CENTRES

Tilbury Leisure Centre
Civic Square, Brennan Road
☎ 0375 856886

SQUASH

Tilbury Leisure Centre
☎ 0375 856886

Special Interests

HISTORIC BUILDINGS

Tilbury Fort
One of Henry VIII's coastal forts, extended in the 17th century.
☎ 0375 858489

MUSEUMS

Coalhouse Fort
Thameside defence fort with aviation and military museum.
☎ 0375 370000

Thurrock Riverside Museum
Tilbury Leisure Centre
Displays on shipping, riverside communities and Tilbury docks.
☎ 0375 856886

Southend Airshow, Southend-on-Sea

Walsingham incorporates both Great and Little Walsingham. The site of the Shrine of Our Lady of Walsingham was built in 1061 by Lady Richeld in response to a command by the Virgin Mary received in a vision. Henry VIII made a pilgrimage to the shrine but later had it destroyed after his quarrel with the papacy. The Slipper Chapel nearby at Houghton is still a place of pilgrimage as is the site of the ancient Shrine.

i Shirehall Museum
Common Place
☎ 0328 820510

Special Interests

ARTS AND CRAFTS

The Textile Centre
Binham Road
Craft shop, hand-printed textiles.
☎ 0328 820009

HERITAGE

Shrine of Our Lady of Walsingham
Holt Road, Walsingham
Pilgrimage site.
☎ 0328 820259

Slipper Chapel
Houghton St Giles
14th century chapel connected with the ancient Shrine of Our Lady of Walsingham, now destroyed. Now the Roman Catholic National Shrine of Our Lady.

Walsingham Abbey Grounds
Remains of an Augustinian priory including the gatehouse, crypt, wells, refectory and East Window arch, site of the Shrine of Our Lady at Walsingham.
☎ 0328 820259

MUSEUMS

Shirehall Museum
Georgian courtroom with original fittings. Local history and pilgrimage display.
☎ 0328 820510

RAILWAYS

Wells and Walsingham Light Railway
Longest 10-inch gauge railway in Britain. 8-mile run.

Waltham Abbey, on the edge of Epping Forest, is the site of an old small abbey and a religious college built by King Harold who is believed to be buried here. Henry II later built a grand abbey to atone for the murder of Thomas à Becket and although much was destroyed during the Reformation the nave, monuments and stained glass remaining are magnificent.

Market days Tuesday, Saturday
Early closing Thursday
Population 16,566

Indoor Sports

LEISURE CENTRES

Waltham Abbey Sports Centre
Paternoster Hill, Broomstick Hall Road
☎ 0992 716194

SQUASH

Waltham Abbey Sports Centre
☎ 0992 716194

Outdoor Leisure

FISHING

Coarse Fishing
For information and permits contact
the National Rivers Authority
☎ 0733 371811
☎ 0473 727712

Chertsey Angling Club
☎ 0932 564872

HORSE RIDING

High Beech Riding School
1 mile from jctn 6 on the M25 between
Waltham Abbey and Loughton
Non-resident holidays in Epping Forest.
BHS approved.
☎ 081 508 8866

ORIENTEERING

Lee Valley Park
Two courses, map packs from the
Countryside Centre, Abbey Farmhouse,
Crooked Mile, Waltham Abbey.

Special Interests

FARM PARKS

Hayes Hill Farm
Working farm. Regular craft
demonstrations.
☎ 0992 892291

Holyfield Hall Farm
Working dairy and arable farm
adjoining Hayes Hill. Tours by
appointment.
☎ 0992 893113

HISTORIC BUILDINGS

Waltham Abbey Church
Highbridge Street
Norman church reputed to be the site
of King Harold's tomb. History
exhibition. Fine Norman nave and
stained glass.
☎ 0992 787897

MUSEUMS

Epping Forest District Museum
Sun Street
Timber-framed building with local and
social history displays and exhibitions.
Herb garden.
☎ 0992 716882

Water Sports

SWIMMING

Waltham Abbey Pool
Roundhills
25-metre pool, learner pool.
☎ 0992 716733

Walton-on-the-Naze is a pleasant seaside resort with a sandy beach, cliffs, a pier and
traditional seaside amusements. It is an attractive old-fashioned town with a small
but lively shopping centre. The backwaters to the rear of Walton are a series of
saltings and little harbours leading into Harwich harbour – worth exploring.

i Princess Esplanade
☎ 0255 675542

Outdoor Leisure

CAMPING AND CARAVANNING

Naze Marine Holiday Park
Near beaches and waterways. 30
caravan pitches, 53 chalets and 3
luxury caravans for hire. Club, lounge,
extensive facilities, no dogs allowed.
Families and couples only.
☎ 0255 676633

Willows Caravan Park
High Tree Lane
5 caravan pitches, 10 caravans for hire,
licensed club, facilities, no dogs.
☎ 0255 675828

FISHING

Sea Fishing
Contact the Tourist Information Centre
for details.
☎ 0255 675542

Special Interests

MUSEUMS

Walton Heritage Centre
Rural and maritime local history in old lifeboat house.
☎ 0255 675257

NATURAL HISTORY

John Weston Reserve
Essex Naturalists' Trust
Clifftop walks, nature trail; fossils, birds, butterflies and moths.
☎ 0206 28678

Naze Nature Trail
Waymarked trail through coastal area rich in birdlife and butterflies. Information board with details of wildlife and events. Leaflet from the Essex Naturalists' Trust.
☎ 0206 28678

Water Sports

YACHTING

Walton and Frinton Yacht Club
Club House, Mill Lane

CAMBRIDGESHIRE

Waterbeach

CAMBRIDGESHIRE

Waterbeach is a small, sleepy Fenland village with the remains of an abbey that has had a fascinating history and opportunities for walking and camping.

Outdoor Leisure

CAMPING AND CARAVANNING

Landbeach Marina Park
Ely Road
650 pitches; facilities.
☎ 0223 860019

Special Interests

HERITAGE

Denny Abbey
Ely Road
Remains of a 12th century church and the 14th century dining hall of a religious house. Run as a hospital by the Knights Templar after being a Benedictine Priory, in 1342 it became a Franciscan nunnery. English Heritage.

NORFOLK

Wells-next-the-Sea

NORFOLK

Wells-next-the-Sea is now inland but with a colourful quayside used by the local shrimp and whelk boats, a local favourite. The town stages arts and entertainment events and there are sandy beaches, nature reserves and pleasant country walks to enjoy.

i Wells Centre
Staithe Street
☎ 0328 710885

Market day Wednesday
Early closing Thursday
Population 2377

Adventure Sports

SHOOTING

Burnham Overy and Norton Wildfowling Association
Peterstone Brickyards, Peterstone
☎ 0328 738908

Outdoor Leisure

BIRDWATCHING

Ilex House Residential Bird Courses
Ilex House, Bases Lane
☎ 0328 710556

Special Interests

GARDENS

Holkham Park Gardens
2 miles west of Wells-next-the-Sea
6-acre walled garden designed by
Samuel Wyatt. Original glasshouses
and unusual species.
☎ 0328 710227

HERITAGE

Binham Priory
5 miles south-east on the B1105
Unique tracery window in west front.

HISTORIC HOUSES

Holkham Hall
2 miles west of Wells-next-the-Sea
18th century Palladian house with
pictures, tapestries, furnishing and
bygones.
☎ 0328 710227

RAILWAYS

Wells and Walsingham Light Railway
Longest 10-inch gauge railway in
Britain. 8-mile run.

Water Sports

WATER-SKIING

Wells and District Ski Club
Lifeboat House
Contact the secretary, Jenny Parker, for
details.
☎ 0362 692059

West Mersea is a pleasant seaside island, close to Colchester, renowned for its
watersports and sailing activities. Yachts are moored at the Hythe where there are
plenty of specialist sailing shops.

Outdoor Leisure

CAMPING AND CARAVANNING

Waldegraves Farm Holiday Park
Quiet family park with boating lakes
and a private beach. 60 caravan and 60
tent pitches, 5 caravans for hire.
Licensed bar and special facilities for
long weekend breaks.
☎ 0206 382898

Special Interests

FESTIVALS AND FAIRS

August
Mersea Regatta

FOOD AND DRINK

Colchester Oyster Fisheries
Home of the famous Colchester
oysters.

MUSEUMS

Mersea Island Museum
High Street
Local and natural history, marine and
wildlife exhibits. Exhibitions.
☎ 0206 383301

NATURAL HISTORY

Colne Estuary
Norfolk Conservancy Council
Foreshore, beach and marshes.
Wildfowl.
☎ 0603 620558

Water Sports

YACHTING

Dabchicks Sailing Club
The Club House, Coat Road

186

Wickham Market

Wickham Market is a straggling village located on the River Deben. Nearby, at Boulge, is the grave of Edward Fitzgerald, the translator of the Rubaiyat of Omar Khayyam, it has a rose bush growing on it that came from Omar Khayyam's grave in Iran.

Special Interests

FARM PARKS

Easton Farm Park
Victorian farm and dairy with rare breed animals. Milking displays, collections of old machinery and bygones.
☎ 0728 746475

MUSEUMS

Easton Farm Park
☎ 0728 746475

Museum of Grocery Shop Bygones
70 High Street
Old grocery shop with 18th century shop fittings and old trade items. Art gallery.
☎ 0728 747207

Wisbech

Wisbech was a port in mediaeval times but as the River Ouse silted up it was diverted into the sea at King's Lynn. The present artificial course of the River Nene from Peterborough halted the decline of Wisbech as a port. The town flourished again when the Fens were drained and it became a market centre for the produce of the most fertile farmland in the country. The port developed important trading links with the Low Countries and the Baltic, links which have fashioned its development. The accompanying prosperity led to the building of the magnificent Georgian buildings that make Wisbech so architecturally distinguished. The Brinks, running beside the river, has been described as one of the most perfect Georgian streets in England.

i District Library
Ely Place
☎ 0945 583263

Market days Thursday, Saturday
Early closing Wednesday
Population 23,191

Peckover House

Outdoor Leisure

FISHING

Coarse Fishing
Fishing on the River Nene. For information and permits contact the National Rivers Authority
☎ 0733 371811
☎ 0480 414581

Indoor Sports

LEISURE CENTRES

Hudson Sports Centre
Harecroft Road
☎ 0945 584230

Special Interests

FESTIVALS AND FAIRS

July
Rose Fair

FOOD AND DRINK

Elgoods and Son Limited
North Brink Brewery
Established in 1878 and supplies fifty
pubs in the Wisbech area.
☎ 0945 583160

HISTORIC HOUSES

Peckover House
1722 merchant's house with an
unusual 2-acre Victorian garden, on the
north brink of the River Nene.
National Trust.
☎ 0945 583463

MUSEUMS

Fenland Aviation Museum
Old Lynn Road, West Walton
Aircraft engines, Second World War
display.
☎ 0945 860814

Wisbech and Fenland Museum
Museum Square
Local and natural history and geology,
decorative arts.
☎ 0945 583817

NATURAL HISTORY

Wildfowl and Wetland Trust
Welney
850-acre wetland reserve. Waterfowl,
wildflowers and butterflies.
☎ 0353 860711

THEATRES

Angles Theatre
Alexandra Road
Georgian theatre built in 1793, used as
a theatre for 100 years then as a school,
a tent makers and recently a live
theatre once more.
☎ 0945 585587

Water Sports

SWIMMING

Hudson Sports Centre
☎ 0945 584230

ESSEX / **Witham** ESSEX

Witham, a small attractive Essex town, has a pleasant village green and some fine old
houses on Chipping Hill. The Knights Templars were based here and more recently it
was the home of the detective novelist Dorothy L Sayers.

Market day Saturday
Early closing Wednesday

Adventure Sports

CLIMBING

Bramston Sports Centre
Bridge Street
☎ 0376 519200

SHOOTING

Bramston Sports Centre
☎ 0376 519200

Indoor Sports

LEISURE CENTRES

Bramston Sports Centre
☎ 0376 519200

SQUASH

Bramston Sports Centre
☎ 0376 519200

Outdoor Leisure

FISHING

Coarse Fishing
Fishing at Witham Lake, Bovington
Mere and Hatfield Peverel, also the
River Stour and Rivenhall Lake at
Kelvedon. For information and permits
contact the National Rivers Authority
☎ 0473 727712

Riding and Pony Trekking

HORSE RIDING

Glebe Equestrian Centre
Mope Lane, Wickham Bishops
Instructional holidays. BHS approved.
☎ 0621 892375

Special Interests

HERITAGE

Cressing Barns
Cressing
Important 13th century mediaeval barns constructed for the Knights Templars and now restored.
☎ 0376 84903

MUSEUMS

Fossil Hall
Boars Tye Road
Reproductions of fossil specimens. Britain's largest specialist geological bookshop.
☎ 0376 83502

Feering and Kelvedon Local History Museum
Maldon Road, Kelvedon
☎ 0376 70307

Water Sports

SWIMMING

Bramston Sports Centre
Swimming, diving and learner pools.
☎ 0376 519200

Woodbridge

Woodbridge is a lively town at the top of the Deben estuary. It grew as a centre for boat building, ropemaking and sailcloth production. It is set in a lovely location and has many fine buildings including a now rare tide-operated mill. Nearby is the site of the famous Sutton Hoo ship-burial, revealed by excavations in 1939.

Early closing Wednesday
Population 9772

Market Hill, Woodbridge

Adventure Sports

SHOOTING

East Suffolk Gun Club
Home Farm, Kettleburgh
☎ 0327 860354

RAF Bentwaters/Woodbridge Rod and Gun Club
RAF Bentwaters
☎ 0394 420225

Outdoor Leisure

FISHING

Coarse Fishing
Fishing on the River Deben (tidal). For information and permits contact the National Rivers Authority
☎ 0733 371811
☎ 0473 727712

GOLF

Waldringfield Heath Golf Club ⁱ₁₈
Newbourne Way, Waldringfield
☎ 0473 36768

Woodbridge Golf Club ⁱ₁₈ ⁱ₉
2½ miles north-west of Woodbridge on the A1152 at Bromeswell Heath
☎ 0394 32038

HORSE RIDING

Poplar Park Equestrian Centre
15 miles east of Ipswich at Hollesley
Riding holidays and hacking. BHS and ABRS approved.
☎ 0394 411023

189

Special Interests

FOOD AND DRINK

Suffolk Cider Company Ltd
Cider House, Bridge Farm, Friday
Street, Brandeston
☎ 0728 82537

GARDENS

Letheringham Watermill Gardens
Letheringham
Formal gardens, riverside walks, 5 acres
of spring bulbs. Guided tours.

HERITAGE

Sutton Hoo
Excavation of a Saxon ship-burial in
progress. The original treasure is in the
British museum, replica treasures are in
the Ipswich Museum. Guided tours
only.
☎ 03943 7673

HISTORIC BUILDINGS

Buttrums Mill
Burkitt Road
Six storey tower mill restored in 1835.
☎ 0473 230000

Woodbridge Tide Mill
Restored tide mill with working
machinery, one of very few in the
country.
☎ 0473 626618

MUSEUMS

Woodbridge Museum
Market Hill
Local and maritime history. Sutton
Hoo ship burial exhibits.
☎ 03943 2178

Water Sports

BOAT TRIPS

Waldringfield Boatyard Ltd
The Quay, Waldringfield
Half day and evening trips through 10
miles of wooded countryside on the
River Deben. Bar, galley, facilities for
wheelchairs.
☎ 047 336 260

SWIMMING

Deben Swimming Pool
Station Road
25-metre pool, sauna, solarium,
sunbeds.
☎ 0394 34763

YACHTING

Deben Yacht Club
Riverwell
☎ 0394 33306

Orford Sailing Club
Orford
☎ 0728 852443

Woodbridge Cruising Club
River Wall

Wroxham is a sailing centre for the Norfolk Broads with their 200 miles of waterways
for sailing and cruising. Boats can either be hired here or joined for trips to experience
and appreciate the distinctive character of the Broads and their wildlife.

i Broads Information
Station Road
Hoveton
☎ 0603 782281

Population 2967

Special Interests

ARTS AND CRAFTS

Willow Farm Dried Flowers
Neatishead
Dried flower suppliers; flower
arrangement workshop.
☎ 0603 783588

HISTORIC HOUSES

Beeston Hall
2 miles north-east of Wroxham on the A1151 at Beeston St Lawrence
Gothic style Georgian country house. Portraits and furniture associated with Preston family since 1640.
☎ 0692 630771

RAILWAYS

Barton House Railway
Hartwell Road
3-inch and 7-inch gauge railways. Train rides.
☎ 0603 782470

Water Sports

BOAT HIRE

Ferry Boatyard Ltd
Ferry Road, Horning
Day launches.
☎ 0692 630392

Moore and Co
Hotel Wroxham car park
Modern motor cruisers and day launches for hire.
☎ 0603 784295

BOAT TRIPS

Broads Tours Ltd
Trips of up to 3 hours in an all-weather launch. Up to 170 passengers in the largest boat.
☎ 0605 32207

Faircraft Loynes
Day launches and passenger boats. Facilities for wheelchairs.
☎ 0603 782280

Tom Phillips
111 Norwich Road
Private skippered trips on the Broads in 25-foot power boat.
☎ 0603 783462

INLAND WATERWAYS

Blakes Holidays Ltd
Narrow boat holidays on the Broads.
☎ 0603 782141

PUNTING

Norfolk Punt Club
Barton Turf
☎ 0493 730338

Wymondham is an ancient town surrounding a 17th century market cross with an octagonal chamber. The church is notable for its two towers built as the result of a 14th century dispute. The town was also the site where Kett's Rebellion began in 1549, a peasants' revolt against encroachments on common land. Kett who led the revolt was later caught and hung in Norwich, his brother suffered the same fate in Wymondham.

Market day Friday
Early closing Wednesday
Population 9152

Special Interests

HISTORIC BUILDINGS

Abbey Church
The Church of Saints Mary and Thomas has two huge towers, the result of a dispute in the 14th century over the use of the church by both the monks and the townspeople. The octagonal tower was built by the monks and the square west tower was built in retaliation by the townspeople.

Wicklewood Mill
Restored tower with original machinery.
☎ 0953 603694

MUSEUMS

Heritage Museum
Middleton Street
Local history.
☎ 0953 603000

191

Useful Information

MAJOR ROADS

A10 London to King's Lynn
A11 London to Norwich
M11 London to Cambridge
A12 London to Great Yarmouth via
     Colchester and Ipswich
A47 Midlands to Norwich
A1   London to Edinburgh road links
     with A604 to Cambridge and
     Colchester

BUS COMPANIES

Eastern Counties
  Norfolk ☎ 0603 760076
  Suffolk ☎ 0473 253734
Eastern National (Essex)
  ☎ 0245 256151 ☎ 0206 571451
United Counties (Cambridgeshire)
  ☎ 0480 453159

MAJOR RAIL ROUTES

Liverpool Street to King's Lynn via
  Cambridge
Liverpool Street to Norwich via
  Colchester and Ipswich
Liverpool Street or Fenchurch Street to
  Southend
King's Cross to Peterborough
Harwich to Liverpool via Peterborough

Bury St Edmunds ☎ 0473 690744
Cambridge ☎ 0223 311999
Chelmsford ☎ 0245 252111
Clacton-on-Sea ☎ 0206 564777
Colchester ☎ 0206 564777
Great Yarmouth ☎ 0603 632055
Harwich/Dovercourt ☎ 0206 564777
Huntingdon ☎ 0480 454468
Ipswich ☎ 0473 690744
King's Lynn ☎ 0553 772021
Lowestoft ☎ 0603 632055
Norwich ☎ 0603 632055
Peterborough ☎ 0733 68181
Southend-on-Sea ☎ 0702 681811
Area Manager's Office: British Rail,
  Anglia Region, 112/114 Prince of
  Wales Road, Norwich ☎ 0603 622255

AIR

Stansted Airport
  internal/external flights
  ☎ 0279 502520
Norwich Airport
  internal/external flights
  ☎ 0603 411923
Southend Airport
  internal/external flights
  ☎ 0702 340201
Ipswich Airport ☎ 0473 718346
Cambridge Airport ☎ 02205 3621/2

SEA

Harwich Parkeston Quay to Hook of
  Holland ☎ 0255 24333
Harwich Parkeston Quay to Hamburg/
  Esbjerg/Gothenburg ☎ 0255 240240
Felixstowe to Zeebrugge
  ☎ 0394 604100
Yarmouth to Scheveningen
  ☎ 0493 842391

COUNTY COUNCIL OFFICES

Cambridgeshire County Council
Shire Hall
Castle Hill
Cambridge
☎ 0223 317111

Essex County Council
County Hall
Chelmsford
☎ 0245 492211

Norfolk County Council
County Hall
Martineau Lane
Norwich
☎ 0603 222222

Suffolk County Council
St Helens Court
County Hall
Ipswich
☎ 0473 230000

TOURIST BOARD

East Anglia Tourist Board
Toppesfield Hall
Hadleigh
Suffolk
☎ 0473 822922